Mastering Operational Risk

PEARSON

At Pearson, we believe in learning – all kinds of learning for all kinds of people. Whether it's at home, in the classroom or in the workplace, learning is the key to improving our life chances.

That's why we're working with leading authors to bring you the latest thinking and the best practices, so you can get better at the things that are important to you. You can learn on the page or on the move, and with content that's always crafted to help you understand quickly and apply what you've learned.

If you want to upgrade your personal skills or accelerate your career, become a more effective leader or more powerful communicator, discover new opportunities or simply find more inspiration, we can help you make progress in your work and life.

Pearson is the world's leading learning company. Our portfolio includes the Financial Times, Penguin, Dorling Kindersley, and our educational business, Pearson International.

Every day our work helps learning flourish, and wherever learning flourishes, so do people.

To learn more please visit us at: **www.pearson.com/uk**

The Financial Times

With a worldwide network of highly respected journalists, *The Financial Times* provides global business news, insightful opinion and expert analysis of business, finance and politics. With over 500 journalists reporting from 50 countries worldwide, our in-depth coverage of international news is objectively reported and analysed from an independent, global perspective.

To find out more, visit **www.ft.com/pearsonoffer/**

Mastering Operational Risk

A practical guide to understanding operational risk and how to manage it

SECOND EDITION

TONY BLUNDEN
JOHN THIRLWELL

PEARSON

Harlow, England • London • New York • Boston • San Francisco • Toronto • Sydney
Auckland • Singapore • Hong Kong • Tokyo • Seoul • Taipei • New Delhi
Cape Town • São Paulo • Mexico City • Madrid • Amsterdam • Munich • Paris • Milan

PEARSON EDUCATION LIMITED
Edinburgh Gate
Harlow CM20 2JE
United Kingdom
Tel: +44 (0)1279 623623
Web: www.pearson.com/uk

First published 2010 (print)
Second edition published 2013 (print and electronic)

© Pearson Education Limited (2010) (print)
© Pearson Education Limited (2013) (print and electronic)

The rights of Tony Blunden and John Thirlwell to be identified as authors of this work have been asserted by them in accordance with the Copyright, Designs and Patents Act 1988.

Pearson Education is not responsible for the content of third-party internet sites.

ISBN: 978-0-273-77874-5 (print)
        978-0-273-77883-7 (PDF)
        978-0-273-77884-4 (ePub)
        978-0-273-79493-6 (eText)

British Library Cataloguing-in-Publication Data
A catalogue record for the print edition is available from the British Library

Library of Congress Cataloging-in-Publication Data
Blunden, Tony.
   Mastering operational risk : a practical guide to understanding operational risk and how to manage it / Tony Blunden, John Thirlwell. -- Second edition.
      pages cm. -- (Mastering)
   Includes index.
   ISBN 978-0-273-77874-5 (pbk.)
   1. Risk management. 2. Opertional risk. I. Thirlwell, John. II. Title.
      HD61.B547 2013
      658.15'5--dc23
      2013020353

Print edition typeset in Garamond 11.5/13.5pt by 3

NOTE THAT ANY PAGE CROSS-REFERENCES REFER TO THE PRINT EDITION

Contents

Preface to the first edition

Risk management has taken a knock over the past few years, as the financial crisis has unfolded. But perhaps the problem was not so much a failure of risk management as such, as its absence from strategic and other decisions.

That is why we believe *Mastering Operational Risk* is both timely and a reminder that good risk management is fundamental to good business management. And, as we show in Chapter 2, good operational risk management can bring real business benefits. It is as much about opportunities as it is about threats: so it demands imagination and the flexibility to adapt to a rapidly changing risk environment.

Operational risk emerged as a risk discipline in its own right in financial services in the early 1990s. However, it was influenced by events in the 'hazard' industries and took on board methods which were already being used in energy, nuclear, space and transport, where operational risk as we now know it, was simply good risk management.

For us, operational risk goes far beyond operations and process to encompass all aspects of business risk, including strategic and reputational risks. Its management is not a complicated science, as much as a very human art which lies at the heart of all business decisions.

Mastering Operational Risk came about because we both passionately believe that there is a need for a book that sets out a practical framework for operational risk management, rather than one which is academic and quantitative in its approach. It has been written by practitioners for practitioners.

Given our professional backgrounds, and given where operational risk management has been developed over the past decade, *Mastering Operational Risk* is grounded in financial services, but the core elements are equally applicable to all sectors and to those who have to make business judgements. Since operational risk covers all aspects of business and involves everybody who works in the business or deals with it, we hope that it will provide useful tips for the beginner as well as the seasoned professional.

The core of the book is a risk management framework which provides a practical structure for managing this most slippery of risks. At its heart lie the critical processes of risk and control assessment and the use of loss events and indicators, all within an overarching governance structure. It tackles head-on the thorny subject of operational risk appetite – for a risk which takes in the unknown unknowns as well as the known unknowns. And although fundamentally this is a book about management, it also covers ways in which operational risk can be modelled and measured. It includes a business approach to modelling operational risk, which places the tool of modelling back in the hands of management, using the fundamental operational risk processes.

Of course, stuff happens which is unavoidable. But unavoidable does not mean unmanageable. That is why we have included chapters on both reputation risk – and how to deal with reputation crises – as well as business continuity. And as so much of operational risk is ultimately down to people failures, people risk is a key risk which is fully covered in its own chapter.

Mastering Operational Risk represents the distillation of two lifetimes of experience in operational risk management, during which we have enjoyed so many conversations with friends and colleagues about taming this exotic beast. A number of them have been kind enough to read individual chapters or in other ways to provide invaluable advice and suggestions: Rees Aaronson, Andrew Bryan, Ian Hilder, Mark Johnson, Charlotte Kiddy, Tim Landsman, Roger Miles, John Naish, Bruce Nichols, John Renz, Nick Symons and Rosemary Todd. To them go our especial thanks. Any sins of omission or commission, though, are entirely our own. Special thanks also to our editors, Chris Cudmore and Mary Lince, who have provided much needed encouragement and guidance.

Finally, we should like to thank our families for their constant support and for having to live lives, probably more than most, surrounded by operational risk.

ACB
JRWT

Preface to the second edition

A few months after the first edition had gone to press the Eyjafjallajökull volcano erupted, causing widespread disruption to air travel, and the Gulf of Mexico oil disaster began. Then a few months after the book appeared, the Japanese earthquake and tsunami caused the Fukushima nuclear disaster. All significant operational risk events and reminders of the scale of the problems which operational risk managers have to face and the scope of operational risk itself.

The events themselves form case studies in this second edition, which has been both updated and revised. The main revisions include raising the difficult issue of operational risk appetite to a chapter in its own right, bringing in thoughts on qualitative modelling in the chapter on Modelling and also revising the chapter on Stress tests and scenarios. The first edition consistently made the point that the fundamental causes of most operational risk failures are down to human factors, in other words people risk. That in turn is often a reflection of the culture of the firm in which people work and so we have expanded the People risk chapter to one entitled Culture and people risk and given guidance on how to embed the right operational risk culture.

As with the first edition, we have been supported and encouraged by many friends and colleagues, some of whom have been kind enough to provide invaluable advice and suggestions, with especial thanks on this occasion to John Barlow, Garry Honey and Charlotte Kiddy. Special thanks as well to the team at Pearson, led by our editor, Eloise Cook, for all their guidance and support. As ever, any errors or omissions are entirely our own.

We have been both delighted and encouraged by the many people who have told us how much the book has helped them as a practical guide to operational risk management which, after all, is what we set out to do. We hope that this second edition is just as practical and just as helpful.

ACB
JRWT

Acknowledgements

We are grateful to the following for permission to reproduce copyright material:

FIGURES

Figures 1.2, 2.1, 3.2, 3.6, 4.9, 4.10, 5.1, 5.2, 5.4, 5.6, 6.1, 6.2, 6.3, 7.1, 7.2, 7.3, 7.4, 7.5, 7.7, 8.1, 8.12, 9.1, 9.2, 9.3, 9.4, 9.5, 9.6, 9.7, 9.8, 9.9, 9.10, 9.11, 10.1, 10.2, 10.3, 10.4, 13.1 and the figure on p.280 courtesy of Chase Cooper Limited.

LOGOS

Figure 4.1 from Balfour Beatty, a registered trademark of Balfour Beatty plc, registered in England as a public limited company; Registered No: 395826; Registered Office: 130 Wilton Road, London SW1V 1LQ. For further information about the 'Zero harm' project, see http://www.zeroharm.bbrce.co.uk/

TABLES

Tables 9.1, 9.2, 9.3, 9.4, 9.5 and 14.1 courtesy of Chase Cooper Limited; Table 10.1 adapted from Information Paper; Applying a Structured Approach to Operational Risk Scenario Analysis in Australia, Emily Watchorn, September 2007, copyright Commonwealth of Australia, reproduced with permission; Table 11.1 from Business Continuity Institute, *Good Practice Guidelines* 2008, Section 1, p.7, The Business Continuity Institute; Gower; Table 16.6 from Honey, G., *A Short Guide to Reputation Risk* (Gower, 2009) © A Short Guide to Reputation Risk, Garry Honey, 2009; Table 16.7 adapted from British Bankers' Association Global Operational Loss Database.

In some instances we have been unable to trace the owners of copyright material, and we would appreciate any information that would enable us to do so.

The authors

PROFESSOR TONY BLUNDEN

Tony has worked in the City of London for over 30 years, primarily within risk management, compliance and related areas in financial services organisations. He is Head of Consulting and a Board member of Chase Cooper.

Tony's areas of focus are the identification and development of clients' need; the development of Chase Cooper's profile and product set; and the provision of both public and bespoke training to clients. Tony has advised and guided over 60 clients, and previous client engagements have included risk frameworks and governance; risk and control assessments; indicators of key risks and key controls; event and loss databases and their use; modelling of operational risk; risk reporting; risk appetite; and stress testing and scenario analysis. He is developing the integration of operational risk data with six sigma techniques in order to bring business benefit through control and process improvement.

Tony has spoken at over 100 international risk and compliance conferences and has appeared on television and radio. He is also a well-known author of articles and chapters on risk management and compliance having published around 30 documents. He is an Honorary Professor at the Glasgow School for Business and Society of Glasgow Caledonian University and a Fellow of the Institute of Chartered Secretaries and Administrators.

JOHN THIRLWELL

John has worked in financial services in the City of London for over 30 years. He was Chief Risk Officer and a director of an investment bank and, for the last 18 years, has been an executive and non-executive director of a number of banking and insurance firms. He was a director of the British Bankers' Association where he was responsible for negotiating the operational risk aspects of the Basel Capital Accord and EU Capital Requirements Directive. He founded and chaired the BBA's Global Operational Loss Database.

He has been chairman of the UK Financial Services and Insurance Committee of the International Chamber of Commerce and has sat on advisory groups on risk and operational risk for the Bank of England, Financial Services Authority, Financial Services Skills Council, Chartered Institute of Securities and Investment and Lloyd's Market Association.

John is well-known internationally as a speaker and writer on operational risk and on risk management and governance and is a Director and Fellow of the Institute of Operational Risk and a Fellow of the Chartered Institute of Bankers. He graduated from the University of Oxford and is chairman of trustees of the Bankside Gallery, London.

SETTING THE SCENE

Part 1

1

What is operational risk?

THE ROAD TO OPERATIONAL RISK

Dateline: Moscow, 19 October 1812

In the face of a deserted city and no capitulation from city or Tsar, Napoleon burns Moscow to the ground and begins the march back to France. Failure to plan for the peculiar logistics of attempting such a long march into Russia and to identify and assess the debilitating effect of snow and temperatures of up to −38 °C result in the loss of nearly all the 420,000 troops of La Grande Armée.

Dateline: North Atlantic, 400 miles south of the Grand Banks of Newfoundland, 23.50, 14 April 1912

On its maiden voyage, RMS *Titanic* hits an iceberg which buckles the hull, causing five compartments to fill with water (the ship was designed to survive if up to four failed) and the ship to sink. Inadequate construction, lack of escalation procedures to handle ice warnings and, critically, inadequate lifeboat provisions lead to the deaths of 1517 of the 2223 on board.

Dateline: Kennedy Space Center, 11.39, 28 January 1986

The failure of a seal in a rocket booster leads directly to the disintegration of the *Challenger* space shuttle only 73 seconds into its flight, with the loss of the lives of the seven crew members on board. The subsequent enquiry identifies poor governance and controls within NASA as fundamental contributing factors to the disaster.

Dateline: Piper oilfield, 58°28N 0°15E, 22.00, 6 July 1988

Inadequate communication about the safety status of a pump causes an explosion on the Piper Alpha oil production platform. Of the 226 men on the platform 167 are killed through lack of safety procedures, including inadequate refuge, coupled with a general attitude of minimum compliance with procedures.

Dateline: Bligh Reef, Prince William Sound, 00.04, 24 March 1989, *Exxon Valdez*

As a result of failures to adhere to appropriate work patterns, to provide navigation watch and, on the part of coastguards, to provide an effective traffic system through the Sound, the *Exxon Valdez* oil tanker strikes the reef, shedding some 40 million litres of oil. The spill results in the collapse of the local marine population and is disastrous to the local economy.

Dateline: Barings Bank Boardroom, 23 February 1995

Barings Chairman, Peter Baring, receives a confession note from his head derivatives trader in Singapore, Nick Leeson. Lack of appropriate controls over trading activity and treasury management, together with inadequate governance and lack of clear reporting lines had enabled Leeson to generate trading losses of $1.3bn, twice the capital of the bank. The 232-year-old bank is forced into insolvency and administration.

The road to operational risk, like the road from Moscow in the winter of 1812, has been long and arduous. In the thirteenth century, when plagues, wars and famine were raging across continental Europe, Thomas Aquinas, philosopher, and saint as he later became, wrote, 'The world has never been more full of risk.' Over 750 years later, people continue to have the same view, but now global warming, terrorism or even the rise of global capitalism keeps them awake at night. And of course pandemics continue to haunt us, whether it is SARS, or avian or swine flu. In October 2010, the UK government published its national security strategy and identified the principal threats facing the country. The Tier 1 threats were seen as: international terrorism, cyber-attacks, a major accident or natural disaster (which included flooding and pandemics) and an international military crisis.[1] *Plus ça change.*

Whether or not the world is more risky, awareness of risk is undoubtedly high. That in part reflects changes in society in which risk assessment and risk tolerance are increasingly democratised. Various forms of activism, whether by consumers or non-governmental organisations, allied to a society which appears increasingly unable to accept personal risk responsibility, mean that we no longer allow risk assessment, and especially risk tolerance, to be left in the hands of governments or 'experts'.

Not that activism is a new phenomenon. In response to social, and therefore political, pressure, often by trade unions or other forms of organised labour, numerous laws and regulations relating to health and safety in workplaces and elsewhere have been coming steadily onto the statute book since the nineteenth century. The first Mining Acts passed into law in 1803.

The interesting thing about these comments and the events at the start of this chapter is that they all form part of what is now known as operational risk. It is a very broad church. As those events show, one of the big problems of operational risk management is that we do not fully know the risks we face now or in the future, but we must act as if we do. Risk management implies that something can be done to reduce, if not eliminate, the likelihood and impact of danger and uncertainty.

But there is always the possibility that something will go wrong, whether through a failure in a process, human failures or simply because something unexpected happens in the external environment. Of all these, the most unpredictable, and the ones most likely to cause serious problems, are human failures and external events. That does not mean that these unpredictable factors are unmanageable, but it does mean that we need to approach operational risk management intelligently, with a humble acceptance of its limitations. If we do not, operational risk management becomes a risk in itself as it falls foul of an expectation that it is in some way a panacea for all our troubles. Risk management means neither risk avoidance nor risk elimination.

Even financial services regulators seem to have recognised the limitations of risk management. In the immediate aftermath of the financial crisis of 2007–9 they shifted their emphasis from risk-based regulation or supervision to the more practical task of outcomes-based regulation. Developing a climate of intelligent questioning is both the challenge and the opportunity for operational risk managers – and probably for regulators as well.

Having said that, risk is an integral part of life which has to be managed. In business life it has been increasingly enshrined in codes of corporate governance since the early 1990s. The Cadbury Report (1992) was the first of these, leading to the UK's first Combined Code on Corporate Governance, which was published in 1999, along with the Turnbull Report on internal controls. Cadbury was closely followed by the Toronto Report in Canada and King Report in South Africa (both 1994) and similar reports and recommendations in Australia and France in 1995. The OECD Principles of Corporate Governance, which were first published in 1999, include the paragraph:

> An area of increasing importance for boards and which is closely related to corporate strategy is risk policy. Such policy will involve specifying the types and degree of risk that a company is willing to accept in pursuit of its goals. It is thus a crucial guideline for management that must manage risks to meet the company's desired risk profile.[2]

The discipline of operational risk management itself probably emerged first in those 'hazard' or 'safety critical' industries or activities where the effect of failure can be catastrophic, whether in terms of lives lost or environments destroyed – nuclear, space, defence, pharmaceuticals, energy and transport. And it also had an honourable tradition in manufacturing, where the management of production lines and health and safety are vitally important.

Against this background, at some time in the 1990s, operational risk emerged in the financial services sector as a term to identify a particular set of risks. Folk memory suggests that its emergence as a separate discipline was triggered by the Barings case in 1995, but it was being considered before that, partly as a result of events and failures which proved to banks that lending might be the least of their worries. Many were also conscious of events in other industries, such as the Piper Alpha rig disaster in 1988.

Not that it was much different for medieval bankers several centuries before. Their businesses failed as much because their communities and customers suffered from war, plague and famine, as they did from imprudent lending to defaulting sovereigns or states. As Thomas Aquinas suggested, operational risk has always been with us.

Before we consider practical ways of managing it, though, we will first establish what exactly we mean in this book by operational risk.

WHAT DO WE MEAN BY OPERATIONAL RISK?

Defining risk

Perhaps the first thing to decide is what we mean by risk. The word came into the English language in the seventeenth century from the Italian *risco* or *rischio*, meaning hazard or danger. Some element of that appeared in a definition given by the Royal Society in 1992, 'the chance, in quantitative terms, of a defined hazard occurring'. This has the merit of introducing the concept of probability or uncertainty, but its accent on defined hazards implies that it concerns 'known unknowns'.

Two other definitions of risk introduce a key element, impact on objectives, which will be a running theme throughout this book. The British Standard on Risk Management defines risk as 'something that might happen and its effect(s) on the achievement of objectives'.[3] This echoes a Standard which had been in use in Australia and New Zealand, AS/NZS 4360:2004, which speaks of risk as being 'the chance of something happening that will impact objectives...'. In the latest international standard this has become 'the effect of uncertainty on objectives' (ISO 31000:2009), which shifts the emphasis back from effect to cause. The subject of risk becomes 'something that might happen'. We are now moving into 'unknown unknowns' territory. Company reports and academic commentators draw a distinction between risks, which are measurable, and uncertainties, which are not.[4] For most people, however, including the authors, the two come together. The measurable and the immeasurable are definitely all part of operational risk.

People often say that risk is a threat to objectives, something which negatively affects those objectives or threatens the factors which make a business successful. However, the two definitions mentioned above, do not speak of threats, they speak of impacts, also known as effects or outcomes. Risk and risk management can be about opportunities as much as threats. As Peter Bernstein has expressed it in *Against the Gods*, when discussing the theories of the eighteenth century Swiss mathematician, Daniel Bernoulli, 'Risk is not something to be faced, but a set of opportunities open to choice.'

In Chinese, the concept of risk is represented by two characters which 'translate' as crisis and opportunity. In fact, the characters for crisis are *wei ji* (危机) and the characters for opportunity are *ji hui* (机会), so it's probably truer to say that the character *ji* forms part of the concepts for crisis and opportunity, which still shows that conceptually the Chinese understood the twin sides of risk many centuries ago.

Loss of one or more key staff, loss of reputation or abandoning a project may well have an adverse financial impact, but even then it is possible that they can result in financial benefit both in the short and medium term. When something happens, it may even help you to achieve and surpass your objectives. Those objectives can be sales, profit, market share or something else, such as the behavioural objectives discussed later (in Chapter 15, Culture and people risk). The disciplines of risk management will mean that you are prepared as much for the upside as for the downside. Risk is not downhill all the way, even if it often feels like it.

Defining operational risk

The question, though, is to decide which of those risks, which of those 'somethings' are we going to put in the box marked *operational* risk, as opposed to other kinds of risk. As we have said, operational risk, as a term, first emerged within financial services in the early 1990s. As awareness of the risks and subject grew, so people looked for a common definition which would describe what they were talking about. The definition of operational risk most widely used now in financial services is the one published by the Basel Committee on Banking Supervision:

Definition	Operational risk

The risk of loss resulting from inadequate or failed internal processes, people and systems or from external events.[5]

Although it was devised for banks and has been adopted within the European insurance industry, it represents a reasonable statement of the scope of operational risk within all industries. In fact, most firms would say that is their definition of business risk, which is true. That is why this book applies as much to non-financial services as it does to financial services.

This definition first emerged from a survey undertaken in 1999 by the British Bankers' Association, the International Swaps and Derivatives Association and the Risk Management Association, with the help of PricewaterhouseCoopers, subsequently written up in *Operational risk – The next frontier*.[6] Up until then, within financial services, operational risk, if it had been thought about at all, was either limited to *operations* risk, i.e. internal processes and systems, or was a negative statement or thought – 'anything which isn't credit or market risk'. In the 1999 survey of more than 50 (mostly) international banks, including nearly 40% of the top 100 banks in the world at that time, less than half had a positive group-wide definition, 15% used the negative statement, and almost all the rest had no specific definition.

The Basel definition has the merit of being positive: it says what operational risk is, rather than what it is not; but it doesn't really tell you what those various groups – people, process, systems, external events – mean in practice. It is a scoping statement. It needs more detail to flesh it out in the shape of sub-categories. Table 1.1 gives some examples of sub-categories of the four key words in the Basel definition.

The Basel Committee classified operational risk losses and came up with the following categories:

- internal fraud
- external fraud
- employment practices and workplace safety
- clients, products and business practices
- damage to physical assets
- business disruption and systems failures
- execution, delivery and process management.[7]

That is not a list of risks, but a mixture of events and effects or impacts. Another categorisation (see Table 1.1) took as its starting point the definition of operational risk and listed risks under those four main headings. But even the Basel Committee limited its own definition by adding a rider that it included legal risk, but excluded strategic and reputational risk.[8]

Sub-categories of operational risk   Table 1.1

People	Includes: fraud; breaches of employment law; unauthorised activity; loss or lack of key personnel; inadequate training; inadequate supervision.
Process	Includes: payment or settlement failures; documentation which is not fit for purpose; errors in valuation/pricing models and processes; project management failures; internal/external reporting; (mis)selling.
Systems	Includes: failures during the development and systems implementation process, as well as failures of the system itself; inadequate resources.
External events	Includes: external crime; outsourcing (and insourcing) risk; natural and other disasters; regulatory risk; political risk; utilities' failures; competition.

Source: Adapted from British Bankers' Association GOLD database

Legal risk – the risk of capricious legislators, of capricious judges and juries, or of finding that documentation is inadequate to sustain a claim against a debtor – is a perfectly legitimate risk to include within operational risk. But it has a sister risk, regulatory risk, which is little spoken of (by regulators), yet which consistently features high in the CSFI's annual 'Banana Skin' surveys.[9] Until recently, that probably reflected irritation with the burden of 'too much' regulation, rather than the biggest genuine threat to the business. Now it might well begin to encompass decisions by legislators and regulators, capricious in the eyes of some victims, which will have considerable impact on business models.

Whilst it might be permissible to exclude strategic risk, i.e. making the wrong strategic decision for the business, it is our view, especially if this concerns poor implementation of strategy, that it is all part of operational risk.

The one outsider is reputation risk, which is not really a direct risk in itself, but is usually the result or consequence of an operational risk failure or, more often, failures. As it is a secondary consequence of another risk, an argument can be made for its exclusion. However, many firms in all industries not unreasonably consider it one of their biggest risks, given the life-threatening damage it can incur (see Chapter 16, Reputation risk). What emerges is that operational risk encompasses practically all the risks of running the business, apart from any which deserve specific treatment.

Of course, another approach to understanding what is meant – or to be more exact, what *you* mean – by operational risk is to ask the simple question, 'What keeps you awake at night?' Or, given that risk can be defined as a threat to objectives, a better question is 'What needs to go right for the business to achieve its objectives?' and think about what might prevent that happening. The answer to either question might be a list like this:

- loss of reputation
- failure of the organisation to change/adapt
- business interruption
- failure to retain employees
- political risk
- product liability
- general liability
- terrorism
- failure of a key strategic alliance
- computer failure.

None is avoidable. Many are transferable, perhaps by insurance (see Chapter 12), but all are manageable to some extent, if only in the sense of the four Ts of: treat, transfer, terminate and tolerate.

The answers to the 'what needs to go right' question also have the merits of both identifying and prioritising the business's key risks. They emerge quite naturally.

As we have seen, one of the glories – and frustrations – of operational risk, like Cleopatra, is its infinite variety. In the words of Michael Power:

> Operational risk is an extended institutionalised attempt to frame the unframeable, assuage fears about the uncontrollable 'rogue others' and to tame the man-made monsters [of the financial system].[10]

That is its continual fascination and challenge.

Operational risk and ERM

In this book, we take the view that operational risk covers all the internal and external sources of operational risk, all those 'rogue others'. It is equivalent in many ways to enterprise risk management (ERM), but certain discrete financial risks, such as credit risk, market risk and liquidity or commodity risk can be hived off from it, as is shown in Figure 1.1.

Operational risks and other financial risks

Figure 1.1

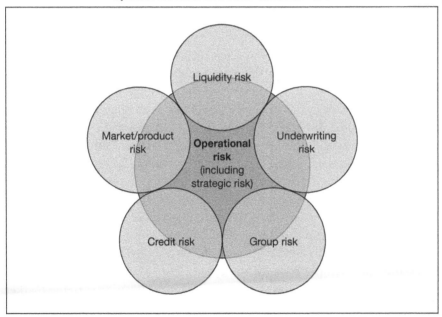

ERM and operational risk management share very similar aims. There are numerous definitions of ERM, but the Risk and Insurance Management Society has published one which chimes with this idea:

Definition	ERM is the culture, processes and tools to identify strategic opportunities and reduce uncertainty. It is a comprehensive view of risk both from operational and strategic perspectives and is a process that supports the reduction of uncertainty and promotes the exploration of opportunities.[11]

ERM undoubtedly covers all the various risk categories. But for us, operational risk is essentially business risk and at the heart of business risk management. That is the view taken in this book, but how you define operational risk is up to you. Your definition must go with the grain of your firm and all firms are different in their business, culture and people. But define it, or scope it, you must, because how you define it will determine how you classify it and assess it and how it is managed in your firm. Your definition is the cornerstone of any operational risk policy.

THE BOUNDARY ISSUE

As can be seen from Figure 1.1, operational risk overlaps with other risks. One of the issues which has to be resolved in positioning a definition is 'the boundary issue'. That reflects the fact that many of the losses which are ascribed to other classes of risk have a strong operational risk component.

Product risk involves the commodity, or market, risk of prices of components moving, but the risks of product quality, design and distribution are operational risks. Supply risk involves the credit risk of the supplier and buyer, but it is rooted in the operational risks of supply chain logistics.

Turning to financial services, it has been claimed, albeit anecdotally, that at least 50% of banks' bad debts are, in fact, operational risk losses, often through failures of documentation which invalidate collateral, whether on retail or wholesale transactions. But they tend to go into the books as credit losses. Similarly, in the market trading environment, a significant number of what are recorded as market losses are operational risk losses: for example, 'fat finger', where the wrong key is struck or an order is mis-typed and you buy when you should have sold, or buy, for example, the Japanese recruitment agency J-Com rather than the cable television group JCom.[12]

Taking the example to a different level from the purely transactional, failure to adequately stress test market risk models against extreme market movements is a form of operational risk. It reflects a failure of internal controls over the stress testing function. Its impact, though, may not be on an individual transaction, but on the general level of market risk to which the firm is exposed and may well feed through into significant losses. Is that market risk or operational risk?

As with so much about operational risk, it is very much up to you and the nature of your firm and how you wish to allocate losses and manage your risks. What is meant by operational risk – how far you push the boundaries out or pull them in – is entirely up to you. Your risk management framework should reflect the ways you work within the firm. In many cases the answer is straightforward, but not where risk categories overlap, which is where most of the risk lies.

The downside of allocating risks by risk type at this higher level is that if you try to extract quantitatively the operational risks which have traditionally been included in credit and market risk data, you add other risks to the problem – the subjectivity of allocation and the breaking of a relatively homogeneous time series of data. Even if you decide that you will keep the boundaries tight – and traditional – you should at least track and record those incidents where an operational failure has resulted in loss. The real object of the exercise is operational risk management, not operational risk measurement.

Operational risk is ultimately about failure of controls – or even lack of controls – so that operational risk management is about establishing and maintaining an effective and cost-effective control environment across all risks. The fact is that operational risk crosses boundaries (and steps on toes) and involves everybody at different levels and in different ways. It gets into the micro-politics, as well as the macro-politics of the firm.

WHY OPERATIONAL RISK IS DIFFERENT FROM OTHER RISKS

Having accepted that operational risk covers a very wide range of risks, it is worth considering whether it is intrinsically different from other classes of risk. The questionnaire shown in Table 1.2 provides a useful way of approaching this.

Operational risk and other types of risk   Table 1.2

	Operational risk	Credit; market; commodity; liquidity; underwriting and other financial risks
Is the risk wholly transaction-based? Is the risk assumed proactively? Can it be identified from accounting information, e.g. the P&L? Can audit confirm that every occurrence of the risk has been captured? Can its financial impact be capped or limited? Can you trade the risk?		

In a very broad sense, the answers to the risks in the right-hand column will be 'Yes' and those under operational risk will be 'No'. Let's look at them in turn.

Transaction-based

Operational risk obviously occurs each time a transaction is undertaken, but it doesn't depend on transactions for its existence. Before a firm opens its doors and transacts any business, it is exposed to operational risk in the guise of, for example, fire, theft or flood. The right-hand column risks are entirely transaction-based.

Assumed proactively

Practically all financial services are about the assumption and management of risk, whether it is a bank lending money, an insurer underwriting or a dealer trading currencies or bonds. With other types of business, management of credit and liquidity risk, and of market or commodity risk, may be an inevitable part of the business, but not the reason the firm is in business. But as we said earlier, operational risk is essentially unavoidable, whether we like it or not. There are exceptions, such as where a firm takes on another firm's processing under an outsourcing arrangement – for a fee. But generally operational risk is something to be reduced and controlled, rather than actively taken on and increased.

Identified from accounting information

If you look through the various types of operational risk, such as the ones listed in Table 1.1, you will certainly find somewhere in the firm's financial information the financial losses (or profits) which result from them, but you will rarely find one of them listed as a line in the general ledger unless, perhaps, that item is fraud. As a result, it is extremely difficult to obtain accurate information on the costs of operational risk. So, for reporting, we have to rely considerably on human honesty and human reporting, rather than data feeds from the accounting system.

This is another consequence of operational risk not being transaction-based. If it were, innumerable bits of data relating to it could be attached to each transaction and it could be comprehensively assessed, analysed and monitored. But it is not. Nor are all its impacts financial.

Can the occurrence of risk events be audited?

It is certainly possible to audit whether an operational risk loss has been correctly recorded – but only if it has been reported. And it's also possible to do this even for ones which haven't been admitted to – provided the auditors are aware of the incident. But you simply cannot guarantee that all operational loss events have been recorded, whatever a firm's policy may be, short of examining every single debit and credit in the books – a rather futile exercise.

Can limits be put on operational risk?

Rarely, mainly because it is not assumed proactively. With other types of risk, you can limit your exposure to an entity, a currency, a maturity, a geographical area and so on. Operational risk, alas, happens. With internal risks, you seek to mitigate likelihood and impact through controls. You can set thresholds and establish a risk appetite. But for the most part (as we show in Chapter 3, Governance), you are unable to prevent risks having the impact that they do. You are establishing a level of tolerance. With external events that is especially true. You may be able to mitigate their effect, but for the most part you can't prevent their happening. Nor can you limit the force of the hurricane which hits you.

Can you trade operational risk?

Again, unlike the other risks, the answer is no. It is true that catastrophe bonds exist (as we explore in the Alternative risk transfer mechanisms section of Chapter 12, Insurance), but these tend to deal with very specific events, such as damage to property caused by earthquakes or hurricanes within a particular geographical area or radius. They don't purport to cover the range of operational risks.

Rating agencies are taking some steps to assess 'enterprise-wide' risk, which is effectively an assessment of the tone and quality of risk management in a firm. But the gradings are limited and certainly far from being able to support a trading market, even if investors wanted one. Credit and market risk, as people have belatedly discovered, are only too readily tradeable.

Operational risk is universal

The final differences between operational risk and other risk types are that every single person in the firm is responsible for some aspect of the risk and operational risk is involved in every single activity which goes on within the firm. It is everywhere and universal, which is why its management should be a paramount concern for the board and senior executives.

All of the above explains why operational risk is intrinsically different from other risks and therefore needs a different toolset with which to manage it, as we shall see in the operational risk management framework which forms the central part of this book.

CAUSE AND EFFECT

There is one further thought about the nature of operational risk – perhaps of all risks. For most types of risk, an event happens and the result is usually a financial loss – or, rarely and tragically, human loss. And that is what people focus on in trying to decide how better to manage risk in future – the effect. Operational risk classification systems invariably identify particular operational loss events or incidents. But that is not what operational risk management is about. It is about understanding fully the chain of causality, the simple sequence of:

CAUSE → EVENT → EFFECT (OR CONSEQUENCE)

Whilst operational risk management is about managing events, it does so through preventative controls and indicators to manage their causes and through detective controls and actions to mitigate their effects. Too often in operational risk management, including in the Basel Accords, causes and effects are confused with events, and people base their risk mitigation on events, rather than on causes. Cause is one of the major concerns of operational risk management. Analysing causes is the best way to prevent operational risk events from happening.

We can see the linkages of the chain by looking at some recent examples from non-financial sector events (see Table 1.3). They provide an interesting catalogue, which again also shows the wide range of operational risk.

Another important element of causal analysis lies in risk interconnectedness. The World Economic Forum publishes an annual Global Risks Interconnection Map.[13] Apart from showing the connections between different risks, it also highlights the systemic nature of many risks. If you apply a similar methodology to your own firm's operational risks, you may well find that a risk which on its own appears not to be especially significant, is in fact a major node, so that if it occurs it can cause a range of other risk events and change your view of the key risks facing your firm and their priority.

The exercise also highlights the simple fact that a risk event can have a number of causes and can give rise to a number of different effects or outcomes, whilst a single cause can trigger a number of different risk events. The chain of causality and its risk management is another important theme in this book.

MEASUREMENT AND MANAGEMENT OF OPERATIONAL RISK

The events in Table 1.3 and those described at the beginning of the chapter highlight one of the problems of operational risk – the sheer range of risks which it covers and the fact that, depending on how it is defined, it often straddles a number of them, rather than being a discrete risk in its own right. The simple fact of 'cause' is another reason why a relatively homogeneous measurement system does not work.

Given the importance of cause and behaviour, as well as the nature of the risks it covers, it is probable that a truly scientific approach to operational risk measurement would probably have to encompass professionals as various as economists (of many shades), engineers, social scientists, behavioural scientists, futurologists and crystal ball gazers, as well as a variety of different types of mathematician. If it is a science at all (as opposed to an art), operational risk is a social rather than a purely mathematical science. When we look at the mathematical aspects, data is thin where it is most needed, i.e. for rare, high-impact events. Probability estimates for operational risk are inevitably affected by behavioural rather than technical factors and, indeed, a major loss will cause behavioural changes and changes to controls which will render past experience less relevant as a guide to the future. There are no groundhog days in operational risk.

The chain of causality and some major operational risk events　　　　Table 1.3

Year	Cause	Event	Effect/consequence
1986	Dangerous design of reactor and control rods; unauthorised changes to procedures; inadequate safety culture.	Chernobyl nuclear reactor disaster	Severe release of radioactivity (four times Hiroshima bomb) across Russia and Europe (60% in Belarus); evacuation and resettlement of 336,000 people; probable 4000 additional deaths from cancer.
1991	Over-dominant chief; complexity and lack of transparency in organisation; lack of internal controls; failure to act on warning signals; inadequate auditing; fraud.	Collapse of Maxwell Communications	Hundreds of millions of pounds stolen from exployees' pension funds of Maxwell companies.
2001	Rise of Islamic fundamentalism; failure of intelligence; inadequate air defence systems; lax airport security.	World Trade Center (9/11) terrorist attack	3000 deaths in World Trade Center; destruction of WTC 1 and 2; second Iraq war; global security crackdown.
2003	New and highly contagious form of atypical pneumonia.	SARS near-pandemic in 37 countries	Air travel restricted; quarantine; disinfectant arrangements.

▶

Year	Cause	Event	Effect/consequence
2003	Failure of alarm system; failure to trim trees which put high-voltage power lines out of service.	NE USA power failure	11 power stations in NE USA offline, affecting 55 million people; water contamination; transport and communications disrupted.
2005	Failure to maintain levees, as contingency against a potentially severe hurricane, allowed water from Lake Pontchartrain to flow into New Orleans. Repeat of flood disasters of 1915, 1947 and 1965.	Hurricane Katrina	Over 1800 deaths; 80% of New Orleans flooded; damage estimated at more than $100bn.
2011	Tropical storm Nock-ten generated the worst flooding experienced by Thailand during its monsoon season, persisting in some areas for four months until January 2012. The effects of the flooding also reflected excessive concentration risk in the sourcing of components for the global automobile and computer industries.	Floods in Thailand	In Thailand, there were 815 deaths, over 20,000 square kilometres of farmland were damaged and seven major industrial estates were inundated. Beyond Thailand, the floods created serious disruption to manufacturing supply chains, which affected regional automobile production and caused a global shortage of hard disk drives which lasted throughout 2012.

Measurement of operational risk has been driven within financial services by the need to ascribe a capital number to it. The events of the financial crisis show how dangerous it is when people believe that there is a mathematically precise answer to the risk problem they have posed – when people place a misguided trust in numbers as a basis, or even a substitute, for rational decision making. Risk management has been in danger of being treated as a kind of alchemy – but the philosopher's stone has not been found, nor will it be. If that is true of the relatively homogeneous, data-rich environments of credit and market risk, how much truer is it in the heterogeneous, data-poor environment of operational risk. As Leibnitz once wrote to his friend Jacob Bernoulli, uncle to Daniel, in 1703, 'A finite number of experiments will always be too small a sample for an exact calculation of nature's intentions'.[14] Nature's intentions are frequently the subject of operational risk.

Operational risk requires a new kind of management and data collection which moves away from existing norms of risk management, especially with regard to low-frequency/high-impact events, which should be its prime concern. Operational risk, and indeed other forms of risk management, should be encouraging managers to open their eyes and ears to other forms of data – information is a much better word – than the purely numeric, even as far as gossip and casual comment. That goes further against the basic laws of probability which demand independent, objective observations of homogeneous events, a long way away from the world of operational risk. Having said that, even actuaries will admit to using quantitative frameworks to structure their 'guesses'.[15] Quantitative analysis undoubtedly has its place, but the actuaries are applying intelligent risk management, which is what this book is all about.

CHALLENGES OF OPERATIONAL RISK MANAGEMENT

Operational risk is a young discipline. It is the softest of risks, difficult to grasp, yet only too familiar. Establishing an effective operational risk management framework in a firm is not easy and open to many challenges. Let us look at some of them.

Getting the board on board

The first task, and the critical one, is to get the board to agree to take operational risk management seriously and for senior management and the board to be involved in devising an operational risk management policy.

If, as we believe in this book, operational risk is effectively business risk, including strategic and reputation risks, it should be an integral part of business strategy and management, the board's primary responsibility. One of the dangers is for operational risk to deal only with internal process risks or to become merely a reporting rather than a management function.

For operational risk management to be effective, it needs to be embraced by everybody and to be integral to all the business decisions made by a firm. That is not to say that it's about risk avoidance. It is about risk assessment and the opportunities which can flow from that. As we say repeatedly in this book, for that or any other approach to be embedded in the firm, it needs to be led and sponsored from the top. And if the board is not sure it is worth it, perhaps they can be asked to read Chapter 2, The business case for operational risk management.

Getting buy-in throughout the firm

Understanding and explaining the benefits of good operational risk management is probably the best way to get buy-in throughout the firm. Because operational risk involves every activity in the firm from the strategic to the minutiae of operational activities, it needs to be embraced by everybody. At an Institute of Internal Auditors conference in September 2008, Professor Mervyn King, chair of South Africa's King Committee on corporate governance, made the pertinent point,

> If you get buy-in you can achieve extraordinary things. But if you don't get buy-in you won't even achieve the ordinary. It's alright to talk about tone at the top, but I like to think about the tune in the middle.

It is the response of everybody in the firm which will make operational risk management effective.

Risk and control assessments and scenario analysis, for instance, will be effective only if they involve people who are at the sharp end of a firm's activities, whether they are customer-facing, part of the support systems or on the board. The more people who are involved in the assessment process and can see practical results and benefits, the more buy-in there will be. They also need to see that they are not wasting their time. If we throw them hundreds of so-called key risk indicators, we are giving indicators a bad name. Which risks are truly key? What are the best indicators which relate to them? Get it down to a workable number of key risk indicators which staff can monitor and use. Likewise with reporting thresholds. We do need to gather information down to a low level, but we have to balance the costs of comprehensive and voluminous reporting with the benefits, and concentrate on the information which best tells us what we need to know.

Operational risk events are very often the results of people failures (see Chapter 15, Culture and people risk). That is why, in Chapter 5, Risk and control assessment, we concentrate on both the design and performance of controls. The design is all about the system and process. The performance of a control is usually about people. If all staff are not engaged, controls will fail and the costs of that can be considerable.

Buy-in comes from communication, especially communicating why we are doing what we do. Why do we assess both inherent and residual risks? After all, the 'reds' amongst the inherent or gross risks tell us where we're most likely to have a disaster. They may, but the chances are that you are doing something about them. So you need to find out and constantly monitor how effective the controls you have in place are to bring them down to an acceptable residual or net level. Explaining and communicating why we are doing what we do in operational risk management means that management becomes clear in its own mind and that other staff will understand the purpose and benefits. That way, we shall achieve real buy-in.

In addition, of course, buy-in can extend beyond the firm. If there are critical third-party dependencies, perhaps agents, sub-contractors or outsourcing suppliers, they need to be part of the communication network and embrace the firm's operational risk standards.

It's common sense, or what we do every day

Operational risk is present in everything we do. It's what we have to cope with all the time, whether as business managers or as individuals. We are all risk managers. And because we do it every day, and are here to tell the tale, we are patently doing it well. We may be. But how do we know? And could we do even better?

There is no great mystery to operational risk management. The fundamentals of identifying, assessing, managing and mitigating risk to an agreed level of risk appetite, are the same in all risk management activity. But if we establish a coherent framework for management, we will understand why some risks are being controlled successfully and where we can put our resources to best use.

Why colours and not numbers?

If it's risk, it must be a number. And, indeed, there's a view that if it isn't a number, you can't manage it. Numbers, even if they are spurious, give the comfort of certainty – dangerously so if they are spuriously accurate. They help to prioritise and focus actions, but it can be unhelpful to go for unjustified precision. The financial crisis of 2007–9 showed, amongst other things, the dangers of relying on numbers whose limitations were not understood.

There are many numbers in operational risk, losses being the most painful ones. But operational risk is not about management by numbers. It is about managing people and circumstances which are constantly changing and where judgements, even when based as far as possible on hard evidence, are necessarily subjective. That's one argument for colours (or words) in operational risk reports, rather than apparently precise numbers.

The other one is that numbers are not as accessible as colours and good operational risk management happens as a result of good communication. In almost every chapter of the framework we show reports which owe their accessibility to the fact that they use colours to tell the story. A picture tells a thousand words. In operational risk, a colour tells a thousand numbers.

So why model it, then?

The answer to that depends on what you expect a model to do. There is often too little thought given to why and how models (and reports for that matter) are being constructed, and how they will be used. In operational risk, a model should be seen as a framework for a conversation. It might even give you the right question, rather than the correct answer. After all, for the most part we are trying to model our ignorance.

At the outset of an operational risk management programme, there will be little hard data on which to model. Even when the programme has been running well for some time, the data is always going to be incomplete and probably imperfect. So what's the point of trying to turn it into something it is not? The answer is that, despite its limitations, modelling can probably get you in the right ballpark, even if it's not an exact science. In operational risk, modelling may not provide the perfect answer, but it can provide a good answer – provided you understand what you're getting.

How can you set a risk appetite for operational risk?

Perhaps the quickest answer is to turn to Chapter 4, Operational risk appetite. Unfortunately, operational risk is not like *The Hitchhiker's Guide to the Galaxy* where fans will remember that the Answer to the Ultimate Question of Life, the Universe and Everything is 42. In operational risk, risk appetite may be a finite number but, because of the range of operational risks and the unavoidability of many, appetite can just as well be expressed in a statement of policy, or by using coloured assessments, or through a range of indicators. So you can set a risk appetite, but there will be different ways of doing it, depending on the risks involved. And remember – setting an appetite will not prevent an operational risk actually happening.

Reporting

The first challenge is to set up a system and a culture in which reporting of events and 'near misses' is what we do, rather than what we try not to do. We will report events, because everybody in the firm accepts and understands that it is only by comprehensive reporting that we can understand what is actually happening; understand what major incident may threaten; and pursue a policy of continuous improvement. If you look at most disasters, whether financial or non-financial, you will find that they generally owe their origin to human frailty of one form or another, of which the most dangerous is the failure to learn. The evidence is all around us, but we choose to ignore it and not to learn the lessons. And another disaster strikes. Intelligent operational risk management demands that we see and analyse the evidence and learn from it.

Once the data is gathered, the next challenge is to ensure that reports up and down the organisation are meaningful and useful; that they highlight the key risks the firm is facing and that reporting of risks, near misses, indicators and so forth is coordinated. Effective reporting should also involve causal analysis so that we can understand what really happened and can work out what to do to control our risks better. All reports, and all the information in them, should lead to action. If a report is not intended to lead to action, drop it.

Just give me the manual

If it were that easy, this book would not be necessary. Unfortunately, it isn't that easy. For a start, as we said earlier, what you mean by operational risk is entirely up to you. In this book we can give you a framework to manage, but only you can decide what it is you are trying to manage. Only you can decide what your risk appetite is. Only you can establish the culture of control – or relative lack of control – in which you wish to operate. Each firm is different; each firm faces different risks; each firm will treat each aspect of operational risk management in a unique way.

And because of the infinite variety of operational risk, there is no universal answer to how to manage it in every case. Indeed, if operational risk is as broad as business risk, it's logical to suggest that there are as many ways of managing operational risk as there are of running a business. There is no universal list of operational risks which applies to everybody. Nor is there a universal list of indicators. Risks are emerging all the time, just as they may recede or disappear as systems, the business or the external environment changes. Even if the list remains constant, the ranking of each risk will be constantly changing.

So there is no standard manual. And even if you write a manual of operational risk controls, processes and reporting procedures, it will be constantly evolving. If operational risk is managed intelligently, it demands constant re-evaluation both of the risks and their controls. It is not a one-off exercise which can be put away for a year, or even more frequently, until it comes up again in the diary. It is part of the everyday process of management, for which a procedures manual is not the answer. It needs to be in the blood.

INTRODUCING THE FRAMEWORK

Having overcome the challenges, it is time to put a management framework in place. As we said above, there may not be a manual which fits every firm, but a framework provides a structure for implementing and embedding operational risk management. Without a coherent framework you simply cannot get to first base.

The framework described in Chapters 3–10 is simple, succinct and straightforward. It covers the six major processes involved in operational risk management, from which any others can be derived. It represents a system which can be understood from the boardroom to the post-room. If there is clarity about what operational risk management entails, there is likely to be an effective and accepted implementation which can then reap the business benefits described in Chapter 2.

The operational risk management framework we use in this book is given in Figure 1.2. It sits within an overall operational risk environment, where each component interacts with the others to build the whole.

Figure 1.2   **Operational risk management framework**

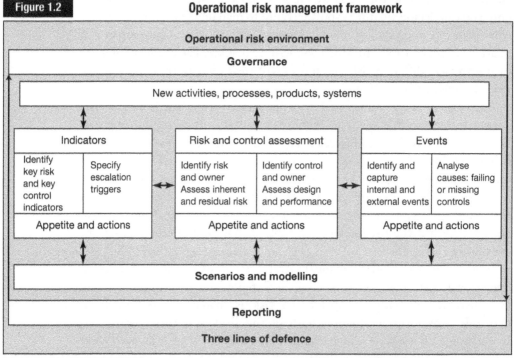

Source: Courtesy of Chase Cooper Limited

Before we get to the chapters where each element is dealt with in detail, it would be good to consider them briefly. Governance (Chapter 3) is the first step in operational risk management. Good governance, through a board approved operational risk policy and appropriate terms of reference for relevant individuals and committees, will ensure that the board and all staff have a clear view of the board's strategy and objectives and of their respon-sibilities. Governance will also involve establishing the principles and main elements of the operational risk management framework.

The other essential to good governance is to ensure that appropriate reports (Chapter 8) are generated to enable everybody from the board down to understand the operational risks to which they are exposed at any one time. Reports on risk should be linked to relevant controls and actions, so that recipients can use them to remedy control failures, review risk appetite and perhaps remove controls. Good reports mean action. They demonstrate a firm's commitment to using operational risk management to enhance the firm's business decisions and continuously improve its performance.

The key to good reporting is to tailor it to the needs of the reader – at every level. Neither governance nor reporting is something which is solely about the board. That is why we use the term 'governance', rather than the board or similar, at the top of the framework. Operational risk management involves everybody. It is not hierarchical.

Having established the environment, we can now move to the engine room of risk and control assessment, recording events and near misses and establishing and monitoring key indicators. Risk and control assessment (Chapter 5) is often the first operational risk management process carried out by an organisation. Initial assessments will almost always be subjective, but even then they can be of significant business value if they are linked to the firm's strategic objectives. As assessments progress and are linked to events and indicators they become more objective. However, a continued focus on the business objectives will help to ensure their relevance, as well as buy-in and use at all levels.

Losses (Chapter 6) often appear to lie at the heart of data-gathering for operational risk. Losses are of little use unless they are analysed to identify causes. Operational risk is about management. Understanding the causes of risk means that you can manage the risks themselves. Merely knowing their number and size is of relatively little value. Finally, within the engine room, indicators (Chapter 7) are invaluable management tools at every level of the organisation, provided they are concentrated on key risks and key controls.

If you look closely at Figure 1.2, you will see that each of the boxes headed Indicators, Risk and control assessment, and Events has, at the bottom, the words 'Appetite and actions'. The framework is a framework for management. It is only worth doing if it leads to management action.

This brings us to scenarios and modelling. Scenarios, of which stress tests are one aspect, are a practical and accessible way of assessing operational risks which, by their nature, are at the far end of the scale of both likelihood and impact. As with most operational risk processes and data, scenarios have to be handled with care (as is shown in Chapter 10). But because they rely on stories involving the real world of work, they can be a powerful means of involving staff and of getting buy-in. Stress tests and scenarios are themselves one aspect of modelling. As we shall see in Chapter 9, all the elements we have discussed in this section can be used in modelling and add significantly to the business benefits which can be derived. Good modelling, using risk and control assessments, for instance, can assist in a cost–benefit analysis of the controls used by a firm and the allocation of resources to new or improved controls.

But before we go into the detail of the framework, we need to get buy-in. Buy-in comes from showing that operational risk management really does add business benefit, which is the subject of the next chapter.

Notes

1 HM Government, *A strong Britain in an age of uncertainty – The National Security Strategy*, Cmd 7953, October 2010.
2 OECD, *Principles of Corporate Governance*, 2004. An index of all codes of corporate governance around the world can be found on the website of the European Corporate Governance Institute at www.ecgi.org/codes/all_codes.php
3 BS31100 Code of Practice for Risk Management.
4 Frank Knight, *Risk, Uncertainty and Profit* (1921; reprinted, Dover Books, 2009).
5 Bank for International Settlements, Basel II: *International Convergence of Capital Measurement and Capital Standards: A Revised Framework – Comprehensive Version*, June 2006.
6 RMA, British Bankers' Association, ISDA, PricewaterhouseCoopers, *Operational risk – The next frontier*, 1999. The original definition read: 'The risk of direct or indirect loss resulting from inadequate or failed processes, people and systems, and from external events.'
7 Basel II, Annex 9.
8 Basel II, para 644.
9 See www.csfi.org for CSFI's various Banana Skin surveys.
10 Michael Power, *Organized Uncertainty* (Oxford: Oxford University Press), 2009, p. 126.
11 Risk and Insurance Management Society; www.rims.org/ERM
12 Jeremy Grant and Michael Mackenzie, 'Ghost in the machine', *Financial Times*, 18 February 2010.
13 http://www.weforum.org/reports/global-risks-2012-seventh-edition
14 Quoted in Peter L. Bernstein, *Against the Gods* (New York: John Wiley & Sons), 1998, p. 118.
15 Ericson, R, Doyle, A and Barry, D, *Insurance as Governance* (Toronto: Toronto University Press), 2003, quoted in Power, p. 13.

2

The business case for operational risk management

GETTING MANAGEMENT'S ATTENTION

If you want to make the case for operational risk to senior management, you need to get their attention. That means talking to their agenda, in other words understanding and addressing their needs. Good operational risk management is fundamentally about informed decision making. If your decision making is better informed, your decisions are very likely to be better. Some of the fundamental elements of informed decision making with respect to operational risk management are:

- understanding the operational risk context of decisions (which is part of governance, see Chapter 3)
- differentiating which risks you are prepared to accept at what level through considering your risk appetite, see Chapter 4
- distinguishing and differentiating your operational risks and how they are controlled (which is part of risk and control assessment, see Chapter 5)
- evaluating and assessing problems in the past (which is part of loss causal analysis, see Chapter 6)
- knowing where you are now (which is part of indicator analysis, see Chapter 7)
- knowing where you might be in the future (which is part of scenario analysis, see Chapter 10)
- allocating capital on an operational risk basis (which is part of modelling, see Chapter 9)
- getting the right information on past events, the present state of the operational risk environment and its possible future state (which is part of reporting, see Chapter 8).

The alternative, of poor operational risk management, will almost certainly lead to the business dying – either slowly or suddenly because of a major operational risk event.

Good operational risk management will also help to instil a culture of continuous improvement and business optimisation. There are a number of links between operational risk management, business optimisation and Six Sigma and Lean management techniques which we will explore later in this chapter (and which are also part of the business outcome from modelling operational risk, see Chapter 9).

OPERATIONAL RISK MANAGEMENT AS A MARKETING TOOL

An additional benefit of operational risk management is as a marketing tool. A good example of this is Volvo which has turned safety into a marketing and sales opportunity. Safety is an attribute which is expected by the motoring public to be built into its cars, as it is an excellent mitigant of a number of motoring risks. However, Volvo has very successfully managed to use an inevitable risk control as a marketing and sales differentiator.

Similarly, in the financial services sector, many firms go beyond the regulatory requirements for the reporting of operational risk within their reports and accounts. The Basel Committee on Banking Supervision, in its Accord published in 2004,[1] aimed to raise standards in banking, in part through increased transparency of reporting. One of the three pillars of Basel II was the disclosure of information about the bank's risk management. However, the regulatory disclosure requirements for operational risk were minimal compared with those for credit risk. It is clear that firms perceive a competitive advantage in making it clear to any reader that they identify, measure, monitor and manage their operational risks thoroughly and so many go into some detail explaining what they do. Where would you rather deposit your money: in a firm which is making a concerted effort in its operational risk management, or a firm which is unable or unwilling to articulate what it does?

International and national accounting rules, and business review rules in the UK, have also joined the trend by requiring increasing disclosure of risk in the annual report and accounts. All of these are designed to bring risk management out into the open. But, again, many firms go beyond the minimum standards and a 'boilerplate' approach and see marketing gain from what was initially viewed as a tedious and oppressive necessity.

BENEFITS OF GETTING OPERATIONAL RISK MANAGEMENT RIGHT

Benefits of getting operational risk governance right

Understanding the context within which operational risk decisions are made is a fundamental element of informed decision making. Good operational risk governance in the business will give increased comfort to the board and senior management that risks which impact on the business objectives are being managed effectively. Good governance provides greater assurance on the effectiveness of internal controls.

Clear operational risk governance is the base for developing an effective and consistent operational risk management framework. It will clarify:

■ the operational risk policy of the firm and ensure that the board approved risk appetite is aligned with its business policy and objectives

■ risk and control ownership and accountability, thus reducing oversights and duplication of effort.

Operational risk is a potential threat to the objectives of the firm. Given that the management of the firm should be driven by its objectives, a better understanding of operational risk will force clarity in the objectives and help to embed better operational risk management within the firm.

However, good operational risk management is as much about opportunities as threats. This means that, for every risk, the opportunities which are implicit in the risk should be explored, as well as the threats to the firm. Intelligent operational risk management enables a firm to exploit risk for its benefit, as well as protecting itself from the risks which are not exploitable.

Good operational risk governance, though, is not only about the existing business and risk environment of the firm. It should mean that discussions about new products, initiatives and business lines include the operational risks inherent in them. If not, major strategic decisions will be taken which are not fully informed.

Benefits of getting operational risk appetite right

It is easy to say that a certain level of risk is inherent in any business. It is nevertheless true. Operational risk appetite statements recognise that there is a trade-off between the amount of operational risk to which a firm wishes to be subject and the returns and costs involved in that level of risk. This involves recognition that financial risks and non-financial risks (such as operational risk) are fundamentally different. It is common (although misguided) to hear a board say that it has no appetite whatsoever for operational risk. Not only does the board have different levels of appetite for business as usual risk and unexpected losses, but other stakeholders have sometimes drastically different levels of appetite for the same operational risks.

The statement of operational risk appetite through capital, risk or indicator measures forces an acceptance that operational risk appetite cannot be easily cascaded down from the board, in contrast to financial risks such as market risk and credit risk. A far clearer understanding of operational risk by the board results from this type of consideration of operational risk appetite. This extends to senior management and assists in the acceptance of accountability for operational risk by the business lines. Regular consideration of a firm's operational risk profile against its operational risk appetite embeds good operational risk management and leads to appropriate mitigating actions being taken, in line with the operational risk appetite.

Benefits of getting risk and control assessment right

It is vital to be aware of your operational risks and the controls that mitigate them. The ability to robustly identify, measure, manage and mitigate the operational risks to which the firm is subject, within a defined and clear structure of risk and control assessment, leads to consistent treatment and reporting of risk across the firm. Comprehensive and consistent information about the level of risk within the firm is clearly essential for the board and senior management to make informed business decisions.

An agreed methodology of risk and control assessment, which is applied across the firm, will also help to bring about a cultural change towards embedding operational risk management within the firm. This assists both senior management and those responsible for managing risk on a day-to-day basis within the business line. Clear assessment criteria will also help to ensure consistent and stable measurement of risk (see Chapter 5).

Risk and control assessments enable you to identify potential risk hotspots and control bottlenecks quickly. They also allow the firm to model operational risk, without having to wait for a number of years to gather accurate and complete operational loss data (see Chapter 9). Risk and control assessments are a simple way of getting the benefits of operational risk management early.

Benefits of getting event and loss capture and analysis right

Learning from previous operational risk problems is a fundamental part of operational risk event analysis. Significant benefit can accrue from identifying the controls which have failed and the subsequent risk events which have happened. This is whether or not an actual loss has been incurred, or indeed a profit has been made. It is common for the same control to have been found to have failed in several parts of the firm. If this information is not captured, no one will connect the incidents together. Nor will they pick up small losses which, repeated a number of times, perhaps in different places, can add up to a much bigger figure.

Reliable loss data can be used as a form of back-testing for operational risk exposure, for instance by identifying data gaps in the risk and control assessments. Risks and their associated control failures, which are detected in the event analysis, should appear in the relevant risk and control assessment as high residual risks and as poor controls – unless, of course, the firm has been going through a period of bad luck!

Comprehensive and consistent capture of events and losses will also aid loss causal analysis by providing a reliable set of data from which to draw tentative conclusions. It will highlight any gaps in the data and show potentially high-loss areas. All sources of operational risk data will be recorded which may show gaps in the risk and control assessment programme.

Modelling benefits a firm through the use of objective (as well as subjective) data, as the losses and events are what have actually happened to the firm. Real events also help to validate the indicators discussed next.

However, loss data is based in the past and future losses are just that: based in the future.

Benefits of getting indicators right

Having analysed the data from the past, it is important to look at where you are now. Indicators provide this information and, in particular, changes to the risk profiles of the firm. Indicators allow the firm to monitor its risks and controls in a way which allows trends to be identified quickly and action to be taken promptly.

Indicators also allow a firm to measure its exposure against its risk appetite, which can be set in terms of indicators. This enables financial resources to be targeted on those areas which will provide the business with the most benefit. Indicators facilitate the setting of realistic and achievable improvement targets to enhance controls and reduce risk.

By monitoring indicators of key risks, the firm may be able to identify oversights and duplication of effort. This will be achieved through being able to evaluate the risk and control environment, monitoring outstanding improvement actions and reviewing the performance of risk owners.

Benefits of getting scenario analysis right

Just as risk and control assessments look to the future, so scenario analysis helps explore alternative extreme, but nevertheless plausible, possible outcomes for a firm. In particular, scenario analysis allows the exploration of the risk and control sensitivities of the firm. It clarifies the interactions of the risks by examining them under stress conditions. It also helps to shed light on the causal relationships between the risks themselves and between controls and risks.

By creating risk and control data points which are outside the firm's usual experience, scenarios compensate for the subjective nature of risk and control assessments and for the lack of internal loss data, which is a frequent problem for firms when assessing their operational risks. Likelihood and impact assumptions are tested by subjecting them to extreme conditions. Similarly, control design and performance assumptions are tested.

Scenarios are an excellent means of getting senior management attention; as a result, they can frequently lead to a reinvigoration of the risk and control assessment process. This is because scenarios should be performed by the senior management team as a whole, so that a complete and realistic review of their effects can be obtained. Scenarios also help senior management to move away from a historic risk management approach, towards a serious consideration of how the firm may look in the future.

Benefits of getting modelling right

Allocating operational risk capital on a risk adjusted basis is a powerful incentive for senior management to manage its operational risks well. Implementing this leading practice in operational risk management also allows the firm to monitor more accurately its exposure against the expressed operational risk appetite of the board, as both exposure and appetite can be expressed in monetary terms.

Modelling allows the possibility of reducing a regulatory operational risk capital charge where this is applicable. A number of modelling approaches are discussed in Chapter 9. The use of an integrated approach to modelling (combining losses with qualitative data) can assist the business in forecasting future losses objectively. The scorecard approach allows the firm to target its resources and controls based on cost–benefit analysis.

Once an operational risk model has been established, operational risk costs can be incorporated into a pricing model. This is often either ignored or forgotten, leading to a lack of understanding of the true costs of a transaction or product to a firm and pricing which can ultimately be ruinous. Many firms in the financial services industry learned this to their disadvantage during the 2007–8 sub-prime crisis. Although this was seen as a credit risk event, it was fundamentally fuelled by the operational risk of failing to understand the relatively complex securitisation products which were used.

Benefits of getting reporting right

Good operational risk reporting allows the firm to develop a common operational risk language which in turn allows operational risk related activity to be conducted on a like-for-like basis. Detailed operational risk management activity can be prioritised, based on consistent scoring across the firm. Good operational risk reporting will also generate management involvement and consensus, which will drive the ongoing identification, assessment and control of operational risk.

Senior management monitoring of operational risk performance will challenge the results of operational risk management activity and further embed the firm's approach to operational risk management. Risk ownership and control ownership can be clarified through good reporting and assist in identifying priorities for enhancing controls and the firm's operational risk profile.

BENEFITS BEYOND THE FRAMEWORK

The benefits of good operational risk management do not just lie in the framework processes. There are also specific aspects of operational risk management which we deal with in later chapters: mitigants to operational risk such as business continuity and insurance; specific risks such as outsourcing risk, people risk and reputation risk.

Business continuity

The benefit of a robust, tested and up-to-date business continuity plan should be self-evident. Fundamentally, it is about survival. Business continuity, or indeed any contingency arrangement, is an essential tool of operational risk mitigation and uses the processes of operational risk in its creation and activation: risk assessment, scenarios and indicators. Just as with any other part of operational risk management, business continuity helps you identify your vulnerabilities. As we shall see in Chapter 11, you need to make sure that you are a survivor. The stakes can be that high in getting business continuity right. And, of course, if you can get back in business quickly, especially if an event occurs which affects both you and your competitors, you will have an immediate competitive advantage. Not having an adequate plan can mean permanent loss of market share or loss of staff and the difficulty and expense of recruiting replacements.

A good business continuity plan might even mean that you can negotiate a reduction in your business interruption policy premium, a point which we pick up next.

Insurance

The fundamental benefit of insurance is, of course, risk transfer at an appropriate cost. Operational risk is the flip-side of commercial insurance since, for the most part, commercial insurance – property, key man, product liability, public liability, directors' and officers' insurance – is there to cover operational risk.

Without an effective operational risk management system in place, it is impossible to assess whether a particular insurance is appropriate, let alone whether the premium represents good value. With a good operational risk reporting process, however, the insured should have the bargaining chips, especially given that insurers are able to spread their risks and so make the deal attractive. Good operational risk information will also enable a firm to decide whether to insure through a captive (as discussed in Chapter 12), which can improve the financial benefits even more.

Outsourcing

Outsourcing is another example where good operational risk management is also good business management. If outsourcing is managed correctly, as we show in Chapter 14, it has the huge advantage of placing the outsourced activity and its associated risks in the hands of somebody who can perform them more efficiently than you: a good example, too, of operational risk management being about opportunities and not just threats.

Outsourcing should enable higher transaction levels, improved speed and quality of customer service and improved financial controls – another aspect of improved operational risk management. And, of course, it should reduce costs and improve profitability. But the primary aim, and most significant benefit, is to make the business and its risk management more efficient.

People risk

As we explain in Chapter 15, our people are not just a firm's greatest asset, but can potentially be its greatest source of operational risk liability. Good people risk management is a fundamental part of good operational risk management. It encourages an environment in which risks are reported, so that lessons can be learned – an environment of continuous improvement. A good people environment will also be one where people are open to change and are able to respond flexibly and quickly to business opportunities, as well as to threats to the business. With good operational risk management in place, people can genuinely become a firm's greatest asset.

Reputation risk

Reputation risk can seriously damage your health and wealth. Since reputation risk almost always results from the occurrence of an operational risk event, it follows that good operational risk management is a vital part of good reputation risk management. If you can prevent a risk happening, you will have no reputation risk to deal with. And if you are the only one of your competitors to have avoided the risk, your reputation will inevitably be enhanced. In Chapter 16 we show some of the many ways in which reputation can be harmed, but we also explain how operational risk management can reduce the chances of reputation risk occurring, as well as how to deal with a reputational crisis if it should occur. The costs of failure and the rewards of success are immeasurable.

BUSINESS OPTIMISATION

Operational risk management is not just about avoiding losses or reducing their effect. It is also about finding opportunities for business benefit and continuous improvement. As we mentioned (in the introduction to this chapter), operational risk management can be used as the groundwork for Six Sigma and Lean management approaches, as shown in Figure 2.1. The just-in-time method of management relies on properly identifying, measuring, monitoring and managing supply chain risks which are part of the universe of operational risk. Additionally, quality circles rely on full and informed operational risk management, as does total quality management.

Figure 2.1   **Interaction of operational risk management and Six Sigma and Lean management approaches**

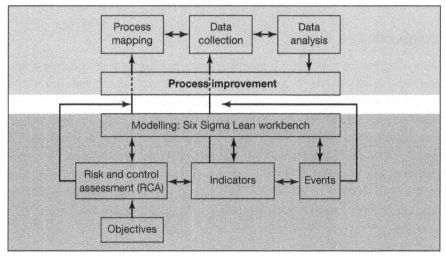

Source: Courtesy of Chase Cooper Limited

The concepts of process improvement and business optimisation are fundamental parts of operational risk management and Six Sigma gives a structured approach. The Six Sigma themes of focus on the customer, of fact-driven proactive management and of unwelcome variations in a process are wholly compatible with good operational risk management and many would argue are, indeed, the same themes as pervade operational risk management. Further, the Six Sigma starting point of process mapping can be very useful to operational risk management and gives business benefit in its own right.

Six Sigma and operational risk management compared

As can be seen from Figure 2.2, the Six Sigma process is iterative both overall and within each pair of stages. In addition, if any stage does not work, the next step in the process is to go back to the previous stage. This forms part of the rigour of the Six Sigma approach. Not only is each stage closely evaluated, but the practitioner/team must repeat the stage using new ideas and solutions if the evaluation does not produce adequate results. This iterative approach seeks to ensure that changes made to business processes have the best chance of delivering the desired positive impact and that the change represents the best return in terms of the improvement achieved.

The overall Six Sigma process

Figure 2.2

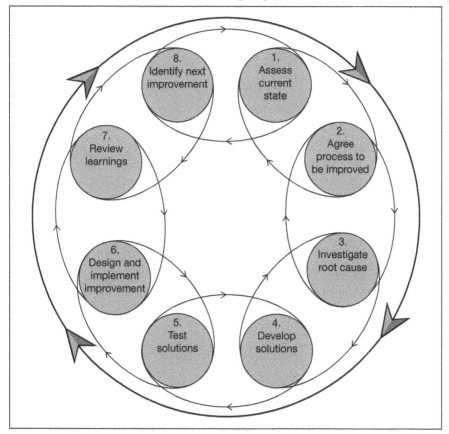

1. Assess current state

As with all stages in the Six Sigma process, this stage has a business focus. The first two stages are to prioritise the process to be improved. This is achieved in the first stage by identifying problems and gaps, and the most pressing needs in the firm. Typically, management workshops are held and affinity charts and interrelationship diagrams are created as a result of brainstorming. The analysis of these results provides insight on which strategic areas will most benefit from improvement. Initially, often six to eight strategic areas emerge that the firm wishes to improve immediately.

The equivalent stage in operational risk management is to identify and assess risks and controls (through a risk and control assessment) and to identify indicators and their thresholds.

2. Agree process to be improved

From the areas identified, the process to be improved can be chosen. Often this is driven by business requirements. Alternatively, there are links between processes such that an improvement to one process can have a beneficial effect on a number of processes. For example, an improvement to the customer take-on process resulting in clearer customer documentation may also improve client liaison, client reporting and client complaint handling. If such an 'upstream' process can be identified, clearly this is a high-priority area. Such an exercise will also aid awareness of the 'downstream' effects of any process improvements. The current performance of the process to be improved is also documented using control charts for the process output over time, so that the improvements can be recognised. This also assists in generating awareness of the scale of the problem, and possibly a target performance level.

The equivalent operational risk stage is to compare the operational risk appetite with the current state using the risk and control assessment and the indicator thresholds from Stage 1.

3. Investigate root cause

Theories as to the root cause of the problem are initially identified through consensus work and workshops, and then through the use of tools, such as cause and effect diagrams, histograms and scatter diagrams. Hypothesis testing may be used and standard statistical tests, such as equal variance analysis, are also key to this stage.

Data is collected to support the root cause analysis and, by using the tools, strong correlations are sought that point to which cause should be addressed as a priority. Root causes are regarded as relevant when the testing shows that the variation within the process (attributed to the proposed root cause) is statistically significant and not the result of natural variation. Note that only one cause at a time is chosen to be improved, otherwise improvement results can be confused due to an inability to apportion the improvements to the relevant root cause.

The equivalent operational risk management stage is event causal analysis, although there may be very few events relating to the particular process. However, such causal analysis will help significantly with the Six Sigma root cause analysis.

4. Develop solutions

In order to develop solutions, this stage of the Six Sigma process will utilise workshops to determine the links to controls and other processes for the identified root causes. Cause and solution diagrams may also be utilised.

This stage also tends to develop further relationships between causes, controls and processes which themselves may point towards solutions. The solutions generated are then prioritised for testing.

Action plans resulting from event causal analysis, and from appetite analysis using risk and control assessments and indicators are the operational risk equivalents of Stage 4.

5. Test solutions

Taking the most promising solution generated in the previous stage, controlled experiments are run to evaluate the impact of the solution. This stage also begins to determine the appropriate implementation of the solution, assuming that it delivers the required improvement/impact.

The modelling of action plans, including modelling of qualitative data, is the operational risk management equivalent of Stage 5.

6. Design and implement improvement

This stage in the Six Sigma process revolves around how to apply the validated change, including items such as: training; implementation and assessment of the pilot; the definition of how the change may be considered to be successful; and involving the business to set a success target (if one has not been already set). Once the pilot is successful, a permanent solution is then put in place, including data collection to show that the improvement continues and has become business as usual.

The equivalent in operational risk is completing action plans, designing new controls and indicators and checking to see if the reduction in risk or improvement in controls expected has, in fact, been achieved.

7. Review learnings

This is the typical debrief of a project, including the following:

- what worked well
- what didn't work well
- tools that were particularly effective
- things that we would like to do better
- learnings from overcoming difficult points
- how we should manage the people side differently.

The operational risk management equivalent to Step 7 is the embedding of the methodology which is, of course, linked to governance. Additionally, operational risk managers at this stage will challenge the methodology and tools used in terms of any improvements that can be made.

8. Identify next improvement

This is a very easy stage in that, typically, the second choice from the original list of required improvements is chosen. This is a very natural step if the firm's business profile has not changed significantly in the meantime. However, if there has been a change, Stage 1 should be repeated.

From an operational risk perspective, a new risk and control assessment and continuing monitoring of losses and indicators will lead to further appetite comparisons and renewal of the cycle.

CONCLUSION

At the business level, a robust and efficient operational risk system will enable managers to react to events more quickly and with greater effectiveness. At the board level, good operational risk management reduces the volatility of performance and facilitates efficient resource and capital allocation.

From an investor point of view, operational risk management encourages and allows an understanding of where shareholder value is being created or destroyed. A good operational risk management system, fully embedded in the business, will prevent any blindness to risk which may affect the profitability of a business line or transaction. Risk and control perception is improved through distilling a risk culture which leads to business optimisation. That will be reflected in a firm's credit rating. And it will also generate a significant regulatory benefit in an improved relationship with the regulator, wherever that is applicable. A further benefit is that if you get it right, you avoid paying the lawyers!

Operational risk management is fundamental to successful business management. It produces true business benefits in its own right. Having established that principle, we can now go on to explore the operational risk management framework in detail and get down to the practical mastery of operational risk.

Note

1   http://www.bis.org/publ/bcbs128.pdf

THE FRAMEWORK

Part 2

3

Governance

GETTING IT RIGHT AT THE OUTSET

Good governance is the starting point for good operational risk management (ORM). Given that risk management (RM) is vitally important to all firms, good operational risk (OR) governance should be one of the board's primary aims and responsibilities. It is essential for the effective embedding of operational risk management into a firm's everyday activity. It is not a rigid set of rules, nor is it a box-ticking exercise, but the basis of good business conduct.

Risk management has also become a focus of investor as well as supervisory attention and investors are increasingly looking to firms for clear evidence of good governance. As we saw earlier in Chapter 1, there are numerous corporate governance codes and requirements around the world which apply to the risk management of any firm, particularly if it is publicly listed. The point of good corporate governance is to establish a system which ensures effective accountability on the part of a board to investors and other stakeholders.

Operational risk governance is about the organisational structure of the firm and accountabilities for operational risk management, including risk ownership. It includes: the risk culture which the firm displays; the attitude of the board and senior management to risk and its risk management staff; and may include awareness sessions for both the board and staff. As was also said in Chapter 1, culture is as much about the tune in the middle as the tone from the top of the firm, so governance is the responsibility of everybody in the firm, not just the board. A firm operating good governance will encourage dialogue and challenge on operational risks up and down the organisation.

The acid test that operational risk is embedded in the firm is how it uses operational risk management methodologies and techniques in its day-to-day management. This is often referred to as the 'use test'. Can the firm demonstrate that operational risks are considered fully when strategy is being set: when a possible merger is being considered for instance; when a new product is being mooted; indeed when any business decision is being made?

Operational risk governance, in common with other forms of corporate governance, is about enabling the board and senior management to guide and direct operational risk strategy and to review its effectiveness. From a practical perspective, this will encompass:

- a framework showing how to identify, measure, monitor and manage operational risks
- a policy document approved by the most senior executive body of the firm
- terms of reference for relevant bodies, departments and persons
- a timeline for tracking and reviewing the development of operational risk processes within the firm.

THE THREE LINES OF DEFENCE

There is no set framework for operational risk governance. It will depend on the culture and structure of each organisation. However, there are basic principles of risk governance which are demonstrated in the classic three lines of defence model shown in Figure 3.1.

The three lines of defence

Figure 3.1

BOARD		
	Risk Committee	Audit Committee
First line of defence	Second line of defence	Third line of defence
Primary risk and control responsibility	Oversight	Independent assurance
Business line management	Risk management, HR, finance, IT, compliance	Internal and external audit
• Promotes strong risk culture • Sets risk appetite; creates risk definitions • Owner of risk management process • Implements controls • Day-to-day risk management by risk takers	• Develops centralised policies and standards • Develops risk management processes and controls • Monitors and reports on risk	• Provides independent and objective challenge to the levels of assurance provided by business operations and oversight • Validates processes in the risk management framework • External audit gives assurance on the financial statements

Business line management

The first line of defence, business line management, is responsible for establishing an appropriate risk and control environment. Establishing and maintaining a strong risk culture, agreeing the practical application of risk appetite and risk definitions, putting in place adequate controls and operating the risk management framework are all part of the day-to-day responsibilities of business line management. Good risk management is fundamental to business success and should be aligned to business objectives. The risk management function is not responsible for risk. That is the primary responsibility of the business, the first line of defence.

Risk oversight

The second line of defence involves those who provide oversight over business processes and risks, and monitor the proper implementation of risk management policies and the risk management framework. They provide advice and support to the business lines on risk management; they challenge the inputs and outputs provided by the business lines in risk measurement and reporting; and they ensure a consistent application of risk management policies throughout the firm. Operating against the background of the board's agreed strategy and risk appetite, they are management's assurance mechanism, providing reports to business line management and to the board. They challenge the risk management information produced by the business lines, such as key risk and control indicators and risk and control assessments.

It is often assumed, because risk management is generally a control function and has an oversight role, that it should be independent from the business to prevent any conflicts of interest or undue influence on its decisions. Whilst that may be true of control functions, such as those involved in counterparty credit risk or market risk, it is not invariably true of the operational risk management function. Operational risk is an integral part of the business. As we said in Chapter 1, it is effectively business risk. It is therefore impossible to dissociate its management from the business and establish an organisational structure where it has the appearance of independence.

The role of the credit or market risk function is to approve and decline risk limits and monitor risk exposures. There is an inevitable tension between the sales or distribution functions and the control functions exercised in respect of market and credit risk which means that the control function should be independent. Credit and market risk limits need independent monitoring or vital controls will be compromised, although even these functions must not become isolated either geographically or otherwise from the business so that they cannot understand the business or access necessary information.

Operational risk thresholds are set by the business, with the assistance of operational risk, and require an in-depth knowledge of the business, both where it is and where it is going. Setting and monitoring operational risk thresholds would inevitably be compromised if the function had to remain in some way independent of the business.

A further example of the difference between the operational risk function and the other risk functions relates to the ability or indeed authority to decline an exposure. This simply doesn't happen with operational risk, where the operational risk function acts more as a specialist adviser to senior management and the board. Whilst it may advise on the quality of mitigants and controls, it does not have the ability to prevent the firm from taking additional operational risk exposure or preventing operational risks from occurring.

Independent assurance

The third line of defence, the audit or assurance process, has two complementary parts – internal and external audit. These functions and their relationship to operational risk management are described in detail in Chapter 13, Internal audit. At this point, it is sufficient to say that internal audit provides independent assurance to the board and senior management on the quality and effectiveness of internal control, risk management and governance systems and processes. External audit's role is to give an opinion on the financial statements.

Board

All three lines, though, come together at the board. The board is responsible for all aspects of risk management: the risks undertaken and managed by the business, ensuring that there is proper oversight of the risks and making sure that financial statements and internal risk processes are properly audited.

Following the financial crisis, the independent Group of Thirty published a report on governance in financial institutions which stated that fundamentally the board was responsible for 'three factors which ultimately determined the success of the firm: the choice of strategy; the assessment of risk; and the assurance that the necessary talent is in place, starting with the CEO, to implement the agreed strategy'.[1] Without a clear strategy, there is no context for risk management. And strategy can be implemented only if the right talents are available. These are all components of people risk management and embedding a risk culture, which we develop in more detail in Chapter 15, Culture and people risk.

OPERATIONAL RISK MANAGEMENT FRAMEWORK

A framework for operational risk makes the practical implementation of governance possible. Figure 3.2 gives a pictorial representation of a framework which shows, at a high level, in one diagram, how a firm will identify, assess, measure, monitor and manage its exposure to operational risks. This is invaluable in communicating to all staff the fundamental elements of the firm's operational risk management processes.

The framework shown in Figure 3.2 is the one we use in this book and which was introduced in Chapter 1. It has the merit of simplicity and concentrates on the essential processes of operational risk management. The various elements work together within the overall operational risk environment.

Governance provides an over-arching organisational structure within the firm's culture. It establishes the three lines of defence discussed earlier. These ensure clarity of operational risk management roles and responsibilities. To be effective, though, governance depends on a monitoring and reporting process which is as comprehensive as possible – the critical links between the top and bottom of the diagram. The information on which reports are based is provided by the various processes at the centre of the framework, which, with reporting, are treated in detail in the chapters that follow.

| Figure 3.2 | A typical operational risk management framework |

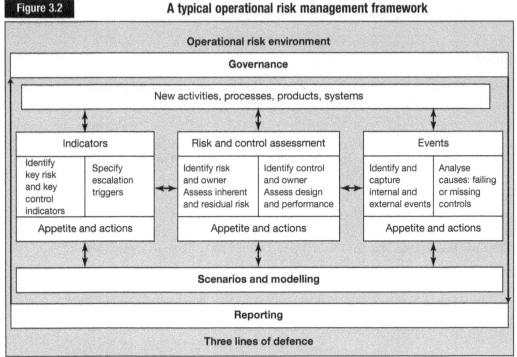

Source: Courtesy of Chase Cooper Limited

Frameworks can take many forms. Framework 'A' (Figure 3.3), for example, is in the form of the familiar 'temple' image. Its three pillars are: strategy and governance, identification and assessment, and monitoring. Within these can be found the elements of the framework shown in Figure 3.2. Framework 'A' shows that a common understanding and embedding of risk management is the fundamental foundation. In this framework, assurance is shown as the key-stone and over-arching process, rather than being part of governance.

Framework 'B' (Figure 3.4), interestingly, separately identifies governance and structure, and strategy and policy. It shows the risk management cycle of risk identification, risk assessment, management and mitigation, monitoring and reporting, but does not identify the processes which are used to achieve that.

Operational risk management framework 'A'

Figure 3.3

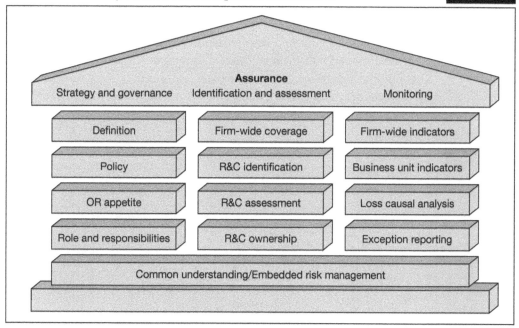

Operational risk management framework 'B'

Figure 3.4

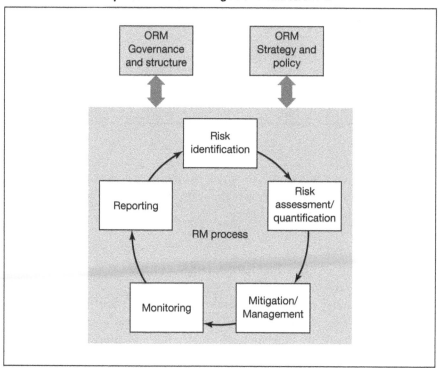

Framework 'C' (Figure 3.5), in common with Framework 'A', makes reference to independent assurance. It also shows the information flows from reporting to strategy/goals and to and from reporting and independent assurance. Once an informed strategy has been agreed, the firm can establish its governance and risk management environment. In addition, Framework 'C' explicitly recognises that action plans are a central part of operational risk management and that they can flow from risks, controls, indicators and loss causal analysis.

Figure 3.5

Operational risk framework 'C'

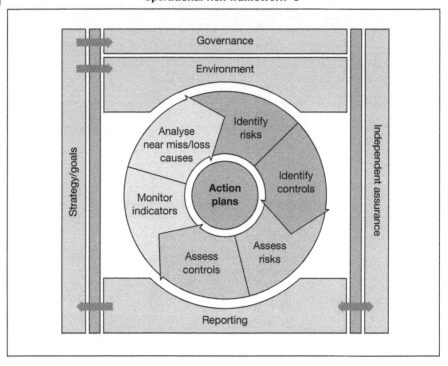

Having agreed on a framework in which the key elements of operational risk management have been identified, the second element of governance is to formulate an operational risk policy.

OPERATIONAL RISK POLICY

A clear operational risk policy supports the organisation in achieving its business objectives. Along with the framework, it also allows the board and senior management to communicate to all staff the approach of the firm to operational risk management. As such, the policy should be approved by the board. The executive or management committee may develop the policy document or, at a minimum, review and comment on it, but ultimate responsibility for approving and implementing it rests with the board.

The contents of an operational risk policy vary from firm to firm and are dependent on the firm's culture and the typical structure of its policies. They will also be consistent with the scale, nature and complexity of the firm.

An operational risk policy should, as a minimum, contain:

- A definition of operational risk. This was dealt with in Chapter 1, where we considered issues such as whether strategic and reputation risks should be included and how the 'boundary' issue is to be dealt with, where operational risk inevitably overlaps other risk types. One further consideration is whether operational risk losses involve only 'direct' losses, i.e. those where there is a debit to the P&L, or whether they include 'indirect' losses, for example, the cost of internal staff, opportunity costs or lost profits caused by an operational risk event (see Chapter 6, Events and losses, What is meant by an event).

- A statement of operational risk appetite. This is often a high-level initial statement which will be broadened and deepened over time as the firm gains knowledge of the operational risk management processes and how these are used in the firm (See Chapter 4, Operational risk appetite).

- An overview of the operational risk management processes. Although this is necessarily high level in a policy, it helps significantly in making clear that the board and senior management are aware of, and have considered how, operational risk management will be carried out by the firm. It should include a short description of each process, together with the links and reinforcements between each process, to show a considered, holistic approach to operational risk management. The various processes will be dealt with in detail in Chapters 5 to 10.

- A statement of the roles and responsibilities of various personnel and departments. It is especially important that the board recognises and actively manages the potential conflicts of interest which exist between operational risk, internal audit and compliance. This point is particularly applicable to any firms where operational risk management was initially carried out by either internal audit or compliance. Clear roles for these three areas must be documented. In smaller organisations, the three functions often overlap. Extreme care should be taken, however, even in small firms, to ensure the independence of internal audit (see Chapter 13, Internal audit).

- A glossary of terms. It is vital that all staff have a clear explanation and understanding of the various terms used in operational risk. Even seemingly innocuous terms such as risk event, control and loss can give rise to confusion if they are not clearly defined and understood.

In addition, policies will often have references to:

- categories and sub-categories of risk and of operational risk
- the role that central risk management plays in the firm (as compared with the risk management units in the businesses)
- how to deal with deviations from policy
- how issues are escalated and resolved
- risk reporting flows of information.

Many of these elements are dealt with elsewhere in the book and risk appetite is considered separately in Chapter 4, but it is worth looking briefly at roles and responsibilities for operational risk management and also giving some suggestions of definitions which might be helpful in compiling a glossary of operational risk terms.

ROLES AND RESPONSIBILITIES STATEMENTS

Clarity about roles and responsibilities is a key part of risk governance and of a good risk culture. It is critical that individuals, committees or other groups understand clearly their role in operational risk management and that everybody with whom they deal is equally clear. The best way to achieve that is to agree with them and write down their responsibilities in a statement. These will include the board, audit committee, executive operational risk committee, the head of operational risk, the business lines, as well as the internal audit and compliance functions. Statements will be approved by the board or other appropriate body.

Examples for each of these are given below, but they are only a guide. How statements of this sort are used will depend not only on the actual responsibilities of individuals within each firm, but also the way in which such statements are expressed and disseminated within individual firms.

Board of directors

The board sets the tone and culture of the firm and also the business strategy and objectives. In addition, it has a vital oversight role. Given this, it is important that its role and responsibilities in operational risk are clearly articulated and understood. The board should:

- articulate the risk and operational risk profile of the firm
- approve the operational risk policy and operational risk management procedures
- ensure that ownership of risks is clear, both to the executives concerned and to those who deal with them

- periodically assess the effectiveness of its operational risk governance practices and oversight
- determine that senior risk executives are qualified, and fit and proper to manage operational risk
- provide oversight of operational risk, and question and insist upon straightforward explanations from senior management
- make sure the information it receives is appropriate and of sufficient quality to support and not hinder its risk oversight role
- receive on a timely basis sufficient information to judge the performance of senior management with regard to operational risk, in particular using the work conducted by the internal audit function, external auditors and the various internal control functions
- implement a programme of ongoing education in operational risk for board members.

Finally, and most importantly, one board director should have particular responsibility for risk.

Audit committee

The roles and responsibilities of the audit committee in relation to internal and external audit are considered more fully in Chapter 13, Internal audit. Increasingly, boards are forming separate risk committees to maintain board level oversight regarding risk management and reporting. The Walker Review of corporate governance in banks, which was instigated by the UK government in the aftermath of the financial crisis, recommended that all FTSE 100 banks and other major financial institutions should establish a board risk committee separate from the audit committee.[2] However, where this is not the case, the audit committee should:

- keep the firm's internal controls and operational risk management systems under review
- receive reports from management on the effectiveness of operational risk management systems and of any tests carried out on them
- review and approve any statements about operational risk management contained in the company's public financial reports.

Executive operational risk committee

The board of a larger firm may have established a risk committee but, failing that, an executive operational risk committee is the most senior body with direct and explicit expertise to consider operational risk management in a firm. The executive operational risk committee is one of the points where lines 1 and 2 of the three lines of defence come together. It should:

- be chaired by the chief risk officer (or the CEO)
- include the head of operational risk
- include representatives from the business lines
- recommend for approval the operational risk strategy and policy
- receive reports, highlighting major operational risks and issues
- advise the board on operational risk appetite and tolerance for future strategy, taking into account the board's overall degree of risk aversion and the current financial situation of the firm; this may include an assessment of emerging operational risks as the business environment changes
- develop quantitative as well as qualitative metrics for risk assessment
- oversee a due diligence appraisal of the operational risks of any proposed strategic transaction, particularly one involving acquisition or disposal – even if operational risk management is or has been part of the project team
- produce a separate annual report on its work, focusing on the governance of risk, the relevance of the committee's work to current and future risk strategy and recognising that there may be a potential overlap with reporting by the audit committee
- recognise that taking external advice is consistent with the board's duty of care, where sufficient skill or knowledge is lacking in a technical area of operational risk.

Head of operational risk

The role of the head of operational risk (or the chief risk officer if the firm is too small to have a separate head of operational risk) is to:

- establish, implement and maintain a framework for identifying, assessing and managing operational risks
- set and agree firm-wide operational risk priorities
- act as the operational risk adviser to the firm, and in particular guide senior management in their operational risk management responsibilities
- establish a process for embedding operational risk awareness
- bring an operational risk focused viewpoint to strategic planning and other activities of senior management
- facilitate the implementation of the operational risk processes, providing coaching and guidance to business line management
- manage the process for setting the operational risk appetite

- monitor and manage the firm's overall exposure to operational risk, including working with the business line and other functions to mitigate operational risk
- ensure a consistent approach to operational risk across the lines of business
- coordinate appropriate and timely reporting of operational risks
- coordinate operational risk input to the risk committee and the board on the firm's risk profile, control infrastructure and any control failings or weaknesses and actions taken
- coordinate input to the regulators on relevant operational risk matters;
- liaise with the internal audit department.

Business lines

The 'three lines of defence' model explicitly recognises the primary role of the business line in managing risk in a firm. Business lines are responsible for the risks they generate. As part of their responsibilities for line operational risk management they should:

- develop operational risk awareness and an operational risk culture within the business line
- own the risks which they generate and their controls
- own the operational risk profile and operational risk appetite of the business line
- identify and assess the relevant business line risks and their mitigating controls in line with policy
- monitor, manage and review their risks
- manage and report incidents, events, losses and near misses in line with policy and guidelines
- keep risk exposures within limits and follow policies when limits are breached, including escalation as appropriate
- support the risk management organisation in recognising and assessing risk, including:
  - fully disclosing known risks
  - being aware of the market environment and its influence on risk
  - recognising and disclosing when conditions or assumptions change
  - accurately represent risk exposures in management information, risk management and other systems
- obtain approval, including from the operational risk function, of new products.

Internal audit

Although Chapter 13 deals extensively with the internal audit function, it is worth commenting, in a chapter on governance, on the confusion there often is between the internal audit function and the operational risk management function. There should not be any confusion if it is clearly recognised that the operational risk function has an oversight role (line 2 of the three lines of defence in Figure 3.1), whilst internal audit is part of the independent assurance process, line 3.

The confusion probably arose from the fact that operational risk started life within internal audit on the basis that it was the only function which understood all the firm's internal processes. Operational risk managers should be involved in establishing processes, with the business line, which cover all aspects of operational risk and providing reports to the board and senior management. It is internal audit's responsibility to review those processes regularly, to assess their effectiveness and to report on the review to the board. Internal audit provides assurance to the board that operational risk is effectively managed.

Of course, there will be liaison between the two functions, but internal audit should not be involved in establishing processes or, for instance, producing scenario assessments. It is there to provide assurance and can hardly give assurance on something on which it has been a party to creating.

Compliance function

There is also often confusion between the roles and responsibilities of the compliance function and those of the operational risk management function, although in this case both are part of the line 2 oversight function (see Figure 3.1). Whilst the compliance function primarily focuses on regulatory requirements, whatever the industry, these are a sub-set of the overall focus for the operational risk management function, which has a broader and more business oriented portfolio. In respect of operational risk management, the compliance function will:

- liaise with the operational risk department on regulatory approaches which relate to operational risk issues
- be involved with all communication and responses to appropriate regulators
- manage operational risk compliance obligations, such as those associated with health and safety regulations or financial services regulatory requirements
- manage operational risk events which are primarily compliance focused.

GLOSSARY

The importance of all staff having a clear understanding of operational risk terms has already been highlighted. One way of ensuring that everybody is speaking the same language is to provide a glossary of terms in the operational risk policy document. Examples of terms and definitions which might be included are as follows.

Action	Process of doing something in order to enhance a *control* or change the *impact* of a *risk event*.	**Terminology**
Control	A preventative or detective feature within a process which has been developed to facilitate action either to reduce or eliminate the *likelihood* of occurrence and *impact* of a *risk event*. A control is directly related to the *cause* or *impact* of a *risk event*.	
Control failure	The malfunction or the overriding of a feature that has been designed to manage the *likelihood* of occurrence or *impact* of a *risk event*. The *control* has therefore been proven to be inappropriate in terms of its *design*, and/or ineffective in terms of its *performance*.	
Design	The manner in which a *control* is intended to operate.	
Impact	The consequences from the occurrence of a *risk event*. Consequences could include elements such as legal liability, regulatory action, loss of damage to physical assets, restitution, loss of recourse and write-downs.	
Incident	Used in business continuity planning to describe the event or circumstance which will trigger a business continuity response.	
Indicator	Something that is observed or calculated that shows the state of a *risk* or of a *control*.	
Indirect loss	The occurrence of a distinct *risk event* which does not directly impact the firm's profit and loss account or balance sheet. This may be loss of sales through loss of an IT system or less growth achieved than budgeted.	
Likelihood	The degree of probability of the occurrence of a *risk event*.	
Loss	The occurrence of a distinct *risk event* that actually impacts the firm's profit and loss account or balance sheet.	
Near miss	Either an event which would have occurred if the final *preventative control* had not worked, or an event which did not result in an actual financial or non-financial *loss* or harm	

▶

	due to the correct operation of *detective* and/or *corrective* *controls* or simply the random nature of events.
Performance	The manner in which a *control* actually operates in real life, and not in theory.
Risk	An occurrence that may cause damage or loss through preventing or hindering the achievement of a firm's objectives.
Risk cause	Factors or dynamics which contribute to, accelerate or lead (directly or in combination with other causes) to the occurrence of a *risk event*.
Risk event	A distinct occurrence which may impact the firm's profit and loss account or balance sheet, either negatively or positively. A *risk event* does not have to have a financial component and may be entirely non-financial in its effect.
Scenario	An imagined sequence of possible *risk events* that are together extreme but plausible.

TIMELINE

The final part of governance is to implement the operational risk framework. The timeline sets out the project timetable which incorporates the six main operational risk processes and also important items such as staffing.

Given the number of interlinking processes in operational risk management, a timeline to identify when each process is expected to be operational is important to the necessarily phased introduction of operational risk management to a firm. In addition, at some stage, the firm will need to implement a software tool to capture and handle the significant amount of data being captured or created. A timeline will assist the firm in deciding when a tool will be useful and when or if it will be indispensable and plan accordingly.

The chart (see Figure 3.6 for an example) will also enable the efficient management and review of the development of operational risk management. Senior management and the board will find that they can more easily understand the implications of changing the speed of the development of operational risk.

If the governance is right, then almost certainly operational risk management will be right. With proper operational risk governance in place, there will be commitment from the top, acceptance through the middle, and policies in place to establish the operational risk framework, which is what we shall cover in the next few chapters.

Example timeline for implementing an operational risk management programme   Figure 3.6

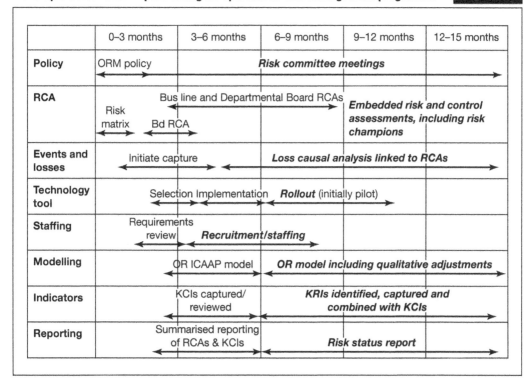

	0–3 months	3–6 months	6–9 months	9–12 months	12–15 months
Policy	ORM policy	*Risk committee meetings*			
RCA	Risk matrix	Bus line and Departmental Board RCAs Bd RCA		*Embedded risk and control assessments, including risk champions*	
Events and losses	Initiate capture		*Loss causal analysis linked to RCAs*		
Technology tool		Selection Implementation	*Rollout* (initially pilot)		
Staffing	Requirements review	*Recruitment/staffing*			
Modelling		OR ICAAP model	*OR model including qualitative adjustments*		
Indicators		KCIs captured/ reviewed	*KRIs identified, captured and combined with KCIs*		
Reporting		Summarised reporting of RCAs & KCIs	*Risk status report*		

Source: Courtesy of Chase Cooper Limited

Notes

1   Group of Thirty, *Toward effective corporate governance of financial institutions*, 2012; www.group30.org

2   HM Treasury, *A review of corporate governance in UK banks and other financial industry entities, Final recommendations*, 26 November 2009; www.hm-treasury.gov.uk/d/walker_review_261109.pdf

Operational risk appetite

RISK APPETITE AND CONTROL APPETITE

It is of course of fundamental importance that a firm's operational risk appetite is identified and its dealings are then monitored against that appetite. A large part of this chapter is about operational risk appetite. However in the latter part of the chapter, we look at how operational risk appetite is partly composed of an appetite for the quality of the controls that mitigate the operational risks to which a firm is subject. By breaking down operational risk appetite into its component parts, we are able to delve further and deeper into a practical approach to operational risk appetite.

RISK APPETITE

Defining operational risk appetite

A typical definition of risk appetite is as follows:

Definition · **Risk appetite**

The amount and type of risk that an organisation is willing to take to achieve its strategic objectives [over a specified time horizon at a given level of confidence].

The clause in square brackets gives more precision and is often included in definitions of risk appetite by more sophisticated firms which are further down the road of risk modelling (see Chapter 9, Modelling, for further discussion). Clearly this broad definition is as applicable to operational risk as it is to other types of risk.

Trying to write a similar definition for operational risk appetite is more difficult. One approach is to look at individual loss categories and to write statements covering these.

Definition · **Operational risk appetite**

Financial crime: The firm has no appetite for financial crime and will implement appropriate measures to control it.

Or

Reputational losses: The firm has no appetite for adverse media coverage and will use every effort to ensure that events that could potentially lead to such events are avoided.

Or

Regulatory risk: The Group has zero risk appetite for regulatory breaches or systemic unfair outcomes for customers. To achieve this, the Group encourages and maintains an appropriately balanced regulatory compliance culture and promotes policies and procedures to enable businesses and their staff to operate in accordance with the laws, regulations and voluntary codes which impact on the Group and its activities. (Lloyds Banking Group plc Report and Accounts 2011.)

Another might attempt to quantify its operational risk appetite as follows:

To manage the firm's operations to ensure that unmitigated losses are no more than x% of profit before tax in any three-year rolling period.

Or

We do not wish to see an operational loss of more than £xxx at the 90th centile.

Or

The firm has no appetite for individual operational risk losses above £x and cumulative losses of £y within a 12-month period. Any individual operational risk losses exceeding £z are to be reported to the Audit and Operational Risk Committee.

All of these definitions acknowledge, as we saw in Chapter 1, that the traditional view of risk appetite – that it should be a hard number and that it should be limit based – is not appropriate for operational risk. Many operational risks are unavoidable and, even if an appetite for loss is agreed, it will be exceeded, despite the controls and other mitigants which are in place.

The intelligent view of operational risk appetite recognises that, whilst there are different ways of mitigating operational risk, thresholds and targets are more relevant to operational risk appetite than hard limits. Appetite can also be expressed using the various processes in the operational risk framework. We shall see how that can be achieved later in this chapter.

Operational risk appetite in the business

Determining the operational risk appetite of a firm is an important component of any firm's operational risk management approach. Used effectively, operational risk appetite will influence the operational risk culture (and vice versa), operational risk operating style and operational risk resource allocation. Operational risk appetite, in common with other risk appetites, represents the firm's view of how much risk can be taken to help achieve business objectives, whilst respecting the constraints within which the firm operates.

Whilst senior management, of course, plays a fundamental role in determining the operational risk appetite of the firm, it should be approved by the board. This sends a clear signal to all staff that the operational risk appetite agreed by the board should clearly govern the activities of all employees. It also defines the boundaries within which the firm's business objectives should be pursued. From an operational risk perspective, this is fundamental, as operational risk identification and assessment is undertaken in relation to the firm's business objectives.

The operational risk appetite of the firm is also important in managing shareholder expectations regarding the amount and type of risk which is accepted. Whilst the appetite of the firm for market risk and credit risk is relatively easy to articulate and quantify, operational risk appetite will include elements which cannot be measured quantitatively, including some risks for which there may be no appetite whatsoever, such as employee deaths or injuries due to poor health and safety procedures.

Risk appetite and risk tolerance

Some firms seek to differentiate between operational risk appetite and operational risk tolerance. This is often explained by reference to the example of theft of the firm's assets. Although there is no appetite for theft in any organisation, many senior managers expect that some level of theft of assets will inevitably occur (if only of pens and paper clips). This level is tolerated even though there is no appetite for allowing theft itself.

An example where there are different levels of appetite and tolerance in differing industries is the risk of 'death or injury whilst working for the firm'. In the financial services industry, as with all others, there is a zero appetite for this risk. Financial services employees, though, are not exposed to the risk of death or serious injury in their normal work, other than as targets for armed raids, so that the outcome is likely to be in line with risk appetite.

The construction industry also has a zero appetite. But it is more likely, in a high-hazard industry, that deaths or injuries will occur. Having said that, and possibly as a result of pressure from customers, employees and the public, construction has put a lot of effort into improving safety over recent years and has significantly reduced the number of deaths. According to the UK Health and Safety Executive, fatalities have fallen from 5.9 per 100,000 workers in 2000/01 to 2.4 per 100,000 in 2010/11. Major accidents have also fallen significantly over the same period.[1]

In 2008, one of Britain's major construction companies, Balfour Beatty, decided to take the process a stage further and introduced the 'Zero Harm' project on its construction sites and throughout the company worldwide. Its stated aim was that, from 2012 onwards, there would be:

- zero deaths
- zero injuries to the public
- zero ruined lives amongst our people.

Balfour Beatty has estimated that approximately half a million people are working on their sites during a 12-month period, the vast majority of them sub-contractors, and that figure excludes the public on and near their sites, for whom they also accept responsibility. The project has an ambitiously low-risk appetite but, as with all the best operational risk management strategies, it is founded on good communication. The 'Zero Harm by 2012' project slogan and logo (see Figure 4.1) – 'Zero Harm by 2012' alongside a large zero in a striking shade of orange – were simple and powerful, and quickly and clearly convey to employees and sub-contractors the company's risk appetite.

Balfour Beatty 'Zero Harm by 2012'® logo[2]   Figure 4.1

Balfour Beatty sees eradicating serious accidents as a competitive virtue and has differentiated them from competitors when tendering for contracts. The common vision is shared by the group's leadership; is constantly communicated at every level, including to sub-contractors who must sign up to it; best practice is freely shared and peer pressure keeps everybody driving towards the target: the benefits of operational risk management in action.

A further example of zero appetite comes from the retail sector where theft of goods is euphemistically referred to as 'shrinkage'. Most firms will set a level of shrinkage that is tolerated by senior management. However, the appetite of the sector can be determined from notices posted around shops which clearly state 'Shoplifters will be prosecuted'.

Whose appetite is it anyway?

Another complicating factor for operational risk appetite is the question: 'Whose appetite is it anyway?' There are many groups and individuals who have separate appetites relating to a particular firm and industry. Typical external groups will include customers, suppliers, investors, regulators and business partners. All of these will have varying levels of appetite, which may be very different. Appetite also ties in closely to reputation (see Chapter 16 Reputation risk, for further discussion). There are natural tensions between the board, senior management and the shareholders which lead to at least three levels of appetite for any firm:

■ Senior management's operational risk appetite is likely to be relatively short term and focused on business opportunities which generate an appetite that is inevitably bullish in nature, i.e. thresholds/targets are likely to be significant in size. An example could be a merger, which will often lead to acceptance of a considerable increase in operational risk to reflect the period of significant change that will be involved. An intelligent senior management will also increase its relevant operational risk thresholds.

■ The board's risk appetite is likely to be longer term in nature and lower than senior management's. Continuing the merger example, the board will state an operational risk threshold, perhaps in terms of the capital it is willing to risk. This may well be exceeded by senior management, even though it is attempting to manage to the board's operational risk policy threshold. The issue will then be resolved, depending on the firm's culture and processes of communication and reporting between senior management and the board.

■ The shareholders' risk appetite is likely to be the lowest of the three and will probably be focused on the smallest possible volatility in earnings consistent with a reasonable return. However, amongst the family of investors, bondholders may have a very different view of appetite to shareholders.

It is important for the board periodically to review and challenge the risk appetite which has been proposed by senior management. Following the review or challenge the board should reconfirm its appetite, with appropriate changes where necessary. During the challenge period, the board should assure itself that senior management has considered all foreseeable emerging operational risks to which the firm may be subject and that appropriate processes and resources are being utilised to manage them.

Within the firm there will also be different approaches to operational risk appetite at each level, so that we need to ask the question: 'At which level within the firm are we considering our operational risk appetite?' In any firm there are at least four levels which have different approaches to operational risk appetite:

- the board, who will frequently seek a risk appetite in terms of capital (either economic or regulatory) and profit
- senior management, who will tend to define operational risk appetite in terms of risk and the action taken to manage and mitigate each risk
- business units, which may well use the classic approach to operational risk management of defining their operational risk appetite through risk and control assessments, key risk indicators (KRIs) and loss data
- business support functions, which mostly focus on KRIs and loss data.

This is shown diagrammatically in Figure 4.2.

Appropriate levels of risk appetite Figure 4.2

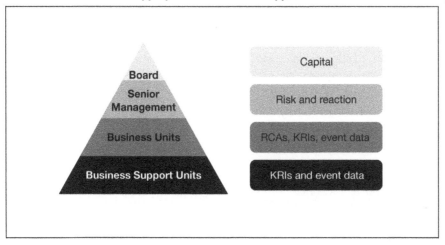

It is natural to wonder whether the risk appetites at the different levels of the firm can be aggregated. After all, credit risk appetites can certainly be aggregated up the firm and broken down throughout the firm from the board level. However, as noted above, the different levels in a firm see operational risk appetite fundamentally differently. This means that easy arithmetical aggregation is not possible for operational risk appetite. It is only when the operational risk appetite can be turned into a figure (preferably a monetary value) that the arithmetic works. In operational risk, this is not possible unless the firm models its qualitative data (see Chapter 9, Modelling, for further discussion).

Reputation risk appetite

One of the challenges which the board should give to senior management is proper consideration of reputational loss. Whilst some firms consider reputational loss as part of the overall impact of a risk event, others consider reputational loss as a separate impact, often using the same scale as is used for risk impact scoring. If this is done, the reputational loss may be greater than, or less than, the impact to the firm from the direct loss from an event. Combining the two assessments will give a total risk loss. However, if the two assessments are kept separate, it is possible that there will be double-counting of some elements.

Expected and unexpected losses

Before looking at different ways of expressing operational risk appetite there is one other point which needs to be considered: which type of operational risk appetite is the firm considering – expected or unexpected operational risk appetite? The expected operational risk appetite reflects the amount of loss to which the firm is subject, assuming that its controls are operating normally. This is effectively 'business as usual (BAU)' and is a relatively easy level of loss to identify and measure, as it is the amount of loss which the firm suffers on a regular day-to-day basis. It is usually provided for in the budget or in special provisions. This expected operational risk appetite can, of course, be back-tested by comparing it with actual attritional losses.

From a strategic perspective, it is more helpful to consider the unexpected loss that a firm may suffer. This is the loss to which the firm is subject when controls fail. It is a much larger figure than the expected loss, as it is usually at a lower frequency and higher severity. It is, therefore, more difficult to identify and calculate. Scenario analysis can be helpful when considering operational risk appetite at an unexpected loss level (see Chapter 10, Stress tests and scenarios). If mathematical models are used in the calculation of unexpected losses, the process will almost certainly be less accessible to most senior management, unless they are given statistical training. Unexpected loss is effectively what a firm's capital and profits are there to absorb.

Different ways of expressing operational risk appetite

Many commentaries on risk appetite state that it should be firmly grounded in the firm's financial reporting. From the perspective of operational risk appetite this is often easier said than done. However, there are a number of ways in which the various components of the operational risk management process can be used to define and manage operational risk appetite.

Absolute figures

At an individual risk level, the main link to the firm's financials is through the amount of loss that the firm is willing to accept in relation to that particular risk. One practical way of expressing the firm's operational risk appetite is therefore through the monetary loss which the firm is willing to accept for each risk to the strategic objectives.

Figure 4.3 shows how a firm may deduce its risk appetite by considering its actual losses against a loss distribution, with the capital determined at a specific confidence level. This can be done at an overall firm-wide loss level or at a loss category level, where sufficient data exists to generate a reliable distribution and its analysis.

Risk appetite in relation to actual loss experience   Figure 4.3

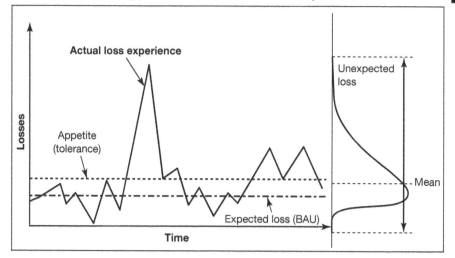

The board may decide that its acceptable risk tolerance lies at the mean of the losses incurred over a given period of time for a particular risk. It can then decide at what point on the curve it should identify thresholds, including for the level of loss it considers unacceptable. Once this is established, risk assessment can be matched to a scale of monetary values as a basis for risk appetite.

Risk and control assessments

As a starting point, low, and following the board's overall risk policy, acceptable, warning and unacceptable levels of annual loss are separately identified for the firm as a whole, probably at risk committee or board level. But wherever they are agreed, it is important that the decisions are made independently of the figures which emerge from the risk and control assessment itself. These loss thresholds are shown at the top of Figure 4.4 and form the basis for the identification of risk appetite by risk.

Figure 4.4

Risk appetite using risk assessment scores (1)

Annual loss thresholds

Low	25,000
Acceptable	100,000
Warning	450,000
Catastrophic	1,500,000

Impact per event (£)

	Lower bound	Upper bound	Mid-point
Low	0	50,000	25,000
Med-low	50,000	150,000	100,000
Med-high	150,000	500,000	325,000
High	500,000	1,500,000	1,000,000

Likelihood of event (per annum)

	Lower bound	Upper bound	Alternative label	Mid-point
Low	0.04	0.10	10% likely in next year	0.07
Med-low	0.10	0.33	30% likely in next year	0.22
Med-high	0.33	1.00	Very likely in next year	0.67
High	1.00	12.00	Several times in next year	6.50

Ranges are assessed for the impact and likelihood of each risk, which are used to calculate a mid-point for each band (see Figure 4.4). It is then a simple matter for the mid-points for impact and likelihood to be multiplied to achieve a heat map which can be coloured according to the appetite levels already identified (see Figure 4.5).

Figure 4.5

Risk appetite using risk assessment scores (2)

Impact		70,000	220,000	670,000	6,500,000
	High	70,000	220,000	670,000	6,500,000
	Med-high	22,750	71,500	217,750	2,112,500
	Med-low	7,000	22,000	67,000	650,000
	Low	1,750	5,500	16,750	162,500
		10% Likely	30% Likely	Very likely	Severe

Likelihood

From the format used in Figure 4.5 it is possible to see immediately which risks in the risk assessment are outside the agreed appetite. At the bottom left-hand corner, the values should be easily ignored as they are so small. If any risks are in the top right-hand corner, immediate action should be taken as these are considerably beyond acceptable levels.

Using risk and control assessments

Another method of setting and managing operational risk appetite, as will be seen in Chapter 5, Risk and control assessment, is to use risk assessment scores which are linked with the quality of the mitigating controls and displayed graphically, as in Figure 4.6.

This graphical representation of risk and control assessment (RCA) scores is constructed through multiplying the likelihood and impact scores for a risk and multiplying the relevant control design and control performance scores. This allows a comparison of the relative levels of different risks and their mitigating controls and enables an implied current risk appetite to be derived.

Risk appetite using risk and control assessment scores Figure 4.6

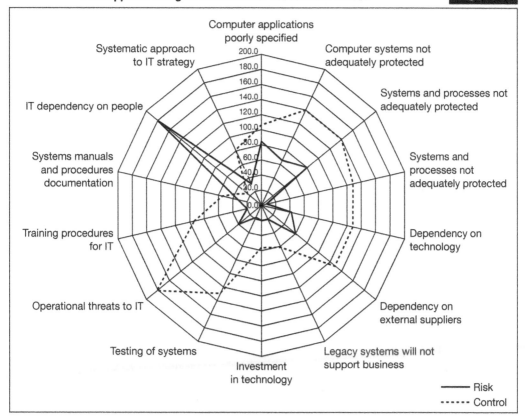

For example, from Figure 4.6, it appears that the risk 'Operational threats to IT' is relatively small at a gross level and is very well controlled. This implies that the firm has a very low appetite for this risk as it has a high mitigation level. If this is not the case, the firm can afford to reduce its controls and free up resources which can be applied elsewhere.

The risk 'IT dependency on people' has been assessed as quite high although the controls have been assessed as relatively poor. The implication here is that the firm has a high appetite for this risk. If this is not the case, the firm should put in place action plans to enhance its controls. These may be drawn from the freed up resources in the paragraph above.

Approaching operational risk appetite in this way means that the firm can adjust its resource application to be more consistent and better fit its actual appetite, whilst keeping its resource spend at a minimum level.

The final and ultimate use of risk and control assessments for expressing operational risk appetite is to model the RCA data (see Chapter 9, Modelling). The output of such modelling is a monetary loss amount which provides the necessary value expression to link with the board's articulation of its appetite in the form of a capital figure (see Figure 4.2 above).

Using indicators

An alternative method for setting risk appetite is through key risk indicators (KRIs). This enables one or more appetites to be set for the same risk depending on the number of indicators identified for that risk. As noted in Chapter 7, Indicators, KRI thresholds explicitly identify a firm's risk appetite. Figure 4.7 shows a green band for the indicator of down to 3 and up to 7. Clearly therefore if the indicator reaches 3 or 7 the appetite for this indicator has been breached. Equally if the indicator reaches 1 or 8 there is a significant breach of appetite resulting in the indicator being in the red band.

As a practical example, consider the bands for the risk 'Loss of IT system' and the indicator 'Number of help desk queries' in Figure 4.8. The boundaries of the firm's appetite around the indicator of 'Number of help desk queries' are very clear (and by implication the management of the risk of loss of the IT system is much clearer than it might otherwise be). The usual number of queries expected is between 7 and 15 per day. If 'Number of help desk queries' is over 25 per day this is a clear signal that the systems are failing the business and that there is a very high likelihood of a loss of the entire system. In this event, there is clearly a senior management problem that requires immediate attention. If 'Number of help desk queries' ever reached those levels it would be likely to be referred to the board as loss of IT system is a typical strategic risk. If 'Number of help desk queries' is 2 or fewer, the firm should question whether or not there may be a problem with apathy in the firm towards the help desk (due to the number of unanswered help desk queries, for example) which may indicate probable likely failure of the IT system too.

Risk appetite using KRI thresholds

Figure 4.7

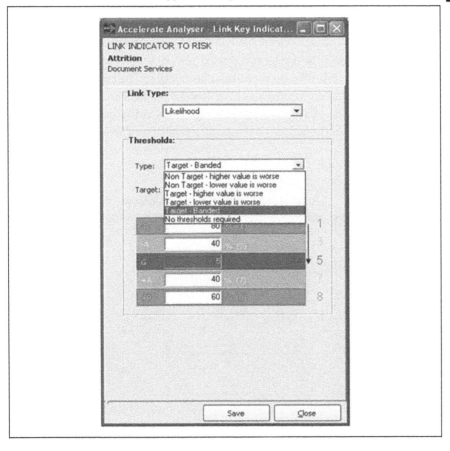

Risk appetite using KRI thresholds for 'Number of help desk queries'

Figure 4.8

Red	Amber	Green	Amber	Red
2 or fewer	3 to 7	7 to 15	16 to 25	over 25

Using numbers of losses

Comment has already been made on the size of loss attributable to an opera-tional risk being one way to express the appetite for that risk. However, an even simpler measure relating to losses is the number of losses. This is a straightforward count of the number of losses relating either to a particular risk or to a category or sub-category of risks.

In Figure 4.9 it can be seen that, by business line, there is a range of between 10 and 79 for the number of losses captured relating to external fraud. It may be that the firm has different appetites for different business lines. For example, external fraud may be more likely in retail parts of the firm, although the impact is likely to be smaller than in the corporate and wholesale parts such as Trading & Sales or Corporate Finance. However, a simple count across the firm can be used for an appetite for external fraud and this may be said to be no more than 20 losses in the period. If this is the case, four out of the eight business lines have exceeded the firm's appetite for external fraud. This may result in an action plan to investigate the relevant controls in the four delinquent business lines, perhaps carried out by internal audit.

Figure 4.9

Risk appetite using number of losses

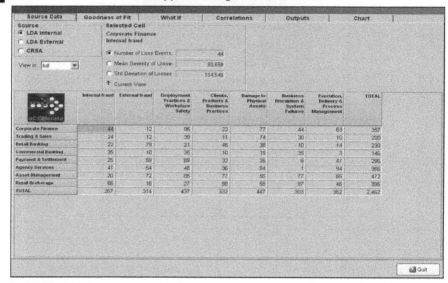

Source: Courtesy of Chase Cooper Limited

Using economic capital

Operational risk appetite, in common with other risk appetites, can also be expressed in terms of the regulatory capital required to support a business line and with reference to particular loss event types. Figure 4.10 gives an example of this and shows the capital required to support the risks allocated to each cell. It can be seen that column 4, Clients, Products and Business, is a significant consumer of capital and that Retail Banking and Trading & Sales have probably exceeded the firm's risk appetite for this loss event type. Additionally, the Payments & Settlement line of business has suffered a massive internal fraud which has also undoubtedly exceeded the firm's risk appetite for this loss event type.

Figure 4.10

Risk appetite using regulatory capital modelling

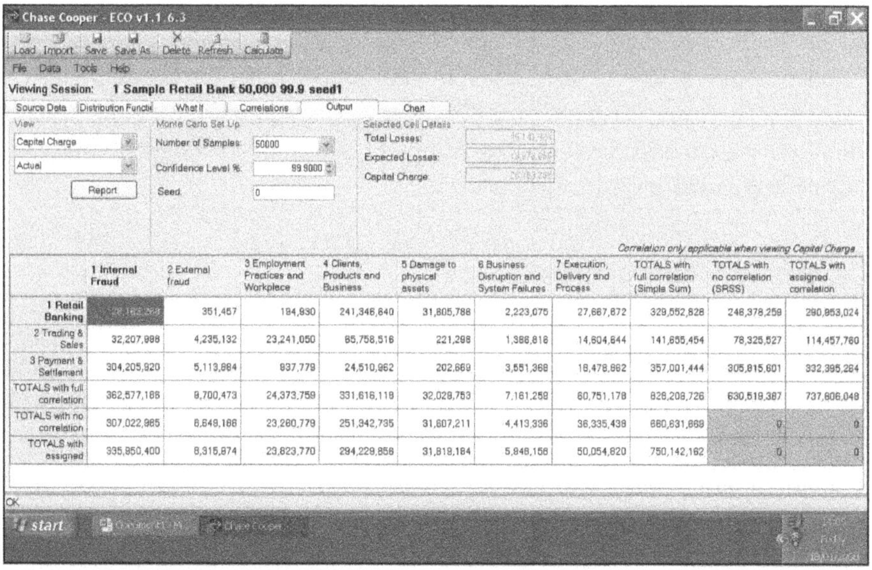

	1 Internal Fraud	2 External fraud	3 Employment Practices and Workplace	4 Clients, Products and Business	5 Damage to physical assets	6 Business Disruption and System Failures	7 Execution, Delivery and Process	TOTALS with full correlation (Simple Sum)	TOTALS with no correlation (SRSS)	TOTALS with assigned correlation
1 Retail Banking	[illegible]	351,457	184,930	241,346,640	31,805,788	2,223,075	27,667,672	329,552,828	246,378,259	290,853,024
2 Trading & Sales	32,207,998	4,235,132	23,241,050	65,758,516	221,298	1,386,816	14,604,644	141,655,454	78,325,527	114,457,760
3 Payment & Settlement	304,205,920	5,113,884	937,779	24,510,962	202,669	3,551,368	18,478,862	357,001,444	305,815,601	332,395,264
TOTALS with full correlation	362,577,166	9,700,473	24,373,759	331,616,118	32,028,753	7,161,258	60,751,178	828,208,726	630,519,387	737,806,048
TOTALS with no correlation	307,022,985	6,649,166	23,260,779	251,342,735	31,607,211	4,413,336	36,335,438	660,631,869	0	0
TOTALS with assigned	335,850,400	8,315,874	23,823,770	294,229,856	31,818,184	5,848,156	50,054,820	750,142,162	0	0

Source: Courtesy of Chase Cooper Limited

CONTROL APPETITE

Some people may think that risk appetite includes controls. However, control appetite is fundamentally different. As an example, consider the risk 'Loss of key staff' and two of its controls 'Performance appraisal' and 'Salary surveys'. The risk appetite for 'Loss of key staff' may be the loss of one key person every three years. This is achieved by a control appetite for performance appraisal that the appraisals are completed every 12 months, and a control appetite for salary surveys that all salaries are within the second quartile. It is therefore clear that risk appetite is linked with control appetite, but that control appetite is completely separate. This is analogous to the link between KRIs and key control indicators (KCIs) (see above Using indicators and Chapter 7, Indicators).

Definition

Control appetite

The amount a firm is willing to spend (in time, money and/or resources) to mitigate a risk(s) to an acceptable residual level.

It should be noted that this definition focuses control appetite internally to the firm. This is in contrast to the definition of risk appetite which can be as much affected by external factors as by internal factors. The definition explicitly recognises that management has a finite willingness to mitigate risks and implicitly recognises that certain risks cannot be mitigated or mitigated further. This is very helpful from a practical perspective as it allows management to focus on controls that can be improved.

The definition above, of course, only covers the business-as-usual control appetite. There are also control appetites at an unexpected level of loss and at an extreme (scenario) level of loss. However, we shall consider the practical business-as-usual level in this chapter.

Describing control appetite

Control appetite can be described in simple terms and it can be modelled. Just like risk appetite, control appetite can be described through the tools that are used in operational risk management. For example, control appetite can be expressed as:

- an acceptable level of control assessment (within a risk and control assessment)
- a reduction in the assessed risk level from gross (inherent) to net (residual) risk
- targets and threshold of KCIs
- reductions in the number and/or value of events and losses
- the monetary benefit that the control makes to the reduction in the risk profile (this can use mathematical modelling of the risks and controls in order to determine a value)
- the money spent on risk profile reduction.

As noted above, control appetite can be analysed in different ways. Consequently, the interpretation of control appetite may vary at different levels of the firm, and this is illustrated in Figure 4.11.

| Figure 4.11 | **Appropriate levels of control appetite** |

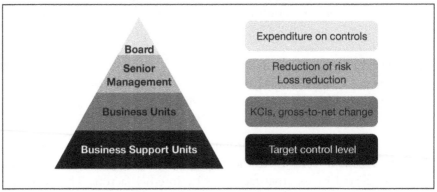

Control appetite also links to internal audit work and to Lean/Six Sigma. As we shall see in Chapter 13, Internal audit is a fundamental part of the operational risk management framework. Internal audit tends to focus on the effectiveness of controls within the firm and its work is therefore valuable in determining what the control appetite of the firm is in reality (as opposed to what the firm says it has as a control appetite). It is often true that controls in an area will be improved following an internal audit as senior management may not have been aware of the poor functioning of certain controls. However, it is also true that (unless action plans are in place *and* being actioned) the current state of the firm's control profile is an accurate reflection of its actual control appetite (notwithstanding what it may say to the contrary).

Both Lean and Six Sigma are concerned with the effective and efficient operation of controls. It may be argued that some Lean practitioners are more concerned with the elimination of unnecessary controls, whilst some Six Sigma practitioners are more concerned with the improvement of existing controls. However, both methodologies rely on control analysis and this is the link to control appetite. From an operational risk perspective, the design of a control is particularly susceptible to Six Sigma analysis as it is often about the processes or systems around the control. And without a good design, it is very difficult to have a defensible low control appetite.

Control appetite is also very useful in eliminating confusion inherent in the current approaches to risk appetite. There are at least three types of risk appetite:

- residual risk appetite
- inherent risk appetite
- stressed risk appetite, which is not applicable to the following discussion.

Taking residual risk appetite first, it is a function of the amount a firm is willing to risk when controls are working. Put into an equation this becomes:

$$\text{Residual risk appetite} = f \text{ [amount willing to risk when controls are working]}$$

Breaking down the right-hand side gives us:

$$= f \text{ \{[residual likelihood value], [residual impact value], [control appetite]\}}$$

as the amount must be a function of the likelihood of the risk occurring, the impact of the risk when it does occur, and the quality of the controls mitigating the risk.

Equally, inherent risk appetite gives:

$$\text{Inherent risk appetite} = f\,\{\text{amount willing to risk when controls have failed}\}$$

$$= f\,\{\{\text{inherent likelihood value}\},\{\text{inherent impact value}\},\{\text{control appetite}\}\}$$

Control appetite is of course simply:

$$\text{Control appetite} = f\,\{\text{amount willing to spend (in money, time and/or resources) to mitigate a risk(s)}\}$$

Breaking down control appetite into its components

Control appetite itself splits into two main parts: causes appetite, which concerns preventative control appetite, and effects appetite, which concerns corrective control appetite (drawing on the four internal audit control types of directive, preventative, detective and corrective; see also Chapter 5, Risk and control assessment).

Causes appetite is linked to management's view of the likelihood of the risk and also splits into two. Preventative controls are often automatic controls. They also often have a significant cost (often IT costs primarily) and occupy a significant amount of management thought and time. They are the immediate, obvious and visible side of the control environment. Thus management's risk appetite is actually often focused on its appetite for the causes of risks. The other part of causes appetite is directive control appetite which is linked to management's willingness to implement governance, as directive controls consist of policies, procedures, committees and the power of the board.

Corrective control appetite is linked to management's willingness to correct for the effects of the impact on the business. Corrective controls are often relatively cheap and unused (until an event happens). They are also therefore often under-rated, do not figure largely in management's thinking and are under-tested. When they are required, it is almost always too late to implement and test them. For this reason, prudent management should consider carefully its effects appetite, alongside its causes appetite.

To conclude the appetite analysis of the four types of control, detective control appetite is linked to management's willingness to identify events once they have happened. However, the focus for action is of course on correction and this is often considered more necessary than detecting the event. In reality therefore there is often only tacit acceptance of the need for detective controls, despite the obvious necessity of needing to detect an event before you can correct for its effects. This leads to a very low level of appetite for spending money on standard detective controls such as reconciliations.

Summary

Control appetite therefore consists of governance appetite, preventative control appetite, effects appetite and (last and least) detective control appetite. Risk appetite therefore breaks down into:

$$\text{Risk appetite} = f \{\text{amount willing to accept as a loss for a given risk reward ratio}\}$$

$$= f \{[\text{likelihood value}], [\text{impact value}], [\text{control appetite}]\}$$

$$= f \{[\text{likelihood value}], [\text{impact value}], [\text{governance appetite}],$$
$$[\text{preventative control appetite}], [\text{effects appetite}],$$
$$[\text{detective control appetite control}]\}$$

$$= f \{[\text{risk assessment}], [\text{control assessment and analysis}]\}$$

Note

1   www.hse.gov.uk/statistics/
2   A registered trademark of Balfour Beatty plc, registered in England as a public limited company; Registered No: 395826; Registered Office: 130 Wilton Road, London SW1V 1LQ. We are very grateful to Andy Rose, Group Managing Director, Balfour Beatty plc, for his time and assistance in explaining the 'zero harm' project. For further information about the 'Zero harm' project, see www.balfourbeatty.com/bby/responsibility/safety/highlights/

Risk and control assessment

AIMS OF RISK AND CONTROL ASSESSMENT

The objective of a risk and control assessment is to identify, measure and monitor the risks and controls to which a firm is subject.

The risk and control assessment can be qualitative, quantitative or both. A qualitative risk and control assessment will be based on value judgements such as high, medium-high, medium-low and low. In contrast, a quantitative risk and control assessment will assess the risks identified through actual numbers, such as percentages for likelihood and monetary values for impact.

Business objectives/processes/activities

A risk and control assessment aims to capture the risks and controls of a firm at the appropriate level. The level required may be strategic, process or activity, as shown in Figure 5.1. A strategic risk and control assessment will derive its risks and controls from the business objectives of the firm and what will prevent the firm from meeting its business objectives. Similarly, the risk and control assessment carried out at the process level will have regard to processes which a firm undertakes and the objectives of those processes. These may be high-level processes, i.e. those carried out at the business unit level, or may be lower-level processes carried out at a departmental level. Processes will ultimately break down into many activities. The risk and control assessment carried out at an activity level will therefore produce a significant number of risks and controls.

Figure 5.1 **Levels of risk and control assessment**

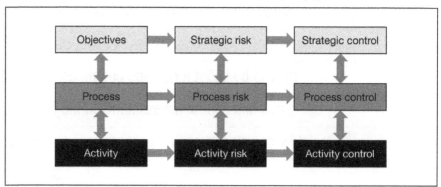

Source: Courtesy of Chase Cooper Limited

Benefits to firms

There are many benefits to firms in carrying out risk and control assessments. These range from a clearer understanding of the operational risks which the business faces, through identifying risks which have insufficient controls, to setting action plans to enhance existing controls and implement new controls. A clear understanding of risks will also point to opportunities for profitable risk-taking and business optimisation (see Chapter 2, The business case for operational risk management).

In detail the benefits include:

- a comprehensive understanding of the business's operational risk profile
- more accurate information regarding the level of risk to the business
- identification of potential risk hotspots and control bottlenecks
- a defined structure to risks and controls, which provides an effective and consistent treatment of risks across the firm and consistent risk reporting
- managing risks and mitigation as a 'portfolio' to help the business make a clear link between risk and performance
- increased acceptance of a risk culture in the business by assisting those who are responsible for managing risk on a day-to-day basis
- embedding risk management processes into the core processes of the business
- communicating the firm's view of its risks and controls to existing staff and new recruits
- enabling risks associated with cross-functional processes to be managed more effectively
- a better response to issues within the business, as the risks are more clearly understood
- further assurance to the board that the statements in the annual report are accurate
- improved business continuity planning
- documentation of risks and controls for use by external stakeholders such as regulators.

PREREQUISITES

Operational risk framework

An operational risk framework is an essential prerequisite for the effective and efficient conduct of a risk and control assessment. A framework provides a clear understanding of the structure and process around the identification of risks and controls and how the risk and control assessment fits into the overall management of operational risks (see Figure 5.2).

Figure 5.2 **Typical operational risk framework**

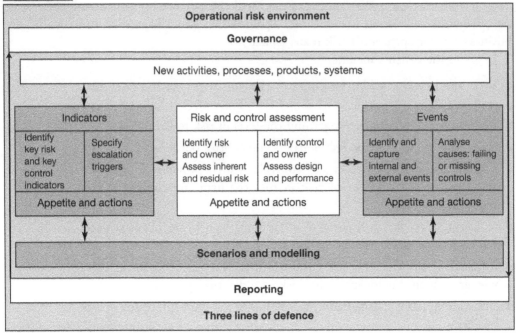

Source: Courtesy of Chase Cooper Limited

As discussed in Chapter 3, the operational risk policy, approved by the board, will state at a high level how operational risk is to be managed. This will include a vision, guiding principles, high-level procedures, strategy and reporting lines. The policy is also likely to give the governance structure within which operational risk is managed, including ultimate and intermediate responsibilities, information flows (both up and down the firm) and how operational risk is used within the firm.

Board commitment and sponsorship

It is important that there is clear commitment from the highest level of the firm before beginning the risk and control assessment. The board should approve the operational risk policy and a full member of the board should have responsibility for the management of risk. Without such sponsorship, a risk and control assessment will not be taken seriously and it is very unlikely that the risks and controls which the firm faces will be fully identified and monitored.

Business objectives

Risk and control assessments should start at a strategic level. It is therefore necessary to have a list of the business's strategic objectives so that the assessment can be carried out in relation to the principal aims of the firm. Without the business objectives to provide a focus, the risk and control assessment will lack an appropriate level in which to place its risks. The result will be a mixture of high-level, process and activity risks, which will give very little business benefit, due to the heterogeneous nature of the risks (and therefore the controls) and the lack of any clear connection with the business objectives relevant to each level.

Process and activity maps

These are not necessary, but if the firm is starting its risk and control assessment at a process level, it is useful that the processes are mapped so that all the processes are captured and the risk points can be seen. This is especially important if the process risk analysis is being carried out at a detailed level or at an activity level. The maps will help to identify where controls may be weak and therefore assist in control analysis. This can also be the start of process improvement, particularly through Six Sigma and Lean analyses. However, whilst it is possible to start risk and control assessments at a process or activity level, it is not recommended as it is very difficult to show quick business wins. Much better is to start at the top at the business strategy level.

BASIC COMPONENTS

Risk events

A risk event is an unchanging and distinct occurrence which may impact the firm's profit and loss account or its balance sheet. An event can have its origin in a number of causes or triggers, which may vary through time (Figure 5.3). An event may also generate different consequences or effects,

Cause, event and effect　　　　　　　　　　**Figure 5.3**

Cause	Event	Effect
Clash of world cultures Lax airport security	Planes colliding with buildings	Many deaths Major buildings claim
Cigarette Lack of sprinklers Poor storage	Building burns down	Loss of building Insurance claim Loss of business
Controls breakdown Markets go 'wrong' way Performance-based pay	Internal fraud	Jail for trader Regulatory fine Loss of reputation

which may also vary over time. However, the event itself is immutable. A risk event is evaluated in terms of the likelihood and the impact of a risk.

Risk owner

A risk owner has direct and explicit responsibility for the management of the risk event. This will ultimately be a board member, but ownership will be delegated down to an appropriate level and individual. Given that operational risk involves everybody in the firm, it could be said that everybody is a 'risk owner'. The identification of a specific risk owner ensures transparency and clarity over the management of a risk. It also enables the firm to judge its concentration exposure in terms of management responsibility for risks, as risk owners generally own several risks. The firm should try hard therefore to identify a single owner for each risk. However, for certain risks, composite owners are unavoidable. These will include a number of strategic risks, which the board will own as a whole.

Control

A control is the element within a process which has been developed to facilitate action to reduce or eliminate either the likelihood or impact of a risk event. A control is evaluated in terms of its design and performance.

Control owner

An owner of a control is an individual with responsibility for executing a control procedure. Several controls can be owned by one individual.

Action plans

Action plans are created in response to a control that does not reduce the risk to within the firm's tolerance for that risk. They modify or add to existing controls so that the risk is within the agreed appetite.

AVOIDING COMMON RISK IDENTIFICATION TRAPS

The first task when undertaking a risk and control assessment is to identify the risks which are to be assessed. That sounds simple enough, but there are a number of traps into which it is easy to fall.

Risk register

A risk register lists all the risks identified by a firm by risk category and may also be known as a risk inventory, a risk library or a risk list. Whilst it is useful to have a full list of risks identified by the firm, it can be constraining in a risk and control assessment, since participants tend to focus on the list rather than on what might prevent the firm from achieving its strategic objectives or the process from being carried out. Given that one of the purposes of a risk and control assessment is to identify the risks, the existence of a risk register begs the question as to how the risks in the register were identified and to what the risks relate. If there is a risk register, put it to one side and start the risk and control assessment from scratch. The register can be used later to check that no significant risks have been forgotten.

Cause/trigger

A cause or trigger is something which precipitates a risk event. The identification of triggers is helpful in recognising risk events and in avoiding confusion between a cause and an event. However, causes are more useful in assisting the identification of an efficient action plan; the prevention of a cause will, by definition, prevent a risk event.

Bear in mind, though, that causes of risk events change over time, so that preventing a cause today will not necessarily prevent the same risk event from occurring tomorrow from a different cause. Just as one cause can trigger many risk events, so a risk event can be triggered by many causes.

Effect/consequence

A risk effect or consequence is an occurrence which is precipitated by a risk event. These are often confused with risk events as they are the most obvious outcome of a risk event actually happening and are often easier to control or manage than the event itself. The control of an effect can give immediate short-term assurance to a risk owner, without having to undergo the more intellectually rigorous and longer analysis of the risk which precipitated the effect in the first place.

Indicators

Indicators show the movement in the likelihood or impact of a risk, in the design or performance of a control, or in the performance of a firm in relation to its objectives or processes. As such, existing key indicators are useful in identifying the risks and controls on which the firm focuses. However, key risk indicators and key control indicators are often mixed with key performance indicators, so a first step is to sort the indicators (see Figure 7.2 and Chapter 7 in general). Although there will be business benefit in sorting indicators into logical and consistent sets, this activity is likely to be outside the scope of a risk and control assessment and will therefore generally be undertaken separately.

Losses

Losses are the monetary result of a risk event occurring. Losses are often collected by firms, particularly in internal audit reports and reports to the audit committee. When loss causal analysis is used, this can again be helpful in identifying the risks which have occurred and controls which have failed. However, the risks will have been identified without any reference to the business objectives or processes and are often couched as control failures relating to causes or effects, rather than as risk events which resulted from the control failures. Again, care must be taken and additional work will probably be required for the analysis to be used in the risk and control assessment.

A firm's losses will only give a historical view of the risk events to which it has previously been subject. It is therefore important to understand that there will be many more potential risk events than are identified by a loss causal analysis. (See also Chapter 6, Events and losses.)

Stress tests and scenarios

A firm which has not yet performed a risk and control assessment will be unlikely to have contemplated stress tests and scenarios. Risk and control assessments give a valuable insight into the likely causes and effects of the risk events about which the firm is most concerned. Without a risk and control assessment it is unlikely that the firm will have separated causes from effects, a fundamental element to building scenarios. (See also Chapter 10, Stress tests and scenarios.)

Link to objectives/processes/activities

A risk and control assessment must be related to a business objective or procedure and must not be performed in isolation. It should start, and often does, as a strategic assessment linked to the business objectives, although assessments can be carried out on processes, activities and projects. The explicit link with business objectives gives the risk and control assessment a focus and enables risks to be identified within a framework and therefore at an appropriate level. Without such a link, it is difficult to relate the risks identified to a specific business area and therefore difficult to identify and provide clear business benefit.

Risk drivers, themes and categories

A risk driver is a single item comprising a collection of closely linked risk causes or triggers, which share an underlying similarity, such as a macro-economic downturn. A risk theme is a set of similar risks, such as fraud. In their first attempts at a risk and control assessment, firms often try to undertake the exercise at this high level, by using combinations of risk drivers and themes (see Assessing risks later in this chapter). This is possible, but has little benefit either to the business or to identifying a firm's risk profile. You need to get down to a granularity which yields business and operational risk benefit, but is not so unwieldy as to provide overwhelming and ultimately meaningless detail.

A risk category is a set of similar risk events, for which there is benefit in treating them as a group (see Table 1.1). This is obviously an advantage, but it is important that they are identified after the risk and control assessment and are not identified beforehand. The risk and control assessment will have been linked to the business objectives, so that any linked risks will naturally emerge from the risk and control exercise and be aligned to the objectives.

Link to products, geographic regions

Similar, or the same, risk event and control pairs often exist between related products (dollar bonds and sterling bonds) or comparable geographic regions (UK and USA). Conversely, some products, such as over-the-counter (OTC) derivatives, and regions (such as Southern Africa) will be more likely to have unique risk and control pairs. A thorough understanding of the firm's business is therefore essential when undertaking risk and control assessments to ensure that links are included.

Frequency of identification

Identifying risks (and their accompanying mitigating controls) should be a part of the firm's day-to-day business life and processes. Risk identification is a normal and natural part of being in business and should not be regarded as something which is done only once every six months or whenever a full risk assessment is performed.

Immutable

As noted above (in Risk events), a risk event is an unchanging and distinct occurrence. Although the causes of an event may change (a building burning down may be caused by different factors), the risk event itself does not change. This enables a consistent analysis to be taken of the gross risk to the business. It also enables the required controls to be viewed consistently for the same risk across a firm, as the firm may develop an ideal set of controls for the risk event. Comparability of the effectiveness of the controls for the same risk across a global organisation is then possible.

Triggers, consequences and control failures

As we have seen (see Cause/trigger and Effect/consequence above), a risk event is precipitated by triggers and itself precipitates an effect or effects. It is important to differentiate between these three connected occurrences so that it is the event which is mitigated and controlled.

If a cause or trigger is wrongly identified as an event, the focus of the assessment will probably be on control failures, rather than on the risk events themselves. Identifying a control failure as a risk event often leads to a new control being put in place to mitigate the apparent control failure, rather than the much more desirable effect of eliminating the failure through remedial action to the control which failed.

If a consequence is wrongly identified as a risk event, the focus of the mitigating effort will again not be the event itself, but rather one of the effects of the event. As consequences change over time, because the external environment changes or because of the effects of the controls themselves, the mitigating controls will become less efficient at reducing the effects of the risk event, through no fault of the controls themselves.

Reputational damage

Reputational damage is generally a consequence of a risk event. As such, there are strong arguments for not identifying it as a risk in its own right. However, many firms view this risk as their most serious and would not give credibility to a risk and control assessment which did not identify reputational damage as a risk. It is therefore important to ensure that double counting does not take place when using a risk and control assessment for quantification of operational risk (see Chapter 9, Modelling).

There are a number of examples of reputation damage in Chapter 16, Reputation risk. In the BP Deepwater Horizon example, BP's small resevoir of public trust and its conduct in the aftermath of the disaster caused a profound loss to its reputation and future business opportunities. But the reputational damage was a direct consequence of failures of risk controls.

Levels and components

Risks can be identified at different levels, for example Business objectives/processes/activities, as shown above. Firms will often struggle with how they will know which risks belong to which level. This question generally stems from a lack of consideration of the subject of the risk control assessment. If risks are being identified at a strategic level, it will be clearly inappropriate to identify risks at the detailed activity level. Conversely, strategic risks are too high level for an activity analysis.

If risks are being identified at the process, business unit or departmental level it is sometimes difficult to know when to stop. The best answer is to make clear reference to the particular process, business unit objective or departmental goal which is being considered. If that seems too difficult, it is often helpful to consider the components of the risk under analysis, i.e. the risks at the next level down. This allows the firm to articulate the detailed risks, whilst continuing to focus on the level under consideration. This will also help a future, more detailed, risk assessment.

Practical examples of levels and their components

Example

Strategic example: Internal fraud

Cause: Invalid claims paid.

Risk event: Internal fraud.

Control: Segregation of duties between claims and finance; escalating claims authorisation limits; quality assurance checks and system controls.

Impact:

- **Direct:** value of frauds (possible sum of multiple loss events).
- **Indirect:** improvements to IT security; cost of review of internal controls.

Process example: incorrect client take-on

Cause: Poor design of client take-on form.

Risk event: Incorrect client take-on.

Control: Automatic postcode check; independent review of input data; written confirmation of details from client.

Impact:

- **Direct:** incorrect booking of client trade.
- **Indirect:** ex-gratia payment to client to compensate for losses; redesign of form.

Activity example: suspense account balance write-off

Cause: Lack of clarity of ownership of reconciliation process.

Risk event: Suspense account balance write-off.

Control: Procedures for regular reconciliation and reporting on reconciliation accounts; follow-up actions on reconciling items.

▶

Impact:

- **Direct:** loss of un-reconciled balance.

- **Indirect:** management time attempting to reconcile accounts; re-engineering the process; opportunity cost through unexpected use of significant capital.

ASSESSING RISKS

Gross/net/target

Risks can be assessed at several levels of mitigation. Gross (or inherent) risk is assessed with no account taken of the controls which exist within a firm. The only controls which are assumed at the gross level are inherent controls such as people's honesty and society's willingness to obey the law. The advantage of assessing risk at a gross level is that there are no assumptions about the quality or existence (or otherwise) of controls. It also identifies the level of loss to which the firm is exposed if and when the existing controls fail.

Net (or residual) risk is assessed after allowing for the existing controls within the firm. This means that there are assumptions about the adequacy and continuing effectiveness of the controls. These assumptions are rarely stated in net risk assessments. If they are stated, they become close to control assessments. The object of this part of the exercise is to assess risks, not controls. The level of loss arising from a net risk assessment is the day-to-day loss which the firm suffers with the existing level of control.

Target risk is the name often given to the final level of expected risk appetite which exists within a firm after all mitigating effects are at the firm's desired level. It is used to assess the impact (and sometimes the effectiveness) of control enhancement plans.

If risks are assessed at a gross level, a control assessment can easily be linked to the risk assessment. If risk is assessed net, the control assessment is already implicit in the net risk assessment and the result will require reconciling back to the explicit control assessment.

Frequency of assessment

How often risk and control assessments are carried out is dependent on each firm's circumstances. Many firms carry out quarterly risk and control assessments, focusing on the risks and controls which have changed during the quarter. These firms will often carry out an annual risk and control assessment going back to the business objective or procedure which formed the basis for the original assessment. Other firms carry out half-yearly assessments at a more detailed level.

The best guide is to consider how frequently individual risks are likely to change. That probably means that it is unlikely that a full risk and control assessment will be performed on a monthly basis unless the risks are likely to change that frequently. At the extreme, an assessment may be carried out several times a day in a department responsible, say, for receiving retail firms' monies and sending out contract notes or policies.

Likelihood/frequency and impact/severity

Once risks are identified, they are evaluated for likelihood (or frequency) and impact (sometimes called severity). Likelihood is reviewed on the basis of how frequently a risk event will occur over a given period (e.g. monthly, three times a year, once in 50 years). Alternatively, many firms find it helpful to think of the percentage likelihood of a risk occurring in one year. A more detailed discussion on alternative likelihood terms and their possible weaknesses is given in connection with Table 10.1.

Impact is reviewed on the basis of the (possible) cost to the firm if the risk event happens. Whilst the term severity is also used by some firms as being synonymous with impact, the word may also be used as a single value for a risk assessment, being a combination of likelihood and impact. This was more common before separate likelihood and impact assessments became widely used.

Expected/unexpected

Risks can also be assessed using the terms expected or unexpected. This refers both to the expected or unexpected likelihood and to the expected or unexpected impact. In practice, both levels give value to a firm. The expected level will give a check on the usual effectiveness of the controls and therefore acts as a check on the provisions or reserves which are made on a regular basis by a firm. It is similar to the net risk level.

The unexpected level gives information about the amount of capital required to withstand a financial shock to the firm from a risk event occurring. This is similar to the gross risk level. The unexpected level is therefore used for assessing economic and regulatory capital requirements.

Qualitative compared with quantitative

Risks can be assessed on a qualitative or quantitative basis. A qualitative assessment will have a range of values which do not comprise figures, for example high, medium-high, medium-low and low. A quantitative assessment will, in contrast, have only figures, although ranges may be used, for example £10m or £10–50m for impact and 10% or 10–25% for likelihood. Some organisations are more comfortable with figures, although it is more common for a firm which is starting its risk assessment process to use a qualitative basis first (high/medium/low or red/amber/green, with no numeric definitions) and then move to a quantitative basis as it gains confidence and gathers objective information about its risks.

Periods for likelihood

The period used for likelihood assessment should be aligned to the level of risk being assessed. For example, an annual period (i.e. the interval in years between the risk happening) is probably inappropriate for an activity risk assessment. Conversely, the use of a monthly frequency would give possibly misleadingly large figures for a strategic assessment based on a five-year plan.

Direct loss or indirect loss for impact

Direct loss for impact is often easier to assess as it is linked to the charge to the profit and loss account. Even when there are no historical figures available, it can often be calculated easily. Indirect loss is much more difficult to assess and inevitably more subjective, as it is based on the total cost to the firm of a risk event occurring. Such items as opportunity loss, for example the loss of additional sales or the cost of redirecting staff to resolve an operational risk problem, are considered in evaluating indirect loss. This means that the indirect loss can often be a larger figure than the direct loss. Firms should be aware of the two levels of loss (direct and indirect) and combine the two to assess the true impact of risk events.

Impact assessed on profit and loss, plan period or shareholder value

A decision is also needed as to which period for the loss it is taking into account. Although multiple years can be considered in an assessment which uses the profit and loss account as a basis for impact, usually only the impact on the first year is evaluated.

Consideration of multiple years often occurs when a firm is using business objectives to be attained over a multi-year plan period as its risk reference. This can give rise to the concept of the net present value of the risk event, although this should be considered only if the firm is comfortable with the concept and already uses it in day-to-day business management.

The largest and most difficult value to assess is the impact on shareholder value, as this is a multi-year indirect loss figure. However, where a firm already uses shareholder value as a concept, its use should be seriously considered, as this is the true impact of a risk event on the owners of the firm.

Impact components

If the firm considers only direct losses, it significantly limits the business benefits of risk and control assessment. By breaking down the impact into separate components, such as financial, people, customer and other stake-holders, it can be easier and more beneficial to assess indirect as well as direct losses.

Loss causal analysis (see Chapter 6, Events and losses) typically analyses the components of the loss and can be used to ensure that the risk and control assessment is consistent with the loss analysis and so delivers business value.

Three/four/five or more scores

Whilst many organisations start their assessment process with three or four levels of scores for likelihood and impact, some use up to ten levels. Unless the firm is skilled in such scoring, it is more than likely that a lot of time will be used discussing whether a risk event is a six score or a seven score. There is usually no material difference between any two adjacent scores when a large number is used and therefore little business benefit in a long discussion on the matter. In any case, the scores are subjective and therefore only give an indication of relativities, not of absolutes.

One interesting question is whether to use an odd or an even number of scores. An even number will force a decision either side of a median value, whereas an odd number will allow a mean value, i.e. four levels might be low, medium-low, medium-high and high, which does not allow a mean score. Some organisations see an even number of possible scores as a benefit as it is often too easy to place a likelihood or an impact on the middle score. Others find it easier to differentiate between low and high if there is only medium in the middle. It can be argued that it is more correct to use odd numbers if the item being scored has a normal distribution as the mean of the distribution is clearly presented, although of course the mean can be inferred when an even number of scores is used. Although there are merits for both odd and even numbers of grades, the foibles of human nature point to an even number of grades as being best.

Use of periods compared with percentages

Technically, there is no difference between using time periods and using percentages for the likelihood of a risk occurring or a control failing. Initially, most people find it simpler to relate to time periods for likelihood (twice during the working week, once every three working months) than to percentages (40%, 1.67% respectively). It is often easier for a firm to articulate its likelihoods as time periods and for the operational risk manager to convert them to the percentages, which will be necessary for modelling the risk and its controls.

Ranges and single figures

Many organisations find it difficult to assess the risk likelihood and impact (and the control design and performance) as a single figure. The problem stems from the character of operational risk, which is naturally imprecise and variable. It is therefore problematic to attribute a single value to a dimension of operational risk assessment. A common way around this is to consider a range of values (£5m–£15m, rather than £10m). Single figure assessment can then be introduced after the firm has gained experience of the assessment process.

How to set the range

Once the decision to choose a range and time horizon has been made, the question arises as to the base used for the ranges. Many firms prefer to use gross revenues on which to base the range of values. These are useful because they can be directly affected by the business (the first line of defence) and therefore encourage embedding of the process. If net profitability is used, it must be borne in mind that it is more difficult for business heads to influence the costs allocated to them and they are therefore likely to be less willing to accept the ranges. However, particularly in industries with a very low profit margin, gross revenues may be inappropriate and profitability may be more relevant.

The beginning point of the highest range is often set at three or four months of gross revenues or profitability, whichever is appropriate. The top end of the lower ranges can then easily be set at one month and one week if four ranges are being used, the full set of four being: above three months; three months to one month; one month to one week; below one week. If five ranges are used, it is common to have an additional small range of two days, making the bottom two ranges one week to two days and below two days. You will notice that the top of each range is a multiple of around three to four of the one below. This is a useful rule of thumb when setting ranges.

One pair (impact/likelihood), two pairs (average and worst case) or three

Whilst most organisations start their risk and control assessments with assessing one pair of scores for a risk (such as impact/likelihood), some choose two pairs (adding average and worst case for each of impact and likelihood). A third level can be added, by taking the assessment of impact and likelihood to an 'extreme worst case'. In mathematical terms, average represents a 50% confidence level, 'business as usual worst case' takes the assessment to a 95% or 1 in 20 confidence level, whilst the third level reaches up to 99.5% or even 99.9% confidence (1 in 200 or 1 in 1000).

Two pairs help the firm to think about the expected and unexpected parts of a risk's distribution without making the mathematical part explicit. Three pairs enable a firm to begin to specify the distribution which constitutes the risk. A very occasionally used alternative is to specify a mean and a standard deviation, although this requires an understanding of mathematics which is generally beyond most managers.

Use of losses to back-test impacts and likelihood

Losses provide a real-life view to guide and challenge the subjective assessments which are made when considering the likelihood and impacts of risks. However, it is important to ensure that the causal analysis of the losses correctly identifies the risks to which the losses relate. The mapping of the risks underlying the losses to the risks which have been identified during the risk and control assessment is difficult but worthwhile as it enables a methodology to be established which tests the assessors' judgement against actual losses experienced by the firm.

This 'back-testing' technique should take account of any changes to the firm. An example might be an increase or decrease in staff numbers, which might affect the relevance of both the frequency and severity of losses to the firm as it currently exists. So when using losses, make sure that the risk profile when the losses occurred is the same as the risk profile at the time of the assessment. If not, adjustments will have to be made.

Heat maps

Heat maps give readily accessible and visual representation of the risk profile of a firm. They are often the first risk report seen by the board and, as such, must be positioned as the start of risk reporting and *not* the final risk report. They are helpful in allowing management to focus on the most significant risks to the firm, in the absence of any further data.

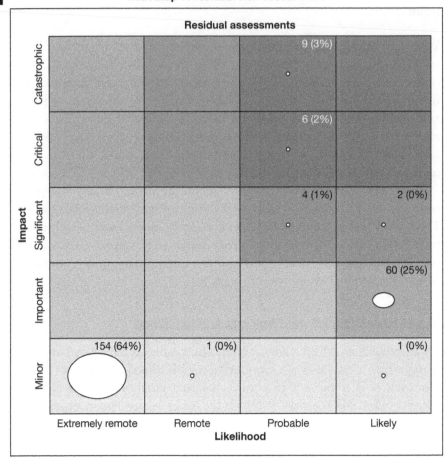

Figure 5.4   **Heat map of residual risk assessment**

Source: Courtesy of Chase Cooper Limited

Heat maps often start as net or residual risk heat maps (see Figure 5.4) and then expand to cover both gross and net risk as the firm develops its expertise in risk assessment, as shown in Figure 5.5 later. Illustrating, by means of a heat map, the reduction to a risk due to the mitigating effect of the controls is helpful in visualising which controls are fundamental to reducing the risk profile.

OWNERS

Different levels

There can only be one ultimate owner of a risk and that person must be at board level. However, the board director responsible for the risk may delegate the management of the risk to another person who in turn may delegate further. This can lead to confusion over who owns the risk. It is likely that those to whom the risk is delegated own only a part of the risk for which the board member is ultimately responsible. However, the risk and control assessment process will decompose the risk down to each level – strategic, process, activity. As a result, the person responsible for a particular process or activity which contributes to the strategic goal of the firm for which the board member is responsible will be clearly seen as the person who owns the risks inherent in the process or activity.

It is often also the case that the CEO is nominated as the owner of most of the risks when a board first considers its strategic risk profile. This must be challenged. Board members should take responsibility for their own risks, for example the sales and marketing director must take responsibility for risks relating to sales and marketing, such as mis-selling.

Risk owners

Risk owners may exist at several levels, although there is only one ultimate risk owner. The owner of the risk is responsible for measuring, monitoring and mitigating the risk, at the relevant level, within the risk appetite set by the board. The actual tasks of measuring, monitoring and mitigation are generally given to another member of staff. This does not reduce or remove the risk owner's responsibility for managing the risk, which is carried out through receiving and actioning reports from the staff to whom the tasks have been delegated.

Control owners

These are the people responsible for managing the mitigation of the risk through the operation of internal controls. Control owners are vital both in designing appropriate controls to mitigate the risk and in ensuring adequate performance of the control in line with the board's risk appetite. They are responsible for identifying any action plans necessary to increase the effectiveness of the control and are also responsible for implementing the action plans.

Liaison between risk owners and control owners

It is essential that there is good communication between the risk owner and the control owner. In an initial risk and control assessment it is often the case that the risk owner scores the control as less adequate than the control owner. This can be due to the risk owner not fully understanding the control, or to the control owner being too optimistic about the control's effectiveness due to a misunderstanding of the risk's likelihood and full impact. Both of these are probably due to a lack of communication between the risk owner and the control owner. With good communication it is possible to design and perform controls to a level which matches the firm's risk appetite, i.e. at the most efficient level for the firm. If necessary, the head of operational risk will challenge and resolve the different scores.

IDENTIFYING CONTROLS

Suitable level

Just as identifying a suitable level of risk can be a challenge, so too can identifying the appropriate level of control. However, as controls are typically identified after risks, it is often easier to set control identification to the appropriate level. If the risk identification has been set, for example, at a business objectives level, the controls which are identified should be at the same level.

It is very easy to identify controls at a departmental or activity level and relate these to the business objectives of a firm. However, this should be avoided as there will be a mismatch between the level of the risks and the level of the controls. Additionally, it is important to identify and then score the strategic controls which are in place to mitigate the risks to the business objectives. If this is not undertaken a firm can be lulled into a false sense of security, believing that its business risks are well controlled by a considerable number of activity or departmental controls.

Independent controls

When identifying controls, we are seeking to identify the independent controls which mitigate a risk. Although there is some point in identifying linked controls, far more business benefit will be achieved through identifying and scoring controls which are independent of each other. Controls which are linked to each other, perhaps in a sequence, are only as good as the preceding control. This means that if the first control in the sequence fails, none of the other controls gives any benefit in mitigating the relevant risk(s). It is therefore vital that controls are checked to ensure that they are independent, otherwise they become another source of false security.

An example of three typical independent controls are those which might be considered to mitigate the risk of 'Failure to attract, recruit and retain key staff', as shown in Figure 5.6 later: 'Salary surveys', 'Training and mentoring schemes' and 'Retention packages for key staff'. Linked controls within this example may be 'Salary increases' and 'Title changes', both of which are linked with 'Salary surveys'.

Mitigating more than one risk

It is often said that a single control mitigates more than one risk. In principle this may well be true. In practice it is unlikely that the application of the control is exactly the same. Often the control is the same, but applied differently by different departments. For example, a staff appraisal is a very common control which mitigates the risk of 'Failure to attract, recruit and retain key staff'. However, the control is likely to be applied differently in different departments and the effectiveness of the control will vary considerably around the firm. The head of operational risk should therefore challenge, whenever it is suggested that a control mitigates more than one risk, in order to avoid two similar controls being mistaken for the *same* control. The risk and control assessment shown in Figure 5.6 provides examples of similar but different controls, such as staff training as a control to improve competencies, and training and mentoring as a control to mitigate key staff turnover. It is important to define not just the control but its purpose.

Controls are only one form of mitigation

Controls are the most common continuing method of mitigating risks. They are completely within the management's sphere of influence and in a firm practising good operational risk management they will be increased or decreased to reflect the sensitivity of the firm to a particular risk. In practice this rarely happens, in part because of inertia. Firms should be alive to change and accept it as part of everyday life, all part of a culture of continuous improvement.

Another method of mitigation for the firm is to transfer the risk to another party entirely, for example through insurance (see Chapter 12, Insurance). This enables a clear cost to be attached to the mitigation through the premium charged by the insurance company. It also explicitly limits the exposure of the firm to the excess, or deductible, applied to the insurance policy. However, there may also be a limit to the loss which the insurance company is willing to suffer and the firm will once again be exposed above this limit.

Another method of mitigation is to remove the risk altogether from the firm, for example by ceasing business in the particular product to which the risk is attached. This is, of course, an extreme move to take but may be justifiable in the circumstances. For example, it was reported that Goldman Sachs withdrew from some markets before its peers during the 2007–9 financial crisis and by doing so considerably reduced its losses.

Types of controls

Controls can be divided into four types: directive, preventative, detective and corrective.

- Directive controls provide a degree of direction for the firm and are typically policies, procedures or manuals.

- Preventative controls act to prevent the risk or event from happening. They are often automated controls, such as guards round a piece of machinery or system checks to prevent limits being exceeded.

- Detective controls act after the risk or event has happened and identify and mitigate the risk which has occurred. Typical detective controls might be the sensors providing warnings of the safety around a piece of machinery being compromised, or reconciliations and monitoring of accounting entries.

- Corrective controls again act after the risk event has happened and mitigate the effects of the event through remedial action. Typical corrective controls are following-up on outstanding reconciliation items or other risk reports and taking action following risk monitoring.

It is helpful to differentiate the controls identified into their various types (see also Chapter 7, Indicators, for a further use of these four types of controls). This enables the firm to assess whether it has a balance of the different types of controls or whether it has a number of, for example, detective and corrective controls but lacks directive and preventative controls. With this imbalance, a firm will be unlikely to prevent a risk from occurring, but may be well placed to minimise the impact of a risk when it does occur. An example of such a risk would be an external event beyond the firm's management influence, such as flooding or a terrorist attack.

Effects of preventative and detective controls on risk likelihood and impact

Analysing preventative and directive controls is particularly important in risk and control assessments as they tend to reduce the likelihood of a risk occurring, whereas detective and corrective controls tend to reduce the impact that the firm suffers. Most risk managers aim to have a balance, where possible, of controls which mitigate a risk before the event and its effects after the event. As illustrated in the paragraph above, this is not always possible.

When a variety of types of controls have been identified, their effects can be assessed on the gross likelihood and gross impact scores. This provides validation and confirmation of net likelihood and net impact scores if the firm has undertaken a net risk assessment. Additionally, the effects can be graphically illustrated on a heat map (see Figure 5.5), a visual representation which rapidly assists management perception and action.

Heat map showing effects of types of control on a risk

Figure 5.5

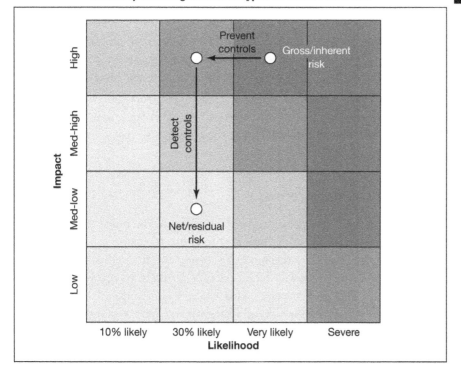

Design and performance

Controls should be assessed on their inherent ability to mitigate risk, their design, and on their actual performance. There are a number of advantages to this method of assessment over the previous methodology of assessing only the effectiveness of a control:

- It enables a control assessment to differentiate between the theoretical and the actual effectiveness of the control. Whilst a control may be theoretically effective, such as a reconciliation performed to mitigate the mis-statement of an account balance, it may not be very effective in reality. It may only be performed monthly, rather than the intended period of weekly, or reconciling items may not be followed up diligently.
- The 4Ws (who, where, when and what) can be used to help the assessment of the design of a control. If the 4Ws are well understood, it is likely that an assessment of the design of the control will be high. However, the performance assessment will then reflect how well the 4Ws are actually carried out.
- The design of a control is often a reflection of the systems or processes underpinning that control, whereas the performance of a control is often

about the people operating the control. Assessing both design and performance enables action plans to be drawn up which enable a control to be better focused. A control which has a poor design is likely to require improvements to the systems or processes relating to that control. A control with poor performance is more likely to require a focus on training, additional people to operate the control, or a different level of skill.

■ The use of two directions to assess a control mirrors the two dimensions (likelihood and impact) used to assess a risk. This facilitates a comparison of the strength of the controls compared with the risk that the controls are mitigating.

Three/four/five or more scores

Just as with risks, some thought must be given to the number of scores for design and performance. Most organisations use the same number of levels for control scoring as they use for risk scoring; if a firm is using four levels for likelihood and four levels for impact, it is likely to use four levels for each of design and performance. This enables easy comparison between a composite risk score of likelihood times impact, and a composite control score of design times performance. Otherwise normalisation of either the risk score or the control score will be required.

The same consideration must be given to using an odd or an even number of control scores as was given for scoring risks. It is even easier to place a control score in the middle of a range. It is however unusual for a firm to have more than four or five levels for control scoring unless a considerable amount of loss causal analysis is undertaken by the firm.

Use of losses

Loss causal analysis is extremely useful in providing objective knowledge of the probable failure of controls, particularly due to poor performance. Even without comprehensive data it is still possible to use losses as a guide to the likely scoring of a control. For example, a control is unlikely to be scored as having a good performance if a number of losses have occurred recently due to its failure. Conversely, no losses occurring in recent times may be an indication of good performance – or simply of good luck.

Use of periods compared with percentages

As with risks, the same consideration should be given to the use of periods compared with percentages. Most people find it much simpler to relate to time periods for the likely failure of controls, for example once a week, twice a month or once every three months. It is often easier for control owners to assess the design and performance of controls using time periods and for the risk manager to convert them to percentages, as required, for monitoring and modelling.

Ranges compared with single figures

Although many firms find difficulty in assessing the risk likelihood and impact as a single figure, it appears to be easier for control owners to relate to single figures or periods than ranges of control failure. This may be partially due to the fact that controls tend to be better understood by control owners as they often operate, or at least review, controls on a relatively frequent basis. The use of a range for the failure of a control may therefore be less helpful than a range for the likelihood or impact of a risk.

Importance and compliance

As well as design and performance being used as an assessment pair for controls, some firms use the importance of the control and how compliant the firm is to the control. The importance is assessed in relation to the mitigation of the risk and the compliance is assessed by not only how well the control is performed, but also taking into account findings of internal audit and compliance. This is a more complex form of assessment and is used by only a minority of firms.

WHAT A RISK AND CONTROL ASSESSMENT LOOKS LIKE

The results of a risk and control assessment will typically look like the example given in Figure 5.6. This contains numeric assessments of risks and controls and identifies the specific controls and both the risk and control owners. Colours or shading help to identify quickly and easily where the greatest risks lie and where to prioritise risk and control monitoring.

ACTION PLANS

Explicit acceptance of risks or need for action plans

When the gross risk has been assessed and the current quality of control(s) for each risk has been scored it is possible to review whether the net risk remaining is acceptable to the firm, or whether there is a need for an action plan to either enhance the control(s) or reduce the risk exposure in some other way.

Figure 5.6

Typical risk and control assessment

ID	Risks	Owner(s) of the risk	I	L	S	Controls	Owner(s) of the control	D	P	E
1	Failure to attract, recruit and retain key staff	SR	4	4	16	Salary surveys	TJ	2	2	4
						Training and mentoring schemes	TB	3	2	6
						Retention packages for key staff	TJ	4	4	16
2	Financial advisers misinterpret/fail to understand the complexity of 'equity release' products	PL AB	4	4	16	Staff training	TB	4	4	16
						Learning gained from previous deals	KW & EL	4	4	16
						Review of individual needs in performance appraisal process	TB	3	2	6
						Procedure manuals for processes	EL	4	4	16
3	Poor staff communication	SR JK	4	4	16	Defined communication channels	ZK	4	3	12
						Documented procedures and processes	EL	3	2	6
4	Failure to understand the law and/or regulations	PL	4	3	12	Internal training courses	EL	4	4	16
						Regular updates from various sources	EL	4	1	4
						External training courses	TB & EL	4	3	12
5	Poor detection of money laundering	PL	4	3	12	AML annual training	TB & EL	3	2	6
						Circulation of BBA awareness circulars	EL & ZK	3	1	3
						KYC	ALL	4	3	12
6	Insufficient funds/deposits to cater for lending activities	CK	4	3	12	Liquidity risk policy	ZK	4	4	16
						Advertising	KW	4	3	12
						Economic forecasting	CK	3	3	9
7	Over-selling credit cards	CK	4	3	12	Staff training	TB	3	3	9
						Credit scoring	EL	4	4	16
						Forward business planning	ZK	3	3	9
8	Over-deployment of management resources on regulatory issues	RU CK	3	4	12	Monthly budget against actual review	TJ	3	4	12
						Corporate governance	CK	4	4	16
						Monthly head of compliance & CEO meetings	CK	2	2	4
9	Failure to capture market opportunities	AB	3	3	9	Competitor monitoring	TB	3	4	12
						Product development	TB	2	2	4
10	Over-dependency on outsourcing	CK	3	3	9	SLAs	CK & EL	4	4	16
						Outsourcing monitoring	CK & EL	4	4	16
						Due diligence	CK	4	3	12
						Policy	CK	3	4	12
11	Weakness in information security system	RU JK	4	2	8	Record retention	ZK	2	2	4
						Information security policy procedure and monitoring	ZK	3	2	6
						Staff training and certification	TB	3	3	9
						Client agreements/marketing	ZK & KW	2	1	2
12	Inadequate or insufficient IT infrastructure to achieve business objectives	JK	2	4	8	Business/strategic planning	ZA & KW	3	4	12
						IT systems performance and capability monitoring	ZK	4	3	12
13	External fraud activities	PL	3	2	6	Anti-fraud training	ZK	4	4	16
						Systems security	ZK	4	4	16
14	Failure to grow staff competencies	SR	3	2	6	Staff training	TB	4	3	12
						Hire of temporary staff	TB	2	2	4
						Appraisals	TB	2	3	6
15	Misaligned employee goals	SR CK	2	3	6	Appraisals	TB	2	3	6
						Corporate governance	ZA	4	4	16
16	Failure to sense and eliminate internal fraud	PL	3	2	6	Criminal background check	EL	3	2	6
						Segregation of duties	ZA	2	3	6
						Staff training	TB	3	2	6
						Fraud monitoring	EL	4	4	16
						Whistle blowing	ALL	3	3	9
17	Unfit or inappropriate new products launched	AB	4	1	4	Staff training	TB	3	2	6
						New products approval process	KW	3	2	6
18	Poor strategic decision making	CK AB	4	1	4	Monitoring of market data	KW	4	4	16
						Research and forecasting	KW	4	2	8
						Monthly Management Forum	ZA	4	3	12
						Marketing strategy review	ZA & KW	3	3	9
19	Inaccessible premises	RU	3	1	3	BCP/M	EL	4	3	12
						Security of floors (to enable loss to be better managed)	ZA	3	4	12
						Building and firm guards	ZA	4	4	16

Key: I = impact; L = likelihood; D = design; P = performance; S = severity; E = effectiveness

Source: Courtesy of Chase Cooper Limited

Action plan details

Each action plan should be linked to a risk and to the relevant control, where appropriate. One possible action is, of course, to implement a new control (rather than enhance an existing control) and therefore it will only be possible to link this to a risk. An owner should be identified for the action plan and this will typically be the risk owner if the action plan is for a new control or the control owner if the action plan is to enhance an existing control. The owner should be notified in writing that an action plan has been raised against their name. A target date should be agreed with the owner and noted in the action plan. Any delay to the date should also be noted with the reason for the delay.

If the action is significant, and will take a considerable time to complete, then a cost–benefit analysis may be appropriate. Part of this analysis may be a consideration of the firm's risk appetite in comparison to the new resultant net risk and may involve mathematical modelling of the existing and proposed risk profiles.

HOW TO GO ABOUT A RISK AND CONTROL ASSESSMENT

Third party review, facilitated sessions, self-assessment

Facilitated sessions for risk assessment are the most common way to begin assessing a firm's risks and controls. Self-assessment by a firm is a common aim. A typical self-assessment will be facilitated by the risk department, with staff from the business line or department being assessed providing a detailed functional knowledge. This will enable a common and consistent approach to self-assessment across the firm whilst utilising the detailed skills and knowledge relating to particular risk areas.

However, there is a lot of merit in assessment sessions being facilitated by a third party, such as a consultant, and by the head of operational risk or the head of risk of the firm. This enables the best of both worlds to be obtained by using someone with outside knowledge of risk methodologies combined with someone with internal knowledge of the firm.

An independent review of risks and controls by a third party provides relatively little business benefit. An outside third party may bring a wider knowledge of risks and controls, but the firm itself should be in the best position to understand its own risks and controls. However, a third party with a wider knowledge can provide benchmarking against similar firms, which can be invaluable in helping the firm to improve its controls and so reduce its risk profile cost-effectively.

Workshops, interviews, questionnaires

Whichever one of the above approaches is used, the methodology can be applied through workshops, interviews or questionnaires. Each of these has different advantages:

- Workshops enable the sharing and discussion of risks relating to an area. The team involved in the workshop is able to spend time agreeing on the risks and debating the impact and likelihood of each risk. This will often be the first time that the team, as a whole, has considered the risks and controls to the area. The workshop can be used as an effective team-building mechanism enabling all attendees to function more coherently in the future due to a shared assessment of the risks and controls. The two major disadvantages of a workshop are the required coordination of diaries to allow all members of the team to attend and the combined time required from the team. Workshops also need to be ably facilitated to make sure that participants have an equal voice and are not dominated by the behaviour or seniority of one of their members.

- Interviews are far more efficient in the use of time required initially as each person is usually able to identify and assess the relevant risks quickly. However, a second round of interviews is often required in order to share the combined risk assessment with each participant. This can quickly degenerate into a considerable number of rounds of interviews unless the process is well managed. There is also relatively little team building when interviews are used.

- Questionnaires can be particularly useful when the team relating to the area to be assessed is widespread. For example, if an international business is being assessed, it may require team members to travel from many different locations if the assessment is by workshop. However, question-naire responses are difficult to collate if a questionnaire is an open one. Conversely, the responses can be too narrow and insufficiently illumi-nating for senior management if the questions are too closed.

One important thing to remember about all of these is their susceptibility to various forms of bias, either in the questions being asked, the experience of the participants, the relevant seniorities of participants or simply the way in which they are conducted. Similar issues arise with scenarios and the topic of behavioural bias is covered in more detail in Chapter 10, Stress tests and scenarios.

Follow-up

A risk and control assessment workshop, interview or questionnaire invar-iably requires follow-up work. This will typically be in relation to further control investigation and testing. Additionally, risk and control assessment participants need further time to consider the scores to be assigned to controls, and sometimes to risks as well. Action plans are another common area requiring follow-up after a risk and control assessment.

Validation of the identified risks and controls (and their scores) can also be obtained by follow-up discussions with peer group members and with internal audit (see also Use of losses to back-test impacts and likelihood above).

Control effectiveness

Once controls have been identified and scored, it is possible to assess their effectiveness in mitigating the risk. Control scores can be directly compared with risk scores although many organisations use pictorial representations such as heat maps (see Figure 5.4) and spidergrams (see Figure 4.6).

USING RISK AND CONTROL ASSESSMENTS IN THE BUSINESS

Link to risk appetite

As we discussed fully in Risk appetite, Chapter 4, Operational risk appetite, when illustrated graphically either in a coloured table or spidergram, RCAs are an excellent way of assessing risks and controls against the risk appetite set by a firm's management for those risks.

Link to provisions/budgets

The expected level of risk impact, i.e. the net or residual level after controls, can be linked to management provisions and budgets as this is the 'accepted' level of loss from a risk and will therefore be taken into account when calculating internal management figures. This level of impact can be regarded as the cost of doing business. Where there is little or no link between management budgets for expected loss figures and the figure indicated as the residual impact on a risk assessment, management should be challenged on the validity of the budget or the residual impact or both.

Using risk and control assessments for quantification

Risk and control assessments can be used for quantification and modelling purposes, as well as internal and external losses. A risk and control assessment is a good indication of the internal control environment, which is one of the four items required for advanced modelling of operational risk (see Chapter 9, Modelling, for more details).

Additionally, risk and control assessments can be used to make clear the effects of a scenario on the risk profile of a firm. A scenario will inevitably change the mitigation effects of controls and may reveal further risks to a firm. These can be reflected in the relevant risk and control assessments (see Chapter 10, Stress tests and scenarios, for more details).

Internal audit

The production of risk and control assessments is of great use to internal audit. A risk assessment identifies areas where management feels much of the controls are perfectly adequate and areas where management believe that the controls require enhancement. Internal audit based on perceived adequate controls can be extremely helpful. If it is confirmed that controls are indeed adequate, remedial action can be focused elsewhere. However, if the internal audit finds that controls are not operating as intended and as believed, the need for remedial action is clear.

WHY DO RISK AND CONTROL ASSESSMENTS GO WRONG?

Risk and control assessments 'go wrong' for many reasons. The most common ones are:

- lack of management buy-in to the risk and control assessment process because there is little perceived business benefit: this leads to strategic risks not being identified and to the assessment process not being taken seriously
- paper overload resulting from too many questionnaires
- lack of feedback from the risk department to the area being assessed
- inflexible software leading to the assessment process being discredited
- failure to link indicators and losses to the identified risks and controls leading to a lack of coherence and consistency in the assessment
- lack of action/follow-up to controls which are viewed as ineffective or to risks which have too few controls.

Of these, the critical ones are: lack of buy-in, lack of feedback and lack of follow-up or action. All are symptomatic of a lack of commitment to operational risk management. If the right management structures are in place, a risk and control assessment will be seen as the simple and valuable process which it is and the problems quoted will either not exist or will be dealt with.

SUMMARY

Risk and control assessments are probably the first step in establishing an operational risk management process. The concepts of impact and likelihood assessments are readily grasped and they can deliver quick business benefit to the risk owners in the business as well as those in either an oversight or independent assurance role.

To be truly effective, they should be linked to objectives at each level of the business. They come with a number of health warnings as this chapter has made clear. There needs to be clarity about the levels of both risks and controls and especially clarity about whether the thing being assessed is a cause, event or effect.

Risk and control assessments, though, are only one tool in the toolbox of the operational risk manager. They should be used in conjunction with loss causal analysis (see Chapter 6, Events and losses), indicators (see Chapter 7) and scenario analysis (see Chapter 10, Stress tests and scenarios), which we shall go on to look at in the following chapters.

6

Events and losses

INTRODUCTION

Events and losses are a fundamental part of operational risk management. They are a clear and explicit signal that an operational risk has occurred. This may be due to the failure of a control, the lack of a control or simply a very unusual event that was not foreseen.

As shown in Figure 6.1, events are one of the three fundamental processes of operational risk management. They provide a valuable objective challenge to the subjective nature of risk and control assessments. They are also often used as indicators of risks and controls (as we shall see in Chapter 7, Indicators).

Figure 6.1	Typical operational risk framework, showing position of events

Source: Courtesy of Chase Cooper Limited

WHAT IS MEANT BY AN EVENT

Typically, the term 'event' is used to describe the occurrence of a risk – whether or not an actual loss is suffered by the firm. Events can be categorised as hard or soft and direct or indirect. Examples of these categories in the event of the loss of an IT system are:

■ a direct hard event is the overtime money paid to the software and hardware engineers to restore the system – this is the money which actually flows out of the firm

■ an indirect hard event is the extra food and hotel bills paid to feed and accommodate the software and hardware engineers whilst they will restore the system – this is also money which has flowed out of the firm

- a direct soft event is the loss of sales that were unable to be concluded – although this is difficult to quantify, it is a direct consequence of the event

- an indirect soft event is less growth achieved by the firm than it had budgeted – this is also difficult to quantify, although it is still a consequence of the event.

Near misses

Events can also be categorised into actual losses or near misses. An actual loss is easy to describe in that it is a debit to the profit and loss account of the firm or the reduction of the value of an asset held by the firm.

There are at least two different definitions of a near miss:

Near miss   **Definition**

1. An event which would have occurred if the final preventative control had not worked.

2. An event has happened, but it did not result in an actual financial or non-financial loss or harm due to either the correct operation of detective and/or corrective controls or simply the random nature of events.

Clearly, in the first definition, there is no actual loss because the risk has not occurred. However, valuable information can be captured by identifying and analysing even this sort of event, since one or more controls have failed in order for a near miss to have occurred.

In the second definition, either a positive or a negative value is attached to the event (a gain or a loss), or there is no financial impact at all, although there may be some non-financial impact. Some firms which adopt the first definition as a near miss characterise the second definition as an incident, to differentiate it from an event which has a negative financial impact. Again, there is significant operational risk management information: preventative controls have failed (or they did not exist) and need to be analysed, whilst the detective and corrective controls may have worked; or the firm may have been very fortunate. As an example, a brick falls from the top of a building on a building site, but nobody is hit or hurt.

Near misses are therefore invaluable for challenging risk and control assessment scores. They are particularly helpful in assessing the performance of controls. If there have been a number of near misses relating to a specific preventative control, the current score of that control should be questioned, especially if its performance is assessed as good or even very good.

Gains and offsets

Operational event profits and gains are just as valuable for challenging likelihood and impact assessments as operational event losses. Of course, in many areas (such as the trading floor) gains and losses should be equal in number. A trader's 'fat finger' is as likely to produce a gain as a loss. However, human nature being what it is, this is rarely seen in reports and is a reflection of a bias in reporting. Many profits are absorbed into the business line, whereas losses are usually identified explicitly.

Inevitably, and throughout most of this chapter, events and losses tend to be spoken of in the same breath. We are primarily concerned with negative impacts, whether they are financial or reputational. In operational risk, however, events which produce gains are just as valuable a source of information because they also represent control failures. Operational risk is not all about adverse consequences. It demands a different risk mindset.

As well as gains being realised when an event happens, sometimes an event will generate offsetting amounts to the actual loss. These may themselves be hard or soft and direct or indirect. For example, if the loss of an IT system prevents a trader from reducing a position which then results in an unexpected profit, there is a financial offset. From an operational risk perspective, the offset should be separated from the costs involved in the loss of the IT system and both should be investigated.

Likewise, recoveries should be separately identified so that the gross loss is known, as well as the net loss. A typical recovery is a claim on an insurance policy. This may be viewed as the operation of a corrective control which transfers the financial loss to a third party outside the firm. Alternatively, recoveries may be obtained directly from a third party. An example of this will be the back-valuing of a payment by a counterparty who has paid late.

Lost data

One of the great problems with operational risk is that it depends on the comprehensive reporting of events and losses, near misses and gains in order to build up as accurate a picture as possible of the scale of operational risk in the firm, or whether controls are effective. However, events and losses are rarely reported fully. Actual losses are the best reported, although even these are frequently incomplete. As noted above, near misses are less frequently reported and gains are rarely reported at all. Considerable amounts of information are therefore in danger of being lost.

One way some firms have successfully tackled the problem of lost data is by making the operational risk function responsible for the insurances of the firm. The head of operational risk (in conjunction with the CFO) then assures the business line heads that any potential loss which is reported to operational risk within 12 hours of first being identified will not be charged to the business line profit and loss, even if it ultimately results in an actual loss. This approach:

- encourages more complete reporting of events and losses
- encourages earlier reporting of events and losses
- encourages near-miss reporting, as events are reported before they become losses
- does not disadvantage the firm, as losses simply move from one account centre to another (business line to risk management)
- results in the insurance buyers in the firm being more fully informed.

DATA ATTRIBUTES

Given the valuable business uses to which events and losses – and gains – can be put (see later, Use of events), the next step in the process is to decide what information should be gathered about the events and losses. The information collected will vary from firm to firm, but there is a minimum set of data attributes which is collected:

- name of the firm in which the event occurred
- geographic location of the event
- business activity
- loss event type, down to a detailed level
- the event start date, discovery date (and end date, if the event has finished)
- description of the event
- causes of the event
- amount of loss and recovery components
- management actions taken.

Name of firm

This may seem obvious, but in a group of companies more than one firm may be involved. Often both the name of the organisation in which the event occurred and the name of the organisation in which the event is detected are recorded as both of these are important from a risk management and control improvement perspective. Additionally, data may be held relating to the firm which will suffer any loss, as this may be different from the firm in which the event occurred and the firm which detected the event. This can happen, particularly in a group, where the firm in which a transaction is booked is different from the firm in which the transaction is originally undertaken and again different from the firm processing the transaction.

Geographic location

Recording where an event happens is important from an operational risk management perspective. There may be control weaknesses which are inherent in a particular location (perhaps due to ethnic culture) or, alternatively, which indicate a better or worse control culture, as compared with other locations. Either way, it is vital to understand each area's control ability so that decisions on improving controls can be taken based on knowledge, rather than take a blanket approach, possibly based on guesswork.

Business activity

Identifying the particular business activity or product line is useful, especially in a group where business units in different companies may be involved in the same activity or in selling similar products. It helps to achieve consistent reporting, both within the group and if external reporting is necessary, perhaps to a government body or regulator, although it is not often that the taxonomy of external reports conform to internal ones. Recording the business activity can also identify units where controls which are operated across a particular activity have failed, or appear to have been particularly successful, and point to improvements which will benefit the whole group.

An example of business activities used by an industry is the table of business lines set by the Basel Committee in its Revised Framework issued in June 2004 (see Table 6.1). These are focused on profit centres (as given by the name 'business lines'). But cost centres are just as valid. Significant operational risk events can occur in, for example, HR, the legal division, IT or even the CEO's office. In fact some of the biggest risks lie at the door of the CEO's office. Examples range from unguarded statements (Ratner) to outright fraud (Enron and Maxwell).

Firms should, of course, draw up their own schedules of business lines or activities. The list given in Table 6.1 is bank-related. In banking, all banks can draw up their own lists, but have to be able to map them to the 'Basel' business lines. Whilst a common taxonomy may help regulators to compare firms and jurisdictions, there is a danger that firms simply adopt the regulators' taxonomy, without really thinking about what is useful for their business.

The Basel business lines are, in fact, often fairly meaningless even to many financial services firms as there are relatively few firms which span a significant number of business lines. Firms which cover only one or two business lines, such as asset managers, are far more likely to analyse the loss data at a detailed level which is relevant to them. They may prefer to categorise loss data by fund type or by each fund. It is common for the trustees of a fund to require notification from the manager of losses which have been suffered by the fund above a certain level, either an absolute monetary amount or a specified percentage of the fund assets under management.

Generic financial services business lines — Table 6.1

Business lines		
Level 1	Level 2	Examples of activity groups
Corporate finance	Corporate finance Municipal/government finance Merchant banking Advisory services	Mergers and acquisitions, underwriting, privatisations, securitisation, research, debt (government, high yield), equity, syndications, IPOs, secondary private placements
Trading and sales	Sales Market making Proprietary positions Treasury	Fixed income, equity, foreign exchanges, commodities, credit, funding, own position securities, lending and repos, brokerage, debt, prime brokerage
Retail banking	Retail banking	Retail lending and deposits, banking services, trust and estates
	Private banking	Private lending and deposits, banking services, trust and estates, investment advice
	Card services	Merchant/commercial/corporate cards, private labels and retail
Commercial banking	Commercial banking	Project finance, real estate, export finance, trade finance, factoring, leasing, lends, guarantees, bills of exchange
Payment and settlement	External clients	Payments and collections, funds transfer, clearing and settlement
Agency services	Custody	Escrow, depository receipts, securities lending (customers) corporate actions
	Corporate agency	Issuer and paying agents
	Corporate trust services	
Asset management	Discretionary fund management	Pooled, segregated, retail, institutional, closed, open, private equity
	Non-discretionary fund management	Pooled, segregated, retail, institutional, closed, open
Insurance	Life	Life, annuities, pensions, health
	General	Property, motor, third-party liability, crime, credit and suretyship, marine, aviation, transport
Retail brokerage	Retail brokerage	Execution and full service

Source: Basel Committee on Banking Supervision, *International Convergence of Capital Measurements and Capital Standards: A Revised Framework*, June 2004, Annex 6

Equally a regional retail bank will find significant business value in categorising its losses by the detailed products it sells to its customers, or alternatively categorising by department. The choice is often determined by the level of risk analysis undertaken by the firm. This will be influenced by, and will influence, the level at which risk and control assessments are carried out.

Loss event type

Classifying losses by business activity or product line is important. But the foundation of operational loss analysis is to be able to allocate losses to loss event types. The difficulty with loss event types is to have enough to be able to break down operational risk losses into sufficient granularity to be useful for effective and intelligent operational risk management, without disappearing into an unwieldy myriad of detailed categories. Those who handle volumes of manual reports can tell you that in any batch, anything up to 30% of entries will contain at least one data element which is incorrectly recorded. The more loss categories you have, the more likely it is that events will be incorrectly recorded, however excellent your instructions may be.

Remember that loss event types are not a substitute for risk types. You need to be clear as to whether you are classifying risks or risk events. Risks are generally 'failures to …' or 'poor …'. Events are the manifestation of a risk actually occurring.

Another example from the Basel Committee is given in Table 6.2. This is a start for financial services firms, but is not detailed enough to provide meaningful management analysis, even if it apparently helps the regulators to understand the operational risk profile of banks. It also confuses causes and effects with the events it is aiming to record.

How you classify loss events both is, and should be, up to you, but always remember that how you classify will affect much of your operational risk analysis.

Dates

It might be thought that the date of an event or loss is a fairly simple piece of data to record. However, it can be difficult to ascertain, particularly if the event occurred several months before detection. Often the only clear date is when the event is discovered. Some events occur over a period of time, in which case it is helpful to record the start and end dates. On the other hand, when an event is first reported, it is often ongoing and it may be a number of months before it is closed and the loss established.

Where the 'event' is in fact a number of separate events linked by a single cause, such as the unauthorised trading undertaken by Nick Leeson at Barings and Jérôme Kerviel at Société Générale, a single date may be inappropriate and a period may work better. In that case, though, it is important to consider the effect on estimates of likelihood, since dates are fundamental to this. In operational risk assessments, even dates are not as simple as they seem.

Generic financial services loss event types   Table 6.2

Basel loss event types	
Level 1	Level 2
Internal fraud	Unauthorised activity Theft and fraud
External fraud	Theft and fraud Systems security
Employment practices and workplace safety	Employee relations Safe environment Diversity and discrimination
Clients, products and business practices	Suitability, disclosure and fiduciary Improper business or market practices Product flaws Selection, sponsorship and exposure
Damage to physical assets	Disasters and other events
Business disruption and system failures	Systems
Execution, delivery and process management	Transaction capture, execution and maintenance Monitoring and reporting Customer intake and documentation Customer/client account management Trade counterparties Vendors and suppliers

Source: Adapted from Basel Committee on Banking Supervision, *International Convergence of Capital Measurements and Capital Standards: A Revised Framework*, June 2004, Annex 7

Description

At a minimum, a brief description of the event should be given. However, some firms require event descriptions which can run to a page or more. Whilst it is helpful to have all the information recorded, this may work against the speedy and timely reporting of events – or even their being reported at all. A well-run firm may have an absolute requirement for a brief description within, say, 24 hours of the event being detected, followed by a more detailed description when sufficient information is available.

Causes

Cause lies at the heart of operational risk management. It is not enough to know that an event occurred or nearly occurred. It is essential to understand why, so that remedial action can be taken. Reporting events and not causes means that they can be counted, but not managed. The cause of an event should form part of the detailed description of an event, although it is more helpful to report it separately. There is a danger, if cause, event and effect are not separately identified, for the loss event type (of the types shown in Table 6.2) to be used as a proxy for causal analysis. There is relatively little loss of business benefit by doing so if the point of the exercise is to provide a consistent basis for assessing risk. But the point is often ignored.

There are certainly benefits to be gained through a more accurate description of the cause of an event and allocating causes to generic causal categories. But the most important information in reports of loss events is to identify the controls which have failed. At least a primary control failure should be identified, although firms should identify secondary control failures as well. A single event is often the result of a number of control failures. Careful causal analysis will identify priorities to enhance or improve controls.

Since a single cause can trigger a number of different risk events, linked risks can also be identified by recording causes, as well as any risk indicators which relate to the event. This will enable a holistic analysis of events to be easily undertaken, which will link together the three fundamental operational risk management processes of risk and control assessments, indicators and event causal analysis.

Amount of loss and recovery components

As noted above, the impact of events can be divided into hard and soft as well as direct and indirect. The hard direct impact, where it exists, is always recorded. The other three categories may be recorded, depending on the relative sophistication of the causal analysis carried out by the firm. It should also be recognised that the final amount of the loss may not be known for a number of months and only estimates may be available when the event is first detected. Alternatively, a first actual monetary value may be available immediately, which may then require changing as the event progresses and more information becomes available.

In a firm which operates in a number of currencies, particularly where an event spans several countries, attention should be paid to the currency in which the event and its subsequent increments are reported. In a group, financial reports are usually anchored back to the head office currency as this simplifies reporting and analysis at the group level. However, currency rates vary over time and account must be taken of this. To prevent the confusion which can occur if the amount of loss from an event is regularly recalculated according to prevailing exchange rates, the simplest practice is to rely on the exchange rate obtaining when the event is first reported. As rates fluctuate, that could, of course, mask the materiality of a particular event, but it has the merit of consistency.

One final issue is where a number of events, possibly relatively small in value, are linked by a single cause, but in aggregate amount to a significant figure. Let us return to the unauthorised trading losses incurred by Barings and Société Générale, through the activities of Nick Leeson and Jérôme Kerviel, totalling as they did US$1bn and €5bn respectively. Did each false trade reflect the failure of a particular – or possibly the same – control, or were they the result of a general cause, 'unauthorised, or fictitious, trading' by the individuals concerned? Do you choose one aggregate amount, which is way down the tail of your loss curve – how the events are often portrayed publicly – or record each of the much smaller events, representing the individual control failures which occurred?

The answer depends on your identification of control failures, or combinations of control failures, but your decision will have a significant effect on your risk modelling. It may also affect any insurance recovery. Does each event fall below the policy deductible, and so is excluded, or is the aggregate sum the amount covered? That obviously depends on the policy wording, but in the end it goes back to the cause of loss.

Actions

The actions recorded can be divided into two types: immediate actions and correct or improve actions. For example, when a laptop is lost, an immediate action will be to disable the laptop's access to the firm's network. This is typical of an immediate reaction to the detection of an event. Following causal analysis of the event, correct or improve actions may be:

- a staff note reminding staff to lock all laptops in the boot of their car when transporting them
- a redrafted policy regarding to whom laptops will be issued
- the purchase of encryption software to be installed on all laptops used within the firm.

There is a clear difference between the two types of actions: immediate damage limitation, followed by considered further action at amending and reinforcing controls or the implementation of additional controls.

Additional information

It is helpful to allocate an owner to the loss so that there is clear responsibility for achieving the actions necessary to ensure that the event does not happen to the firm again. Where a transaction or trade is involved, the unique transaction or trade number is recorded, together with any relevant client details. This is, of course, important if the event has a loss attached to it which may be passed back to the client.

Figure 6.2 **Example of a loss capture form**

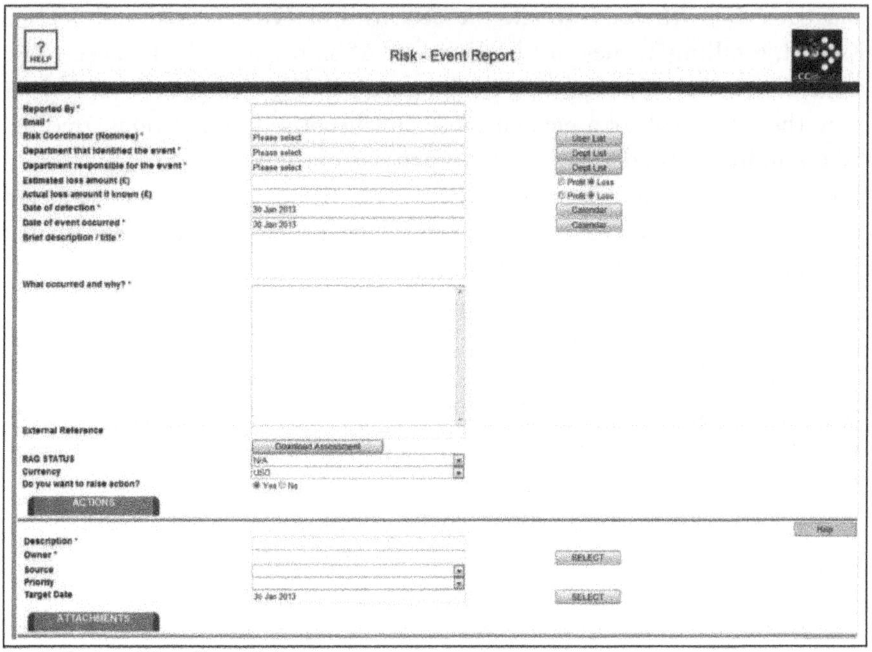
? HELP

Risk - Event Report

Reported By *
Email *
Risk Coordinator (Nominee) * — Please select — User List
Department that identified the event * — Please select — Dept List
Department responsible for the event * — Please select — Dept List
Estimated loss amount (£) — Profit ● Loss
Actual loss amount if known (£) — Profit ● Loss
Date of detection * — 30 Jan 2013 — Calendar
Date of event occurred * — 30 Jan 2013 — Calendar
Brief description / title *
What occurred and why? *
External Reference — Download Assessment
RAG STATUS — N/A
Currency — USD
Do you want to raise action? — ● Yes ○ No

ACTIONS

Help

Description *
Owner * — SELECT
Source
Priority
Target Date — 30 Jan 2013 — SELECT

ATTACHMENTS

Source: Courtesy of Chase Cooper Limited

Internal and external notifications may also be necessary: internally to the firm's compliance, fraud or health and safety department, for instance; or externally, to a regulator or government authority, depending on the type of event that has occurred. And, of course, operational risk management must be notified if they are not already aware. All of these various elements come together in the type of loss reporting form shown in Figure 6.2.

WHO REPORTS THE DATA?

Some firms allow anonymous reporting of losses, although most require the name of the person who detected the event. But the person who reports the event may not necessarily be the person who detects it. Some firms require the name of the person's manager and will send an automatic e-mail to the manager as validation and confirmation of the event. That can, however, discourage whistle blowing, which can be a useful source of identifying potential or actual high-impact/low-frequency events.

In a firm with the right operational risk culture, it is understood that reporting events is not about blame, but about learning. As Andrew Hughes puts it in his book on the BP Texas City oil refinery disaster, *Failure to Learn*, 'Blame is the enemy of understanding'.[1] Many firms have a loss reporting form on their intranet which is available to all staff. In this case, staff are encouraged to report events as they happen.

An alternative is for the operational risk leader or champion within the detecting department or business line to make the report. The advantage of this approach is that an operational risk leader will have some training in operational risk and will probably be a user of operational loss data. This should mean that the data will be of a higher quality compared with data submitted by an untrained person. However, there may be a time delay compared with a submission by the employee who discovers the event.

Reconciling losses to the general ledger (or an audit) will provide valuable confirmation and validation of the accuracy of reporting. However, it will not identify events where there is no financial impact or, of course, events which have not been reported – the lost data mentioned earlier.

REPORTING THRESHOLD

The reporting threshold, the level down to which a firm seeks to capture operational risk events, is a cost–benefit decision. The Basel Committee has set a threshold of €10,000 for loss reporting by banks. It is interesting that, in a recent survey of over 100 banks from around the world, most had a threshold of €5000 or below.[2] A number of firms, including banks, have a policy to report all losses, no matter what size.

The operational risk management departments of many firms which have set a size limit generally monitor losses down to a lower level, since several smaller losses can add up to one larger loss which is above the reporting threshold. In this way continual small control failures are captured before they turn into a significant value. Weak signals can often demand strong action.

Many firms believe that capturing small losses costs more than the benefit achieved. However, a reporting threshold above zero will prevent a significant amount of control failure being captured, including the majority of operational loss events which in fact have a zero financial impact. These, and events where there have been small losses, will be picked up by successfully implementing a zero reporting threshold. Although large losses will still be captured and can be analysed, it is easily arguable that the firm will miss data today which could prevent a large loss from happening tomorrow.

Setting the reporting threshold is therefore a significant issue, the consequences of which should be properly understood by at least the risk committee and preferably the board.

USE OF EVENTS

Causal analysis of events is critical for effective operational risk management. The analysis can be used to challenge risk assessments and control assessments, to validate indicators and to assist in the production of scenarios and stress tests. Additionally, losses can be used in mathematical modelling for economic capital allocation and for regulatory capital calculation.

Causal analysis and controls

The start of the causal analysis of an event is typically to determine which control or controls have failed. There are often a number of preventative controls whose combined failure has led to an event occurring; some detective controls may also have failed. It is important to determine the main controls which have failed as this aids the design and implementation of action plans to prevent the risk from occurring again.

Sometimes a risk has occurred because appropriate controls were not in place. This is, of course, relatively easy to fix. However, it may be that it is acceptable to the business for the risk to occur or that the implementation of controls to prevent the risk occurring is regarded as too expensive. If so, it is important that management understands and explicitly approves the acceptance of the risk.

Risk and control assessment

Once the main controls which have failed have been identified, scoring the design and performance of the controls can be challenged with the objective data of the event. In particular, if the performance of the control has been rated as very effective, the frequency of failure for that control should be challenged if it has failed more than once in an agreed period. Although the design of a control is more difficult to challenge directly through events, it is still possible to draw some tentative conclusions through causal analysis and therefore to challenge this rating, as well as the performance rating.

The analysis of an event, whether or not a financial loss has occurred, will also assist in challenging and validating the likely scoring of a risk in a risk and control assessment. Looking at impact, it may be that an event has occurred, but there has been no apparent impact. A check should nevertheless be made to confirm both the impact and impact assessment shown in the risk and control assessment and the risk owner asked to justify their assessment.

On the other hand, if there have been a series of impacts of similar value, this is a good indication that the impact of the risk should be assessed at that level. The risk owner may, however, feel that the firm has been fortunate in managing the impact of the risk well and that a higher value is justified; or that the firm has for a variety of reasons been poor at managing the risk recently and that a lower value remains appropriate because systems and controls have been tightened. Either way, the firm has challenged the subjective risk assessment scores and created greater awareness of the value of both event causal analysis and risk and control assessments.

Turning to the frequency or likelihood assessment, if three events of a certain risk have occurred in the past five months and the likelihood of the risk has been assessed as low, it is important that the owner of the risk is challenged. It can often be easy simply to say that the firm, at least in relation to this particular risk, has been experiencing a period of bad luck. However, it is more likely that the assessment of likelihood has been unduly optimistic and that the scoring of the likelihood should be revised upward.

Luck is a seductive and dangerous concept, which has no place in the cold light of risk management. An event may be extremely random, and a concatenation of events even more so, but they nevertheless happened. That may feel as if the gods are against you, and it's all unfair and unreasonable, but all events need to be recorded and your assessments adjusted. Don't ignore an event because 'it was a one in a thousand year event' or a 'once in a lifetime' event. 'Once in a lifetime' events have a nasty habit of happening rather more often than that. Outliers may not in reality lie as far out as we would like them to.

Indicators

Events and losses can also be used to validate indicators. If an indicator shows that a control is starting to fail or that a risk is more likely to happen, some events will be expected to occur. If the events do not occur, the indicator must be challenged in case it is not as relevant to the risk as was originally thought. It should be borne in mind that a failure of one control will not necessarily cause a risk to occur, as other preventative controls may be in place and working. Whether or not this is the case can easily be seen from the risk and control assessment.

Equally, events and losses can be used to validate indicators of detective controls. In a similar way to the validation of preventative controls, the size of the events and losses is a guide to how well the detective control indicators are performing. This is shown in more detail in the discussion on Figure 9.6 in Detective and corrective control testing in Chapter 9, Modelling.

Scenarios and stress testing

A significant use of events and losses is in the creation and validation of scenarios and stress tests. The occurrence of real-life events is a very useful pointer towards the construction of plausible but extreme scenarios and stress tests. By combining several events (each of which may occur on a reasonably regular basis) the more extreme event can be built. Developing a scenario in this way often leads to scenarios that are more easily accepted by management.

EXTERNAL LOSS DATABASES

Up to now, we have been considering event information which is gathered from within the firm. However, as can be seen from Figure 6.3, there are three main sources of losses which are available for causal analysis. A firm's own losses are inevitably the primary source of loss data. But there are two other sources of loss information which are external to a firm and which can yield valuable and different information to operational risk management.

Dealing first with information from competitors, a number of consortia exist which capture the internal losses of a number of firms, on a sectoral, national or international basis. Each consortium manager then anonymises the data and redistributes the anonymised data to all its members. The oldest such consortium in the financial services sector is the British Bankers' Association's Global Operational Loss Database (GOLD) loss database, which started in 2000.[3] Consortium databases are a good example of the art of the possible. They often comprise only hard, direct losses, rather than indirect loss amounts, because that increases consistency and eliminates internal subjective assessments, including information which may be price sensitive. But they provide valuable additional events, especially towards the tail of the loss curve.

This type of data is inevitably of a similar type to a firm's own loss data in that it ranges from high-frequency/low-impact to medium-frequency/medium-impact events. As such, it provides valuable validation and confirmation of a firm's own loss data. In addition, it can provide an early warning of losses which have occurred to a competitor but are not yet occurring to your firm. Given this warning, a firm is able to reassess

Sources of losses

Figure 6.3

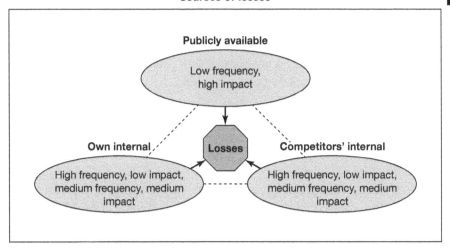

Source: Courtesy of Chase Cooper Limited

its own controls in relation to the risks being suffered by its peers and possibly reduce or even eliminate the approaching losses relating to those risks.

A different type of loss database captures publicly available loss and event data. These events are typically reported on the internet or in the media and are of such a size or consequence that they are impossible to hide. Such data is, by its nature, relatively rare, although it is the most valuable source of data as losses of this size will rarely appear in a firm's own data but are of a size which could cause a firm to collapse. You can collect the data yourself, or save some of the effort by subscribing to a firm offering that service and which may be able to investigate further and provide a more objective analysis than the information given in the press.

Finally, government agencies, such as the Health and Safety Executive, or industry bodies, provide industry-wide information on events. As with all the other external information, this is useful in helping firms to benchmark their own performance and the quality of their controls.

Some health warnings on external data

Cultural differences – controls and risk appetite

Different risk cultures and risk appetites can distort the data. Often the conclusion of an analysis is that 'the event could not happen here'. Whilst in all probability that may be correct, it should be questioned carefully rather than accepted casually. External data is more difficult to analyse, because the precise control environment cannot be known. Such data is nevertheless worthy of committing time and analytical resources to, as it is vital to avoid what are often significant losses.

Data completeness

The completeness of data in an external loss database is a major challenge to anyone using the data for causal analysis. In a database consisting of competitors' internal losses, it is worth bearing in mind that the quality of reporting by competitors may not be up to your standard. Although most firms belonging to a consortium try hard to report all of their losses, no firm can be certain that it has captured all losses above the consortium reporting threshold.

In addition, the larger the loss to be reported the greater the temptation to reduce the size of the loss in case it is discovered which firm has incurred the loss (despite the anonymisation of the data). There is also the temptation to report only public knowledge, which may be very different from reality. One final problem concerns losses which are subject to a court or insurance settlement. The terms of the settlement often prohibit its publication in any form beyond the parties concerned – another example of lost data.

Given that a legally binding obligation to report a loss to the consortium is almost impossible to enforce, most consortia impose a moral obligation on a firm rather than a contractual obligation. But, as we said above, we are dealing with the art of the possible.

In a public loss database there will never be complete capture of data, because the range of media from which reports are gleaned is worldwide, but it will nevertheless provide information about large losses which, by definition, are outside your experience.

Data consistency

A linked problem is the quality and consistency of the data. Even if the data approaches completeness (which is highly unlikely), it is important that the data is of good quality. It is inevitable that the quality of the data will vary by consortium member with some members contributing the minimum required and others giving significant amounts of information. It is not uncommon for a significant percentage of data initially submitted to the data consolidator to be returned to consortium members because the data requires cleaning or further enhancement before it can be used by the consortium.

In a loss database recording public losses, knowledge of the control environment relating to each loss is very variable. This inevitably leads to a problematic quality of data, when using it for causal analysis or modelling purposes, as data consistency is vital to a meaningful analysis of either causes or capital assessments. Public information is also unlikely to tell the whole causal story, if only for good competitive or reputational reasons.

Scaling

One of the most significant problems with external loss data is how to scale the loss with respect to another firm. For example, the Barings loss was in the order of US$1bn. Barings was a well-respected City of London bank with a strong pedigree, although not large by international standards. It had a number of offices (although, again, not a large number) around the world and dealt in a wide variety of financial instruments. How should Deutsche Bank, for example, consider the loss that Barings suffered? Clearly, Deutsche Bank is a much larger bank than Barings and so could possibly suffer a much larger loss. But how much larger? What multiplier should Deutsche Bank use? Should it be based on the comparative number of staff, gross revenues, profitability or something else which is in the public domain?

On the other hand, Deutsche Bank has more resources to hand, as it is a very much larger bank. Maybe the loss that it could suffer from poor segregation of duties should be smaller than US$1bn. After all, segregation of duties is a fundamental control that is an absolute requirement for the boards of many firms whatever the industry. Additionally, large banks' operational risk controls are generally perceived to be better than those of smaller banks, notwithstanding the large operational losses suffered by a number of large banks over the years. In which case, how much smaller? Possibly an inverse of the ratio of the number of staff, gross revenues or profitability?

A pragmatic approach is to scale each loss with respect to the particular factors that influenced the loss, if these are known. For the Barings loss, a firm might first take into account the number of its branches which are small enough to have a segregation of duties problem. This is because, in a small unit, it is often impossible for complete segregation of duties; they tend to be concentrated on the unit manager as there is no one else who has the experience and authority to carry out supervisory controls. Having established the number of relevant branches, a further analysis is then made of the types of products handled in those branches and their value. By combining the two factors, it is possible to assess the likely effect of a similar incident on the firm concerned.

Using this method demands little detailed research about the precise size or financials of the loss suffering firm, information which will probably be historic and of little relevance. It avoids using probably spurious correlations between firms by simple numeric multipliers of sales turnover or staff. It also has the advantage that changes to the risk environment of the firm, such as more or less small branches in the future or changes in the product range, will naturally be reflected in the value of the potential risk impact. It doesn't even require knowledge of the precise amount lost by Barings. You only need to know that the risk event happened and apply this knowledge to the firm's risk and control profile, from which a value is easily deduced. Go back to the causes, not the numbers.

The main disadvantage of the pragmatic approach is that you need to examine each loss in order to determine what the relevant risk factors are. However, the relevance of the result far outweighs the time required for this additional work, which will be required anyway if several high-level factors are captured for each loss such as number of staff, gross revenues and profitability. Such an examination is required only once for each loss and then additionally for new losses as they are captured.

USING MAJOR EVENTS

As noted above, major events, whether internal or external, are particularly valuable for operational risk management as these can cause the loss of the entire firm. Of course, after a major event, many firms will carry out an audit of the specific controls which failed (or are perceived to have failed) and therefore caused the event, and take remedial action. But special audits can be delayed for good business reasons and not all firms will carry out an audit. This nevertheless begs the question: 'How valuable is the historic data relating to a major event?' The answer is that major events are of use to conceptual, rather than numeric, analysis in trying to get to the true causes of the events.

TIMELINESS OF DATA

Event data degrades over time as the acceptable level of control environments and people's perceptions of control environments change. For example, as IT environments change, manual controls will also change. Automated controls are also frequently updated as software improves. So, any analysis of loss event data must be careful to take the current environment into account.

SUMMARY

Events, being what has actually happened, are probably the only hard facts we have in operational risk to make judgements about the future. However, as we have seen, the information we gain from them comes with a number of health warnings. The data will never be complete. As events occur, they inevitably affect behaviour, whether individual or corporate, which means that even if we have captured information comprehensively and accurately, its usefulness degrades over time.

The information gained from events validates and supports risk and control assessments, the levels of indicators and scenarios, and is fundamental to assessing capital requirements. But we should be careful that it does not bear too great a load of expectation.

Notes

1   Andrew Hughes, *Failure to Learn* (Sydney: CCH Australia Limited), 2009.
2   Basel Committee on Banking Supervision, *Loss Data Collection Exercise*, 2008; www.bis.org
3   www.bba.org.uk/content/1/c4/65/05/GOLD_Brochure.pdf

7

Indicators

WHAT DO WE MEAN BY KEY?

Key risk indicators (KRIs) are a fundamental part of any comprehensive operational risk management framework and yet many firms seem to be puzzled and confused by them. The confusion might be less if they were called IRKs (indicators of risks which are key) or IKRs (indicators of key risks). They are definitely *not* 'key' risk indicators as this leads to far too many indicators.

Many firms have identified several hundred indicators and are trying to manage their businesses by using this number of KRIs. However, it is highly questionable whether any business can truly have or indeed manage that number of indicators of key risks – or have the number of key risks which will give rise to several hundred indicators.

Other firms have striven for a very small number of indicators which will tell them about the well-being of the firm overall. This approach brings to mind a doctor trying to assess the complete state of your health only by taking your blood pressure, by measuring your pulse and by listening to your heart – clearly a good place to start, but definitely not to finish.

As can be seen in Figure 7.1 indicators are one of the three fundamental processes of operational risk management. Indicators of risks which are key can provide vital early warning signs to enable threats to the business

| Figure 7.1 | Typical operational risk framework, showing position of indicators |

Source: Courtesy of Chase Cooper Limited

and its objectives to be managed before they happen. Such indicators are typically called leading or predictive indicators. They give the current risk and control levels, as opposed to historic or future values.

As indicators give today's levels of risk, they also enable trends in risks and their associated controls to be investigated and analysed. This trend analysis can help to predict events before they happen. It can also signal that escalation criteria have been breached and so trigger management action.

KEY PERFORMANCE INDICATORS AND KEY RISK INDICATORS

It is important to differentiate between key performance indicators (KPIs) and KRIs. KPIs are commonly used in business to assess the current level of performance. Perhaps the most commonly used KPI is the profitability of a business. From a risk perspective, profitability tells us about the state of the firm's entire risk exposure and its control performance in the most recent period. However, it is a poor indicator of key risks as it tells us very little about any particular key risk and nothing about how to modify the risk exposure. The profit figure by itself gives no disaggregation by key risk (or by control performance) and therefore little opportunity to manage the firm by adjusting its risks. KPIs are about the performance of the business and are typically linked directly to the business objectives. Examples of KPIs are: sales, revenues, profitability, total costs, staff costs, premises costs and IT costs. Some, though, can also act as KRIs. Examples could be: market penetration (risk: poor distribution network), or board and senior management turnover (risk: loss of key staff). By comparison, KRIs tell us about changes in the likelihood or impact of a key risk and can be linked to a risk and control assessment (RCA).

KPIs, KRIs and KCIs

Figure 7.2

K Risk I

Change in likelihood or impact, linked to RCA

KIs

K Performance I

Change in business performance, linked to business objectives

K Control I

Change in design or performance, linked to RCA

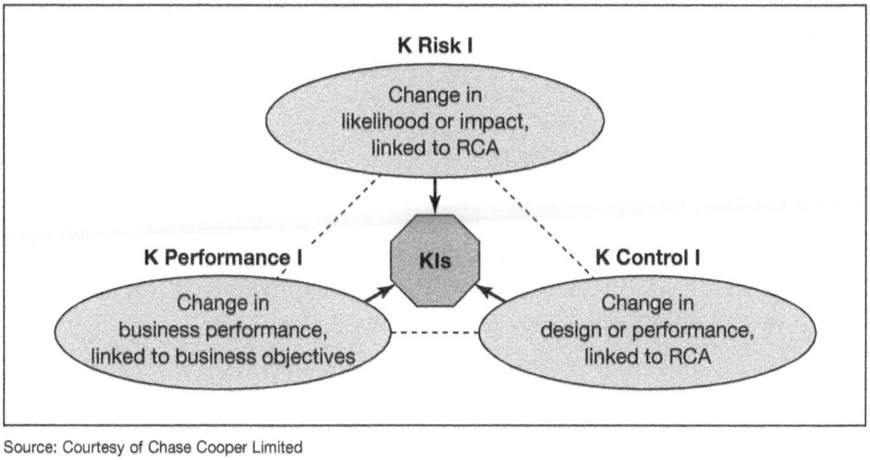

Source: Courtesy of Chase Cooper Limited

Figure 7.2 shows how KPIs and KRIs relate to each other and also how they relate to a third set of key indicators, key control indicators (KCIs). KCIs tell us about the change in the design or performance of controls and again can be linked to a risk and control assessment. KCIs fall into two categories: indicators of those controls which mitigate individual key risks and indicators of those controls which mitigate a number of risks.

ESTABLISHING KRIs AND KCIs

Approaches to identification

Management support is essential for establishing indicators of risks which are key. There are various approaches to identifying indicators of key risks and key controls. Some of these are more likely than others to attract management support and drive. They are:

- using a blank sheet of paper
- using existing management information
- using an existing risk and control assessment.

Blank sheet of paper

Many firms start their identification of KRIs by starting with a blank sheet of paper and setting down all the indicators they are able to articulate. This has the advantage that there are no preconceptions, but it ignores any previous risk management work, in particular risk and control assessments.

Given that senior management should have been involved in the production of the relevant risk and control assessments, this approach sends a clear message that the risk and control assessment is of limited and narrow value, rather than being one of the three linked and fundamental operational risk management processes.

It also makes it difficult to identify which indicators are the best to manage the key business risks. Additionally, the indicators are identified in isolation and are not directly related to a risk.

Existing management information

Using existing management information has several advantages:

- It uses business metrics which are well known and understood. This means that senior management will be comfortable with the indicators and more willing to take decisions based on them.
- The data is more likely to be accurate as it is in current use.
- There is an implicit link to identified risks and controls as most managers intuitively know their major risks and the controls that mitigate them.

This intuitive knowledge leads to a natural match between the information used to control the business and the risk profile of the business, as represented by the risk and control assessments.

However, there is no explicit link to specific key risks. It is therefore harder to identify the indicators of key risks from indicators of normal risks. This approach also makes it difficult to identify which indicators are significant, although it can be argued that all metrics which are used on a monthly basis by senior management should be significant.

Existing risk and control assessment

This approach has the advantage of using risk and control data which have already been agreed and are linked to the business objectives (or processes), assuming these have been used to identify the risks and controls, which they should have been. It therefore builds on previous risk management work and reinforces that work as being valuable and key in its own right.

Identification of key risks is relatively easy with this approach. Typically, a key risk is identified as a risk with a gross/inherent high-impact score and a gross/inherent high-likelihood score. If this approach identifies only a few key risks, it is often expanded to include all risks which have a high impact, with no attention being paid to the likelihood score.

Having defined the key risks, it is also easy to identify one category of key controls, i.e. any control which mitigates a key risk. Another category of key controls is any control which mitigates several risks, since the failure of this control may have a significant effect on the firm. In Figure 7.3, a firm may consider the key risks to be risks 1 to 3, although 4 to 7 may also be counted as key. Then 11, 17 and 18 are also assessed as having a high impact, but their likelihood is considered low, so it is probable that the firm will not consider them as being key. All controls of risks 1, 2 and 3 will be considered as key controls. Additionally, 'Appraisals' and 'Staff training' mitigate more than one risk and so may also be considered key.

Having identified the key risks, it is now relatively easy, using knowledge of the business, to identify indicators of the key risks which tell you about the changes to their likelihood or impact and to the design or performance of a key control. A good indicator will be easy to access and easy to understand. Many risk indicators, typically around 60–70% of indicators of key risks, are already being tracked somewhere in the firm. Although getting access to the relevant Excel spreadsheet or database can initially be difficult, it is worth persevering as data already in use is generally of a far better quality than new data.

It is common to identify a considerable number of indicators for each key risk. The challenge is to find a small number of indicators which convey information that is useful to the business, preferably using existing management information. Ideally, there will be one or two indicators for the likelihood and impact of a key risk and one indicator for each control which

Figure 7.3

Typical risk and control assessment

ID	Risks	Owner(s) of the risk	I	L	S	Controls	Owner(s) of the control	D	P	E
1	Failure to attract, recruit and retain key staff	SR		4	4	16	Salary surveys	TJ	2	2	4
							Training and mentoring schemes	TB	3	2	6
							Retention packages for key staff	TJ	4	4	16
2	Financial advisers misinterpret/fail to understand the complexity of 'equity release' products	PL	AB	4	4	16	Staff training	TB	4	4	16
							Learning gained from previous deals	KW & EL	4	4	16
							Review of individual needs in performance appraisal process	TB	3	2	6
							Procedure manuals for processes	EL	4	4	16
3	Poor staff communication	SR	JK	4	4	16	Defined communication channels	ZK	4	3	12
							Documented procedures and processes	EL	3	2	6
4	Failure to understand the law and/or regulations	PL		4	3	12	Internal training courses	EL	4	4	16
							Regular updates from various sources	EL	4	1	4
							External training courses	TB & EL	4	3	12
5	Poor detection of money laundering	PL		4	3	12	AML annual training	TB & EL	4	3	12
							Circulation of BBA awareness circulars	EL & ZK	3	1	3
							KYC	ALL	4	3	12
6	Insufficient funds/deposits to cater for lending activities	CK		4	3	12	Liquidity risk policy	ZK	4	4	16
							Advertising	KW	4	3	12
							Economic forecasting	CK	3	3	9
7	Over-selling credit cards	CK		4	3	12	Staff training	TB	3	3	9
							Credit scoring	EL	4	4	16
							Forward business planning	ZK	3	3	9
8	Over-deployment of management resources on regulatory issues	RU	CK	3	4	12	Monthly budget against actual review	TJ	3	4	12
							Corporate governance	CK	4	4	16
							Monthly head of compliance & CEO meetings	CK	2	2	4
9	Failure to capture market opportunities	AB		3	3	9	Competitor monitoring	TB	3	4	12
							Product development	TB	2	2	4
10	Over-dependency on outsourcing	CK		3	3	9	SLAs	CK & EL	4	4	16
							Outsourcing monitoring	CK & EL	4	4	16
							Due diligence	CK	4	3	12
							Policy	CK	3	4	12
11	Weakness in information security system	RU	JK	4	2	8	Record retention	ZK	2	2	4
							Information security policy procedure and monitoring	ZK	3	2	6
							Staff training and certification	TB	3	3	9
							Client agreements/marketing	ZK & KW	2	1	2
12	Inadequate or insufficient IT infrastructure to achieve business objectives	JK		2	4	8	Business/strategic planning	ZA & KW	3	4	12
							IT systems performance and capability monitoring	ZK	4	3	12
13	External fraud activities	PL		3	2	6	Anti-fraud training	ZK	4	4	16
							Systems security	ZK	4	4	16
14	Failure to grow staff competencies	SR		3	2	6	Staff training	TB	4	3	12
							Hire of temporary staff	TB	2	2	4
							Appraisals	TB	2	3	6
15	Misaligned employee goals	SR	CK	2	3	6	Appraisals	TB	2	3	6
							Corporate governance	ZA	4	4	16
16	Failure to sense and eliminate internal fraud	PL		3	2	6	Criminal background check	EL	3	2	6
							Segregation of duties	ZA	2	3	6
							Staff training	TB	3	2	6
							Fraud monitoring	EL	4	4	16
							Whistle blowing	ALL	3	3	9
17	Unfit or inappropriate new products launched	AB		4	1	4	Staff training	TB	3	2	6
							New products approval process	KW	3	2	6
18	Poor strategic decision making	CK	AB	4	1	4	Monitoring of market data	KW	4	4	16
							Research and forecasting	KW	4	2	8
							Monthly Management Forum	ZA	4	3	12
							Marketing strategy review	ZA & KW	3	3	9
19	Inaccessible premises	RU		3	1	3	BCP/M	EL	4	3	12
							Security of floors (to enable loss to be better managed)	ZA	3	4	12
							Building and firm guards	ZA	4	4	16

Key: I = impact; L = likelihood; D = design; P = performance

Source: Courtesy of Chase Cooper Limited

Examples of risks, KRIs, controls and KCIs

Figure 7.4

	Risks	Risk indicators L = Likelihood I = Impact	Controls	Control indicators
1	Failure to attract, recruit and retain key staff	L: Staff turnover (annualised)	–Salary surveys	Employer salary survey ranking
		L: Offer/acceptance ratio (percentage)	–Training and mentoring schemes	Training costs
		L: Employer survey ranking	–Retention packages for key staff	Staff turnover
		I: Client complaints (per week)		
		I: Error rates (per week)		
2	Financial advisers misinterpreted/fail to understand the complexity of 'equity release' products	L: Time spent on each client	–Staff training	No. of staff attending the training courses
		I: No. of complaints (per month)	–Learning gained from previous deals	
			–Review of individual needs in performance appraisal process	No. of staff queries
			–Procedure manuals for processes	Time from last update (by month)
3	Poor staff communication	L: No. of general meetings/ newsletters (per month)	–Defined communication channels	No. of internal newsletters published
		I: Staff morale (survey)	–Documented procedures and processes	No. of access to intranet pages where documented procedures and process are displayed
4	Failure to understand the law and/or regulations	L: No. of front office queries to compliance office (per month)	–Regulator registration	No. of Regulator visits
		I: No. breaching the law (per month)	–Regular updates from various sources	No. of newsletters published from compliance department
			–External training courses	No. of newsletters published by the staff after attending training courses
5	Poor detection of money laundering	L: Refer to controls	–Anti-Money Laundering annual training	No. of people NOT attending Anti-Money Laundering course
		I: No. of times money is laundered (per year)	–Circulation of British Bankers' Association awareness circulars	No. of circulars distributed compared to number of circulars received
			–Know Your Customer	No. of potential clients rejected due to Know Your Customer

Source: Courtesy of Chase Cooper Limited

mitigates the key risk. In this way it is possible to achieve a manageable number of indicators which will give a good picture of the current risk profile of the firm, such as the one given in Figure 7.4.

TARGETS AND THRESHOLDS

As noted above, establishing targets or thresholds linked to an indicator can be very useful in setting escalation criteria for management action and in assessing trends in indicators. Thresholds should be set by reference to the business needs, and willingness to take a specific risk or to accept a level of control failure. The starting point is the required risk profile for the business. It is poor practice to set thresholds with reference initially to the available data.

In the example shown in Figure 7.5 a mean target has been set of 5 with a green band of 4 to 6. The indicator has bands on both sides with an amber band of 3 or 2 on the lower side and a value of 7 on the upper side. These bands represent a breach of risk appetite. 1 or below is in the lower red band and 8 or above is in the upper red band. At this level there has been a significant breach of risk appetite. This is an example of an indicator which is bounded on both sides and which has uneven bands.

| Figure 7.5 | Threshold setting |

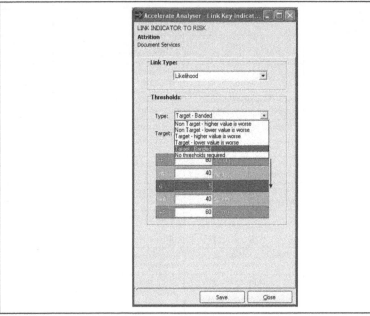

Source: Courtesy of Chase Cooper Limited

It is also common for indicators to have one-sided bands, for example a green band of 0 and 1, an amber band of 2 or 3, and a red band of 4 and above. Indicators can also be binary, that is, they move directly from a green band to a red band. An example of this type of indicator might be the number of fatalities on a construction site where the contractor will have a green level of 0 and a red level of 1 or more.

Clearly these bands should be linked to the appetite of a firm. For example, for the key risk 'Loss of key staff' an indicator may be 'Key staff turnover' and the bands agreed as in Figure 7.6.

| Figure 7.6 | Thresholds for 'Loss of key staff' risk and risk appetite for 'Key staff turnover' |

Red	Amber	Green	Amber	Red
under 5%	5% – 9%	10% – 15%	16% – 20%	over 20%

A firm may be willing to accept a key staff turnover of between 10% and 15%. The management of key staff turnover at this level may be delegated to the relevant head of business. This level is considered to be normal and acceptable for the business.

Key staff turnover between 5% and 9% and between 16% and 20% may be regarded by the business as inconvenient and, for the upper range, expensive but nevertheless tolerable. These levels of key staff turnover may be notified to an appropriate senior manager or group, such as the risk committee, so that action can be taken to bring key staff turnover back to the green band, if this is considered appropriate.

Key staff turnover over 20% may be regarded as too expensive for the business, both in terms of loss of corporate knowledge and of recruitment costs. It will probably also result in disruption to the business and mean that some months go by before stability and cohesion are restored to senior management. Key staff turnover under 5%, though, may also be considered to be a 'red' indicator, as being at too low a level for the business, since fresh ideas and new approaches are often brought in by new key staff. Low key staff turnover can also be a reflection of a senior management cadre which is relatively overpaid and complacent. These levels of key staff turnover would probably be notified to the board as well as the risk committee.

Validation of thresholds through experience

Thresholds can be validated through reviewing previous indicator data, where it is available, and through a review of the losses incurred by the firm which are relevant to the specific risk or control. Additionally, threshold validation can sometimes be achieved by examining peers' or competitors' losses.

When looking at validation data, however, remember to allow for data which changes in different periods. For example, the number of non-productive days due to staff absence will be higher in the summer, when holidays are traditionally taken, than in the spring or autumn.

PERIODICITY

Indicators can be tracked over various lengths of time (e.g. daily, weekly, monthly or annually). Most typically, risk indicators are recorded on a monthly basis although indicators of risks which are at a transaction level are often daily or even intra-day. The periodicity of an indicator is largely irrelevant to using it for managing a risk. Much more important is how frequently the risk changes.

An indicator linking a risk to a daily process or activity clearly requires recording on a daily basis, for example an indicator which records whether or not daily reconciliations of a bank account have been completed. Equally, an indicator linked to a risk which is annual in nature needs recording only on an annual basis, for example an indicator linked to the completion of an annual regulatory return. However, the majority of indicators are recorded on a monthly basis as this frequency gives the best balance between the effort required to record the indicator and good management of the risk. Examples are staff turnover and staff attendance at training courses, each of which may reflect the level of competence of the workforce.

IDENTIFYING THE LEADING AND LAGGING INDICATORS

As noted at the beginning of this chapter, risk indicators are sometimes able to show when risks are more likely to occur; they can give early warning signals before risks happen. The challenge for operational risk management is to identify which indicators are most likely to give the early warning signals, in other words the ones which act as effective leading indicators. Clearly, indicators that the risk is more likely to happen, likelihood indicators, are a good place to start as these provide warnings before the risk event has occurred. Equally, indicators about the impact of a risk event are lagging indicators and will tell you about the effect of the risk when it has happened, and the likely size of the impact. However, there is not necessarily a correlation between an indicator's numeric value and the final size of the impact. Indicators tell you that the world may have become riskier, but not by how much.

For control indicators, a helpful technique is to use an internal audit methodology of classifying controls. This divides controls into four categories:

1. Directive controls – controls which mitigate a risk through direction (e.g. policies, procedures, terms of reference).
2. Preventative controls – controls which mitigate a risk through preventing it happening (e.g. guards round a piece of machinery).
3. Detective controls – controls which mitigate the impact of a risk (e.g. fire alarms or accounting reconciliations).
4. Corrective controls – controls which mitigate the impact of a risk through correcting the effects of an event (e.g. disaster recovery site).

It is clear that indicators of preventative controls are leading indicators, whereas indicators of detective controls will provide information about the likely size of an event and are lagging indicators. The good risk management practice of having a balance of directive, preventative, detective and corrective controls to mitigate a risk is therefore very helpful in identifying leading and predictive control indicators. This technique also provides a valuable challenge to the management of risks in that the risk owner is able to see whether or not the mitigation of the risk is balanced with a similar number of controls operating before and after the event has occurred (see Identifying controls in Chapter 5, Risk and control assessment).

ACTION PLANS

Collecting and monitoring indicators is of no use unless action is subsequently taken. A firm will clearly wish to take action if a leading indicator shows that the risk is more likely to occur. Action plans raised by indicators will be similar to other management action plans in that they will include the objective to be achieved through completion of the action plan, the expected date of completion, the owner of the action plan and other typical items. However, there will also be reference to the control which is failing (if applicable), the risk which has been identified as more likely to occur and the possible impact to the firm if the risk does occur. These points, which are linked explicitly to an indicator, will be helpful in preparing a cost–benefit analysis for the action plan.

DASHBOARDS

Indicators are commonly reported on dashboards, an example of which is given in Figure 7.7. As can be seen, a Red (R)/Amber (A)/Green (G) status column is very common together with a trend indicator. These two columns provide a quick view and guide the dashboard user as to which indicators to focus on first. It is also common to record the most recent three periods and to have an average of the most recent three in order to smooth the volatilities in the indicators.

In Figure 7.7, the 'Overtime hours' has a 'red' status and is of concern because of its actual level, although it is at least trending down. 'Complaints received' requires attention because, although it is at 'amber', it has doubled in this period. Additionally, although the 'Temporary staff' percentage is trending down, the change from the last period is relatively small.

Combinations of indicators can also tell stories. For example although the risk of 'Accounts not KYC [Know Your Customer] compliant' is stable and within the green band, the number of customers has increased significantly in this period whilst the 'Overtime hours' and 'Temporary staff' percentage are both trending down. These last two indicators may be indicators of how well the control of 'Operations KYC review' is performing in mitigating the risk of 'Accounts not KYC compliant'. This leads to the conclusion that 'Overtime hours' and 'Temporary staff' are likely to be leading indicators for the risk of 'Accounts not KYC compliant'.

Figure 7.7

Example of a KRI dashboard

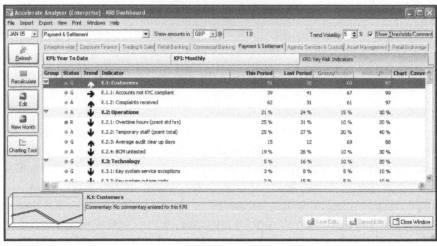

Source: Courtesy of Chase Cooper Limited

SUMMARY

Indicators are valuable not only in monitoring business performance, but in identifying changes in a firm's risk environment and in the effectiveness of risk controls. They are a fundamental part of the operational risk management process and an essential part of monitoring operational risk appetite.

The important thing to remember is that a KRI is an indicator of a key risk and a KCI an indicator of a control which relates to a key risk. If that is understood, the number of indicators will be manageable and the business will see them as valuable, thus helping to achieve buy-in for the whole operational risk management process. Another tip to encourage buy-in is to use, as far as possible, indicators which are already being used by the business. Inventing new ones, or failing to involve the business in identifying and establishing indicators, will be counter-productive and a waste of energy and goodwill.

Having considered the three fundamental processes of operational risk management, it is now time to 'advance the framework' and look at various aspects of modelling and reporting operational risk data.

Part 3

ADVANCING THE FRAMEWORK

Reporting

WHY REPORTING MATTERS

Looking at Figure 8.1, it is clear that there is little value in carrying out the processes in your operational risk framework without good reporting. Informed decision making flows from good operational risk reporting. Without it, poor decisions are far more likely or, even worse, result in no decision making at all. It can be only too easy to drown in operational risk data, and so be unable to produce information and reports which support effective action plans to improve or protect your operational risk profile.

Good operational risk reporting is more difficult than it looks. With the widespread use of Excel everyone thinks that they can write good reports. However, little consideration is given to the fact that operational risk information is often complex and presenting it to a broad and diverse audience is not easy.

| Figure 8.1 | Typical operational risk framework, showing position of reporting |

Source: Courtesy of Chase Cooper Limited

COMMON ISSUES

Relevance to the audience

Operational risk reports may be directed at heads of departments, heads of business lines, risk committees or the board. There are clearly differing needs in this broad church of users. At one extreme, the board will generally require a report giving headline risk information and highlighting exceptions and will assume, unless told otherwise, that the rest of the risk profile is acceptable (or at least not unacceptable). The board will not be interested in a report which details all the operational risk data available to the firm. However, it may well ask for specific and detailed information on a particular area. Indeed, such a request shows that the board is fully involved in the operational risk management of the firm and has read and digested the regular summary exception reports.

A CEO or head of business unit is unlikely to be interested in the detailed activity level risks referred to in Chapter 5, Risk and control assessment. Equally, the supervisor of a unit within a department will have little interest in business level or process level risks. For an operational risk report to be of use, it must capture and report on risks, controls, indicators and losses which are pitched at the level of detail for the recipients of the report. Data must therefore be in a form in which it can be tailored and presented to answer the needs of a variety of audiences at any point in time.

Understanding of operational risk terms

Significant effort is needed to ensure that there is a common understanding of the terms used in an operational risk report. This will typically involve management awareness programmes, as well as a glossary in the operational risk policy document (see Chapter 3, Governance). Even with this done, it is advisable to make sure that the terms used in the reports are clear, in common use throughout the firm, and mean the same thing to everybody who reads them. For example, the term 'severity' may confuse a reader if 'impact' is the common term used in the firm.

Communication of key messages

Report producers often assume that the reader has the same knowledge of operational risk as they do. This is rarely true. In addition, most senior management have considerably less time to read and digest a report than the producer of the report took to produce it. Attention must therefore be given to making sure that the report communicates the key messages. This can be done in a variety of ways, often by techniques such as highlighting or using colours, but take care not to overuse colours (see Shading later in this chapter).

Use of quantitative and qualitative information

As we have seen in various chapters in this book, operational risk management generates both quantitative and qualitative data. A particular challenge for operational risk reporting is, therefore, that of collecting, aggregating and interlinking both quantitative and qualitative data in reports. With a little bit of forethought and planning, it is possible to generate reports which enable this to happen naturally (see Report definition and Dashboard reporting later in this chapter). Regrettably, most operational risk reports comprise only either quantitative or qualitative data; the interlinking challenge is conspicuous by its absence.

For example, it is very common to have a report which contains qualitative information about the risks and controls relevant to a particular business unit, without any reference to the quantitative information provided by key risk indicators and losses relating to the same unit. Whilst the head of a department or business line may wish to know all his or her risks and controls, this is likely to be the only audience which requires that information in isolation. Other users will want information from all the key operational risk management processes.

Data collection and quality

A common (but misplaced) view in operational risk management is that reports are not worth producing until the quality of the data is acceptable. Data quality may be poor because it has not all been collected (e.g. the complete collection of losses is notoriously difficult, as seen in Chapter 6, Events and losses); or because operational risk management is not embedded in the firm (e.g. risk and control assessments may not yet have achieved acceptance).

Reports which contain data of suspect quality should be clearly annotated. They may still provide useful information, but they should also be used to show the advantages which would accrue if data was of better quality. Whilst such an approach works up to a point, it should be treated with caution. By replaying poor-quality data in reports to the producers of the data and their seniors, you are in serious danger of compromising acceptance of good and effective operational risk management throughout the firm.

BASIC PRINCIPLES

What does this number mean? Why is it at that level?

These key questions often arise from reading an operational risk report. Most operational risk reports are seen on a monthly basis and there can be an assumption that the reader will remember the values given in the previous month's report. That is unlikely. The report will almost certainly be one of many that the reader reviews. Context must therefore be given to a particular number or information it contains, either from other numbers in the same report or from a comparison with the previous period, expected range or agreed appetite.

Should I do something about it?

A good report should not simply give values but should guide the reader as to whether or not action is required. Indeed, if a report does not point to some form of action or decision, its existence should be questioned. Too many reports are regularly produced whose purpose is long forgotten or whose practical use has disappeared, if there was one in the first place. The pointer to action can be explicit, as in a key indicator report showing that an indicator is in the red band (see Chapter 7, Indicators), or implicit, as in a report showing the risk appetite alongside a column of values. All reports, though, should highlight the need for action or at least a decision on action. As we have said before, if they don't, drop them.

Timely reporting

A report is only useful if it is produced in a timely fashion. If a report frequency is set as monthly, it is likely that the values in the report will or may change on a month-by-month basis. It is therefore no good producing a monthly report three or four weeks after the end of the month as it will have relatively little value. Time has moved on and it is almost time for new values to be calculated for the end of the following month. Equally, there is no point setting a report frequency of daily or weekly if the values only change on a monthly basis. Untimely reports like this will be ignored by management and will actively work against embedding good operational risk management in a firm.

Reports continuously evolve

Operational risk reporting is, by its nature, a continuously evolving process. This stems in part from the firm's operational risk profile being itself in a state of continuous change and in part from the dynamic nature of good reporting. The questions raised by, and asked of, an operational risk report are likely to change as the risks, controls and indicators themselves change. This will undoubtedly have an effect on the structure of the report and on the data contained within it. Indeed, it could be argued that if an operational risk report has not changed its structural detail in five or six reporting periods it is not doing its job efficiently.

A related problem is that reports can easily grow in both length and number. If additional information is asked for, or even a new report is requested or suggested, it can be useful to remember the mantra 'one in, one out'. A new report will only be accepted if an existing report is deleted from the pack. It's a useful challenge to establish what information really matters to the people for whom the report is intended.

Risk ownership

Any risk report should enable management to take ownership of the information. This may be done explicitly, with a risk owner clearly identified, or implicitly through the identification of a department or business line. Either way, and linking with the point above about identifying actions, a good operational risk report will precipitate effort to correct or enhance the operational risk profile of the firm by the person who owns the risk which requires action. An alternative, of course, is that the report shows that all risks are within the firm's risk appetite and that no action is required. If this is the case, it is debatable as to whether or not the risk appetite of the firm is too conservative. Even a report indicating that no action is required can prompt a useful challenge.

Identifying and treating non-compliance

Allied to this, a report should identify where there is non-compliance with either internal or external policies or regulations, and what action is going to be taken to bring the firm back to compliance. This is, of course, fundamental and echoes the point above about a report for the board identifying exceptions. The board will also want to know what is being done about the exceptions by whom and by when. If the exceptions have been authorised, the report should show by whom and at what level.

Incentives to deliver operational risk strategy

Operational risk reports play a key role in clearly identifying the operational risk strategy and how it is being achieved. A number of organisations use operational risk reports as an input to senior management and staff incentives. If a department or business unit is doing its part in delivering the operational risk strategy, this will be reflected in the operational risk reports. As we discuss in Chapter 15, Culture and people risk, remuneration should reward good performance, including non-financial aspects as exemplified by good risk management. Pay should, in part, reflect good operational risk management performance, which will be demonstrated both in and by good operational risk reports.

Define the boundaries

The boundary issue discussed in Chapter 1 – knowing what is included or excluded in the firm's definition of operational risk – also has an effect on reporting. It is particularly important that the interdependencies of market, credit and operational risks are recognised in operational risk reports. As an example, a loss from a 'fat finger' event may have been viewed as a market risk event five years ago. It is now almost certain to be viewed as an operational risk event and care must be taken not to double count it in the market risk losses as well as in the operational risk losses – or to lose it altogether if definitions change in the interim. A further example, from the world of credit risk, is the inability to perfect a lien over collateral deposited with the firm. This is now likely to be viewed as an operational risk event, rather than a credit loss, which would have been the case a few years ago.

This particular problem will be largely overcome if definitions of market risk, credit risk and operational risk are clear. Additionally, a firm may develop a boundaries document which explores these points and clarifies, through a number of examples, the firm's approach to risk boundaries.

Integration with other processes

Operational risk does not happen in isolation. There are a number of other processes which are tangential to operational risk management. These include performance measurement, compensation, audit and planning. Operational risk reports should take these other processes into account and should not repeat conclusions drawn from them. Instead, a good operational risk report will, for example, add to audit conclusions and indicate risk acceptable actions which can be taken on audit points. Repeating conclusions in different reports is likely, at best, to lead to resources being wasted as a number of people seek to solve the same problem and, at worst, to cause confusion and the possibility that nobody resolves the problem.

REPORT DEFINITION

Before a draft design or prototype report is considered, it is important to define the report. A definition of a report is usually a single sheet of paper, which typically contains the following:

- Name of the report. A clear name is preferable to a report code; a report named 'Risk and control assessment' is self-explanatory, as opposed to one headed 'ORM1'.
- Objective(s) of the report. This is often a difficult topic but a clearly stated objective helps considerably in ensuring that the report is effective in use.
- Distribution list of recipients. This will help to ensure that the report is targeted at the right people and contains the right level of data.

- Names of fields to be used. This will help to ensure that only the fields required for the report are on the report, i.e. that there are no extraneous data items on the report.

- Calculations required in each field (before the report is printed). This makes clear the calculations to the IT staff who will be producing the coding for the report; it also helps the person requesting the report to think through the requirements and therefore eliminates unnecessary manipulation of the data.

- Manual actions to be performed in each field (to obtain the final report). These are any additional actions which may be required before the report is ready to be used; there should be very few manual actions, if any.

- How to use the final report (including typical actions resulting from the final report). This is a crucial part of the report definition; it further clarifies the report objectives in a practical manner. The act of thinking through in detail how the report will be used challenges the report requestor in terms of the necessity of the report and its differences with existing reports. This section may even lead to other reports being reconfigured or eliminated.

It is only after a report definition has been completed that a design or prototype should be considered. These will, of course, be guided by the definition which will remain a crucial document throughout report coding and production.

REPORTING STYLES AND TECHNIQUES

Different styles are useful for different reports and desired outcomes. Using the same set of data (see Table 8.1) we will now consider the effectiveness of different reporting styles.

Table 8.1	Basic loss data					
Loss type	Jan	Feb	Mar	Apr	May	Jun
Internal fraud	50,000	60,000	55,000	45,000	70,000	80,000
External fraud	70,000	100,000	45,000	35,000	25,000	20,000
Employment practices	40,000	20,000	5,000	3,000	15,000	20,000
Business practices	80,000	40,000	120,000	100,000	30,000	20,000
Damage to assets	30,000	5,000	7,000	10,000	2,000	18,000
System failures	35,000	25,000	45,000	15,000	18,000	30,000

Pie and bar charts

If the loss data just for January is reported on a pie chart (see Figure 8.2), it is difficult to see which 'slice' of the pie is bigger, without further information.

Basic pie chart

Figure 8.2

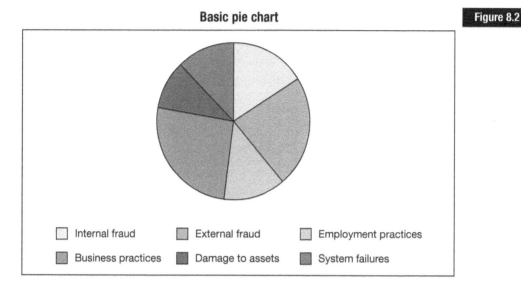

Internal fraud   External fraud   Employment practices

Business practices   Damage to assets   System failures

Further context can be given in terms of percentages for each slice – see Figure 8.3 – together with clearer labelling – see Figure 8.4 – which makes for much easier reading.

Enhanced pie chart

Figure 8.3

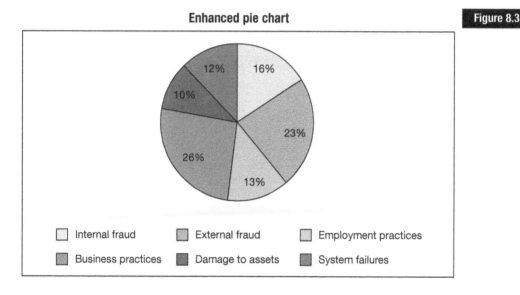

Internal fraud   External fraud   Employment practices

Business practices   Damage to assets   System failures

Figure 8.4

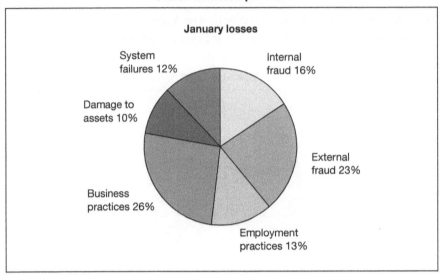

Further enhanced pie chart

January losses

Alternatively, even a simple bar chart will enable easy comparison of the size of loss types (see Figure 8.5).

Figure 8.5

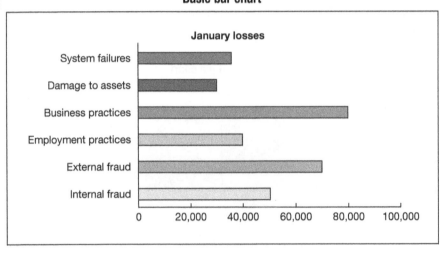

Basic bar chart

January losses

2D or 3D

There has been a trend towards three-dimensional reports. Whilst this look is '21st century' the 3D reports do not always give information clearly or quickly, as can be seen in the 3D column and line charts shown in Figures 8.6 and 8.7 which use the data given in Table 8.1.

3D column chart

Figure 8.6

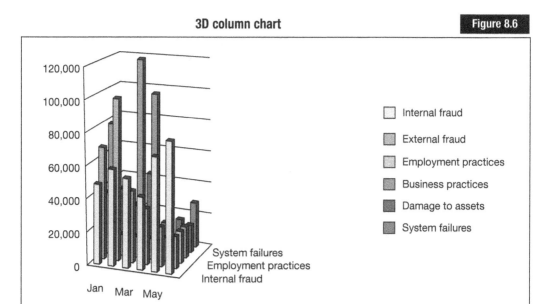

3D line chart

Figure 8.7

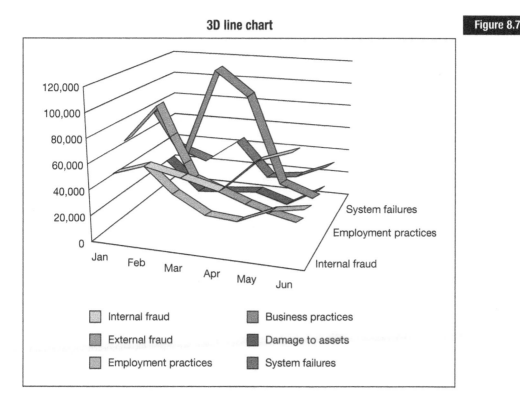

In Figure 8.6, a great deal of information is obscured by the columns in the front. In Figure 8.7, information is again difficult to access. This is in contrast to Figure 8.8 which is a 2D line chart.

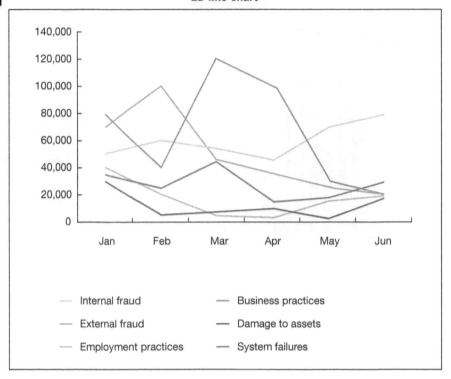

Figure 8.8   **2D line chart**

Although there is a considerable amount of information in this chart, it is still possible to understand it quickly and therefore be able to draw an informed conclusion as a basis for action.

Shading

It is easy to shade a table to indicate the status of a cell and to include possibly spurious accuracy through decimal values. Figure 8.9 is more cluttered and more difficult to extract information from than Figure 8.10.

Figure 8.9   **Losses for six months, showing thresholds**

Loss type £	Jan	Feb	Mar	Apr	May	Jun
Internal fraud	50,000.00	60,000.00	55,000.00	45,000.00	70,000.00	80,000.00
External fraud	70,000.00	100,000.00	45,000.00	35,000.00	25,000.00	20,000.00
Employment practices	40,000.00	20,000.00	5,000.00	3,000.00	15,000.00	20,000.00
Business practices	80,000.00	40,000.00	120,000.00	100,000.00	30,000.00	20,000.00
Damage to assets	30,000.00	5,000.00	7,000.00	10,000.00	2,000.00	18,000.00
System failures	35,000.00	25,000.00	45,000.00	15,000.00	18,000.00	30,000.00

Losses for six months, highlighting red cells only

Figure 8.10

Loss type (£000s)	Jan	Feb	Mar	Apr	May	Jun
Internal fraud	50	60	55	45	70	80
External fraud	70	100	45	35	25	20
Employment practices	40	20	5	3	15	20
Business practices	80	40	120	100	30	20
Damage to assets	30	5	7	10	2	18
System failures	35	25	45	15	18	30

In Figure 8.9, the eye is pulled to the masses of light and medium shaded cells, rather than to the important information highlighted in dark tint, which stands for red cells. In Figure 8.10, loss amounts have been reduced to round £ thousands and only the dark-tinted (red) cells are highlighted, the information which most concerns the reader.

DASHBOARD REPORTING

Many reports feature in other chapters of this book. These focus on the chapter topic, for instance risk and control assessment, indicators, events and losses. However, it is important to draw the threads together so that a comprehensive and cohesive approach can be taken to managing operational risk. Such a report will show the major items of interest to the reader (and as noted above these will be different for different readers). A report giving a range of information, often in different formats to suit the particular topics being reported, is usually called a dashboard. Two examples of a dashboard report are given in Figures 8.11 and 8.12.

The risk performance report in Figure 8.11 gives the top four risks for the firm. (This is commonly produced for the top 10 or top 15 risks.) The indicators and events/losses for these top risks are given too, so that an overall operational risk picture is available. Actions and overall rating (on the right-hand side) can be agreed at the risk committee. This report can then be distributed to board members as a summary of the firm's operational risk status for its top risks.

Figure 8.12 provides summary risk information on the top operational risks of the firm at a more detailed level of loss event type and extends the analysis in Figure 8.11 to include more complete data on indicators and losses, as well as more information on risk and control assessments. Whilst there may be a loss of detail in any summary, salient information is brought out by different display formats. The summary table at top left provides a good use of colour which draws attention to risks which require action, as well as providing a clear indication of indicator trends, which is developed in the bar chart at top right. The spidergram at bottom left is an effective way of highlighting relative levels of risks and controls. The column and line chart at bottom right provides a clear visual summary of the more detailed loss information just above it. In addition, this report provides directional information in terms of arrows relating to the KRIs. It is, however, important to remember that, for particular KRIs, down can be good or bad. So, arrows are often coloured green or red to indicate whether the direction of travel is good or bad.

Looking in more detail at Figure 8.12, we can see that the first four risk categories are all at the same high inherent level. However, closer examination shows that, although the first two categories have a relatively small number of losses and indicators which are entirely acceptable, the third category, External Fraud – System Security, has a low level of losses but has three indicators which are at a stressed level. Furthermore, there is no action outstanding against this category. The fourth risk category, Business Process Failures – Account intake/Acquisition, has seven losses although its indicators are also all acceptable. For the set of the first four risk categories, numbers three and four require further investigation.

Figure 8.11   **Dashboard report: risk performance**

Risk performance report MMM/YYYY									
	Gross level		Net level		Performance		Appetite		Overall	
Risk	Impact	Like'h'd	Impact	Like'h'd	Actual	Trend from previous	Target	Better (Worse)	Action/ Summary	Rating
Failure to attract, recruit and retain key staff	H	H	M-H	M-L	Turnover 17%	Down 5%	15%	(2%)	Investigate poor survey result	
					6th in survey	Up 1 place	1st/ 2nd/3rd	(3 places)		
					30 training courses	Up 10	20 places	+10		
Poor staff communication	H	H	M-H	L	1 general newsletter	Level	1 general newsletter	Level	See action above; no further action	
					Morale 3	Up 1	Morale 4	(Down 1)		
Failure to understand the law and/or regulations	H	M-H	M-H	M-L	1 internal update	Down 1	2 per month	(Down 1)	COO to investigate poor performance	
					0 courses/ 3 months	Down 1	1 course/ 3 months	(Down 1)		
					1 fine in 12 months	Up 1	0 fines in 12 months	(Up 1)		
Poor detection of money laundering	H	M-H	M-H	L	10 staff o/s training	Down 5	0 staff outstanding	(10 staff)	Chase outstanding staff	
					15 SOCA reports	Down 3	10 SOCA reports	Up 5		

Figure 8.12

Dashboard report: operational risk summary

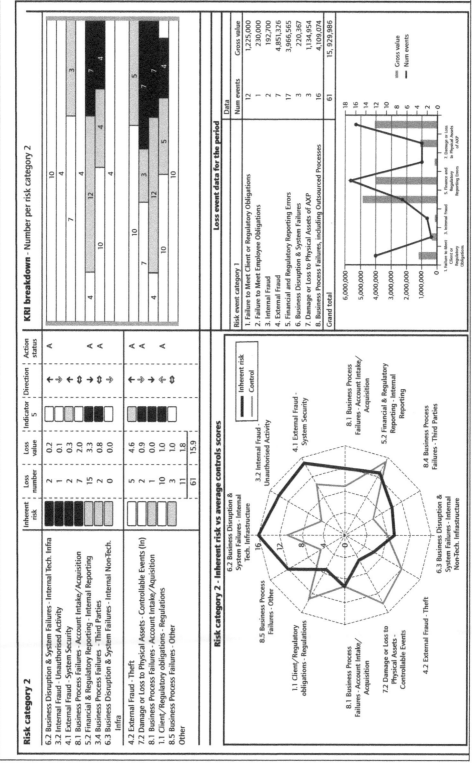

Risk category 2

	Inherent risk	Loss number	Loss value	Indicator 5	Direction	Action status
6.2 Business Disruption & System Failures - Internal Tech. Infra		2	0.2		←	A
3.2 Internal Fraud - Unauthorised Activity		1	0.1		⤳	
4.1 External Fraud - System Security		2	0.3		←	
8.1 Business Process Failures - Account Intake/Acquisition		7	2.0		⇕	A
5.2 Financial & Regulatory Reporting - Internal Reporting		15	3.3		→	A
3.4 Business Process Failures - Third Parties		2	0.8		⤳	
6.3 Business Disruption & System Failures - Internal Non-Tech. Infra		0	0.0		⤳	
		61	15.9			
4.2 External Fraud - Theft		5	4.6		⤳	A
7.2 Damage or Loss to Physical Assets - Controllable Events (In)		2	0.9		→	A
8.1 Business Process Failures - Account Intake/Aquisition		1	0.0		→	
1.1 Client/Regulatory obligations - Regulations		10	1.0		←	A
8.5 Business Process Failures - Other		3	1.0		⇕	
Other		11	1.8			
		61	15.9			

KRI breakdown - Number per risk category 2

Loss event data for the period

Risk event category 1	Data	
	Num events	Gross value
1. Failure to Meet Client or Regulatory Obligations	12	1,225,000
2. Failure to Meet Employee Obligations	1	230,000
3. Internal Fraud	2	192,700
4. External Fraud	7	4,851,326
5. Financial and Regulatory Reporting Errors	17	3,966,565
6. Business Disruption & System Failures	3	220,367
7. Damage or Loss to Physical Assets of AXP	3	1,134,954
8. Business Process Failures, including Outsourced Processes	16	4,109,074
Grand total	61	15,929,986

Risk category 2 - Inherent risk vs average controls scores

The fifth risk category number 5.2, Financial & Regulatory Reporting – Internal Reporting, has a lower level of inherent risk but 15 losses totalling 3.3 million. In addition, its indicators are totally unacceptable with 7 being red, 12 being yellow and only 4 being green. The one redeeming feature of this risk category is that there is at least an action outstanding. However, there is clearly considerable remedial work to be actioned urgently for this risk category.

SUMMARY

Good reports are essential to good operational risk management. Key information must be easily accessible and delivered in such a way as to support informed business decisions on the firm's operational risk profile. That sounds easy and obvious, but is not so easy in practice. It is only too easy to be overwhelmed by information which is not focused on readers' needs. That can include too much information, information which is not relevant to the reader and information which may be relevant, but is not presented in a way which is readily understandable. With operational risk, readers can be at every level of the firm, so the range is wide.

All of those issues of communication and understanding are just as pertinent when it comes to modelling operational risk, the subject of the next chapter.

9

Modelling

ABOUT OPERATIONAL RISK MODELLING

Much has been written about the mathematical modelling of operational risk. Unfortunately, almost all of the writing has been very mathematical and with very little focus on the business benefits. It is almost as though the modelling of operational risk should be sufficient in itself as an intellectual exercise. Modelling appears to be divorced in some way from the reality of the business world. Yet there are considerable benefits which can be derived from modelling and you do not have to wait for several years until you have collected sufficient loss data. Modelling of operational risk can start as soon as the first risk and control assessment is completed and it can help challenge and validate the data in that assessment.

As shown in Figure 9.1, modelling can use data from any one or more of the three fundamental operational risk processes. It can change the qualitative data obtained from risk and control assessments into monetary values and be used to make sense of the plethora of loss and indicator data. In addition, when probabilistic modelling is used, it provides vital validation of these processes by enabling management to challenge the conclusions reached deterministically.

| Figure 9.1 | Typical operational risk framework, showing position of modelling |

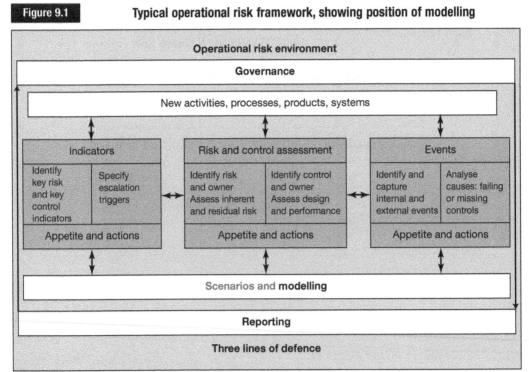

Source: Courtesy of Chase Cooper Limited

Modelling of operational risk can be used to determine the economic capital required to support the operational risks to which a firm is subject, as well as to calculate regulatory capital requirements. By calculating capital by business line and loss event type, modelling enables the capital to be allocated to business units easily and fairly and supports a risk adjusted return on capital approach to business management.

In using mathematical models care has to be taken to understand the limitations of both the input to and the output from the model, which are considered in detail in the next section.

PREVIOUS APPROACHES TO OPERATIONAL RISK MODELLING

Operational risk modelling has matured over the years. To see how it has developed, and learn some lessons from the issues which have arisen in its development, it is instructive to look at the efforts of the financial services industry. Between the late 1990s and 2004, when the Revised Basel Accord was issued, the financial services industry experimented with a wide variety of modelling approaches for operational risk. The Basel Committee identified three broad approaches:

- internal measurement
- loss distribution
- scorecard.

Internal measurement approach

The internal measurement approach (IMA) was first floated by the Basel Committee in early 2001. It was a deterministic approach based, to some extent, on the more advanced credit risk capital calculation and therefore provided a consistent methodology for advanced credit risk and operational risk calculations. The approach relied on a firm having a comprehensive and complete database of losses experienced by it over a considerable number of years. Its core was based on the popular deterministic method of calculating the annual effect of a risk occurring: the annual likelihood of the risk occurring multiplied by the value of the impact. Both the annual likelihood and the value of the impact are calculated using a loss database of a firm's own losses.

The Basel Committee extended this approach by dividing impacts into seven loss event types and eight business lines (see also Chapter 6, Events and losses), giving a 56-cell matrix. Additionally, each firm was required to identify an exposure indicator which related to the scale of the firm's activities in a particular business line. The regulator provided a factor which translated the firm's expected loss into a capital charge for each cell. This factor was based on industry-wide data and would in effect take each expected loss and increase it, such that it became an unexpected loss. The combination of the factors of this approach resulted in a formula which was summed for each cell in the matrix, i.e.

$$\sum(PE \times LGE \times EI \times \gamma)$$

where PE is the probability of an event over some future horizon, LGE is the average loss given an event occurs, EI is the exposure indicator for that particular firm and γ (gamma) is the expected/unexpected translation factor supplied by the regulator.

This is broadly consistent with the credit risk approach of using the PD (probability of default) and LGD (loss given default) together with an EAD (exposure at default).

Although this approach is easy to understand as it is deterministic, there are several significant disadvantages:

- Before applying this approach, a firm must collect losses in all areas for a number of years. This means that no firm is able to use this advanced method of calculation for its operational risk capital until it has collected sufficient losses. Given that there are 56 cells and that at least 30 losses are required in each cell for statistical significance to be achieved, a firm will have to collect several thousand losses before each cell is sufficiently filled from a mathematically coherent perspective.

- Even if the firm has collected many losses, the quality of the data is still suspect unless there is a clear methodology for collecting losses which is consistently applied by the firm over a number of years.

- Allied to the first two points is the fact that very few firms which collect loss data are confident that they have captured all operational losses (see Chapter 6, Events and losses).

- The approach assumes that the firm continues to operate in the same way that it has done in recent years. There are also assumptions that the firm's operational risk approach, appetite and methodology will remain constant in order to generate comparable data.

- This approach implies that past losses are a good indication of future requirements of operational risk capital. It is well known (and financial services regulators require firms to make the point in a footnote to their advertising) that the past is no guide to the future. This is in part due to changes in controls which are made as a management reaction to operational risk losses and in part to the ever-changing external environment.

- This approach assumes a fixed and stable relationship between the losses experienced by the firm in the past and the unexpected losses which may be experienced by the firm in the future (the gamma, γ). As the losses collected are generally of the high-likelihood/low-impact type, this is the equivalent of extrapolating a curve which is derived from high-likelihood/low-impact losses (that is around the 40th to the 60th centile) out to the very high centiles (e.g. 99.9). Such an extrapolation is clearly suspect, without using data which is closer to the very high centiles, and takes no account of a particular firm's risk profile, which may be better than the industry's generic profile. Additionally, the relationship between expected and unexpected losses is rarely linear.

Loss distribution approach

In some ways, the loss distribution approach (LDA) is similar to the IMA, even though external losses could arguably also be used and a probabilistic methodology was directly applied. It was first raised by the Basel Committee in September 2001. In this approach, the firm estimates the likely distribution of operational risk losses over some future horizon for each loss event type/business line combination, i.e. the 56-cell matrix noted above.

As the distribution is estimated either by reference to an existing loss database or derived through, for example, Monte Carlo simulation, there is no need for a gamma factor. Indeed, the distributions could vary by cell as a specific distribution may be deemed to be more appropriate for a particular loss event and business line combination.

This approach also neatly removes the IMA disadvantage of the assumption of the relationship between expected and unexpected losses, by deriving distributions directly from the data, from a combination of the data and simulations of the data, or from prior knowledge, perhaps gained through knowledge of the experience of other firms.

A capital charge is derived from the value at a high centile of each of the 56 distributions which is to produce an overall capital figure. Mention was made of the potential to use less-than-full correlations as it was recognised that simple summing assumes a perfect correlation. The values from all cells relevant to the firm are then added together. Mathematically:

$$\sum VaR_{le,bl}$$

where $VaR_{le,bl}$ is the value at the required centile of the selected loss event (le) and business line (bl) cell.

One serious flaw of the LDA is that it did not recognise that it is mathematically incorrect to sum VaRs from different (and possibly very different) distributions. However, the approach could be mathematically correct if an expected shortfall figure was used instead of the VaR, as the expected shortfall is an average of all the VaRs at and past the relevant quantile.

The first five disadvantages for the IMA (see p. 168) are equally valid for the LDA.

Scorecard approach

This is named after the balanced scorecard approach to management practised by a number of large firms. It takes a more qualitative view of operational risk capital than the IMA and LDA. It is intended to reflect improvements in the control environment which may reduce the frequency and/or the severity of future operational risk losses. Changes to the risk profile may be reflected through indicators of particular risks or the results of, for example, risk and control assessments. Given the use of qualitative data, the results of this approach must be rigorously challenged through the use of both internal and external loss data.

A fundamental difference between a scorecard approach and the two approaches above (based solely on loss data) is the inclusion of forward-looking data derived from discussions with business line staff and reviewed by a central risk function. The discussions and review often form part of the risk and control assessments, as it is these which can easily be used to identify expected risks to the firm in the future and its control environment.

A further difference using the scorecard approach is that the capital is calculated from a single VaR value taken at the required quantile from a single distribution created using the firm's or the business unit's entire data. This has the advantage that it does not sum VaRs.

The advantages to this approach include the following:

- If a firm acquires or disposes of a business or commences or ceases trading in a new product, an assessment of the risks (and the capital required) can be included immediately due to the forward-looking element of this approach.

- Forward-looking risk and control data can be used to compensate for a lack of loss data.

- There is, in theory, no need to wait for a number of years in order to collect sufficient data. The inherent nature of this qualitative forward-looking data is that it is refined and modified over time as management becomes more confident with its risk methodology and as the firm's risk profile changes.

- Although the data is subject to business judgement assumptions, the assessment of risks and controls is often performed on a realistic worst-case basis. This yields data that is significantly towards the high centiles and therefore the data used in a scorecard approach is inherently more representative of data which can severely damage a firm, than data solely from losses.

There are, however, a number of drawbacks to this approach:

- The major assumption that business judgement is a good indicator of the future capital requirements of the firm: the events of 2007–9, particularly in the banking part of the financial services sector, show that this assumption is just as flawed as the assumption that the past is a good guide to the future. (See also Recognising and mitigating natural biases in Chapter 10, Stress tests and scenarios.)

■ The quality of the forward-looking data can vary widely depending on the extent of line management commitment. Some management can be very willing to dedicate time and effort to determining a comprehensive set of risks and controls. Others will view it as an intrusion into their everyday work and may delegate the risk and control assessment to inappropriate or inexperienced junior personnel. This is, of course, a reflection of an unacceptable risk culture in the firm.

■ Whilst the two loss data based approaches derive distributions from the data, the scorecard approach often requires a distribution to be assumed for the probabilistic modelling. Distributions have different sizes and shapes and this can affect the capital requirement. This drawback can be overcome by taking capital requirement readings at whatever quantile is used from a variety of distributions, as the modelling can be repeated using as many different distributions as the firm sees fit.

Summary of the three approaches

A summary of the three approaches is given in Tables 9.1 to 9.3. These tables highlight a number of issues and limitations which need to be considered when modelling operational risk.

Assumptions analysis   Table 9.1

	IMA	LDA	Scorecard
Past is guide to future	Y	Y	N?
Business judgement is guide to future	N	N	Y
Detailed accounting analysis is accurate	Y	Y	N
Low-frequency, high-impact data is sufficiently available	Y?	Y	N?
(Un)expected fixed relationship	Y	N	N
Likelihood/impact distributions	N?	Y	Y

Source: Courtesy of Chase Cooper Limited

As can be seen in Table 9.1, the assumption that the past is a guide to the future is clearly made in both the IMA and LDA. However, the scorecard approach could also be challenged in that whenever the future is assessed, there is at least an inherent bias towards what has happened in the past.

Equally, the assumption that 'business judgement is a guide to the future' is clearly made in the scorecard approach although the only way that the other two approaches could be accused of making this assumption is through the derived capital requirement which of course applies to the future.

As the data for the IMA and LDA are from losses experienced by the firm, there is a clear assumption that those losses are recorded in an analysis by the firm (most usually in the accounts/general ledger of the firm) and that this analysis is accurate. The scorecard approach is likely to use losses suffered by the firm as a form of back-testing and therefore the assumption of accuracy is considerably less important.

As the IMA explicitly assumes a fixed and stable relationship between the firm's loss data and capital requirement, the use of low-frequency/high-impact data is less important, although it will add to the accuracy of the capital requirement if it exists. In contrast, the LDA makes no such assumption in terms of a fixed and stable relationship and therefore the availability of low-frequency/high-impact data is of much more significance. Again, although the scorecard approach does not use loss data directly, its availability for back-testing is useful and therefore sufficient high-quantile data will again add to the accuracy of the derived capital requirement.

The only approach which assumes a fixed relationship between existing losses and unexpected losses is the IMA. In terms of distribution assumptions, the IMA does not use a distribution, being a deterministic method for calculating capital, whereas the scorecard approach definitely assumes distributions in its probabilistic modelling. The LDA may assume distributions in the higher quantiles and also may assume a particular distribution is the best fit for a particular loss event type/business line cell.

Table 9.2 **Data analysis**

	IMA	LDA	Scorecard
Objective (past)	Y	Y	N?
Subjective (forward looking)	N	N	Y
Quality analysis by	Finance	Finance	Management
Quantity available	Low?	Low?	Tailored
Collection time	Long	Long	Short
Source	Accounts	Accounts	Management
Use of external data	Direct	Direct	Indirect

Source: Courtesy of Chase Cooper Limited

Table 9.2 analyses the characteristics of the data in the three approaches. Clearly, the IMA and LDA both use objective (i.e. past) data and the scorecard approach may use it in assessing the future. Equally clearly, the scorecard approach uses a subjective analysis of the risks that may be suffered by the firm and of the controls that may be used to mitigate the risks. Both of these are forward-looking although possibly influenced by past events.

Any quality assurance on the data will probably be provided by internal audit for the IMA and LDA loss data whereas quality assurance on scorecard data can only be provided by internal audit at a process level.

Although some cells in the Basel 56-cell matrix will have considerable loss data, other cells will have very little loss data, if any. This means that the statistical analysis in the LDA in particular may be poor due to a low quantity of data. In comparison, the scorecard approach data will be tailored to that which is required if line management can be engaged in the process.

To have sufficient data for loss event modelling you need at least 30 data points for each risk, or combination of risks, which you are trying to model. The time it takes to collect that amount of data is therefore as long as you need, but could well be at least five years or longer for relatively rare risks. Timescales such as these significantly affect the ability of a firm to start using advanced modelling. And, of course, even five years of benign activity tells you little, as we have seen with credit data in the period preceding the 2007–8 sub-prime problems. On top of which, old data can be largely irrelevant, since the internal and external environments will almost certainly have changed.

Although the collection time for scorecard data is much shorter (as long as it takes to complete sufficient risk and control assessments), the need to challenge the scorecard data through the use of appropriate and sufficient loss data means that the scorecard approach is similarly constrained to a five year minimum period as with the IMA and LDA. However, the scorecard approach can be used by the business to gain significant benefit before this time has elapsed (see Obtaining business benefits from qualitative modelling later in this chapter).

The source of losses will ultimately be a value which is recorded in the accounts in the IMA and LDA whereas management will provide the data for the scorecard approach.

The use of external data can be either direct or indirect in the LDA or IMA, whereas the scorecard approach will use external data both for back-testing and possibly for the generation of relevant high-quantile risks. Direct use of external data in the LDA or IMA is dependent on appropriate conditioning of the data, such as scaling (see Chapter 6, Events and losses).

Table 9.3	Other factors		
	IMA	LDA	Scorecard
Capital charge calculation	Standard factor	Individual percentages	Single%
People – training	Significant	Significant	Significant
People – accessibility	Difficult	Difficult	Easy
Rapid business value	N	N	Y
Efficiency of controls	Indirect	Indirect	Direct
Cost reduction support	Indirect	Indirect	Direct
Transparency	Low	High	Medium?

Source: Courtesy of Chase Cooper Limited

Other factors come into play, apart from the nature and quality of assumptions and data. These are shown in Table 9.3. The capital charge calculation in the IMA is deterministic and uses a standard factor. In the LDA, individual VaR values are used and then summed to produce an overall capital figure for the firm. In the scorecard approach, a single value is taken from the overall distribution for the firm.

Training people to use any of the three approaches is a significant exercise:

- The IMA requires a significant amount of training as loss data must be captured firm-wide over a number of years in order to produce an accurate value for the capital required. It also requires considerable acceptance across the firm that comprehensive collection of internal loss data is a worthwhile use of resource. This acceptance requires commitment from everyone in the firm. This is difficult to obtain for capital modelling purposes in that the resultant control gaps will almost certainly have been closed and the capital suggested by the losses is therefore historic rather than that required to provide support for future problems.

- The LDA also requires a significant amount of training as, again, loss data must be captured firm-wide, together with an understanding of probabilistic approaches applied to operational risk amongst risk management and senior management.

- The scorecard approach requires significant training for line management in order that its assessments are comprehensive and consistent, as well as an understanding of probabilistic approaches applied to operational risk.

The IMA can be difficult to assess as a concept because it incorporates a large amount of data and exposure indicators, together with a translation factor supplied by the regulator. The LDA may be inaccessible for many staff due to its probabilistic approach for extending known losses into high quantiles for a capital requirement. In contrast, the scorecard approach may be easier for management as it is based on management's view of the risks which are likely to be faced by the firm and the controls that will mitigate those risks.

Neither the IMA nor the LDA is able to give rapid business value, as considerable time is required to collect the data. However, the scorecard approach may give rapid business value, as the collection time for data is much shorter.

The efficiency of controls is tested indirectly through the IMA and the LDA as control failures lead to losses and therefore there is an implicit link to the capital required. As the scorecard approach directly assesses the quality of the controls, it can also be used to challenge the efficiency of the controls by comparing the mitigating effect to the cost of controls (see later in this chapter, Obtaining business benefits from qualitative modelling).

In the same way the IMA and LDA can be used indirectly to support cost reduction, whereas the scorecard approach can be used directly to support reduction.

The transparency of the three approaches is hotly debated. It can be argued that the IMA has a low transparency because of the use of exposure indicators (determined by the firm) and translation factors (determined by the regulator or an industry body). Equally, the LDA uses the firm's own losses (albeit probabilistically) and it can therefore be said to be transparent. Whilst the scorecard uses management's own view of its forward-looking risks and of its controls, the probabilistic approach may be viewed as lacking transparency.

TOWARDS AN INCLUSIVE APPROACH

By considering the advantages and disadvantages of the above approaches, it becomes clear that a firm must take into account internal losses, external losses, the business and internal control environment, and scenario analysis, within a comprehensive approach to modelling. This neatly combines the quantitative and qualitative approaches. Alternative approaches which are also possible but are less elegant are a loss distribution approach with a subsequent qualitative adjustment to the capital outcome, or a scorecard approach, with a subsequent quantitative adjustment to the capital outcome.

Is there a difference between good operational risk management practice and an inclusive modelling approach?

It is often assumed that there is a significant difference in the work required from the operational risk department and the business between good operational risk management practice and the sophistication implied by an inclusive modelling approach. However, good modelling governance incorporates most of the qualitative requirements for good practice as is shown in Table 9.4.

Table 9.4

Qualitative governance standards

Governance standard	Inclusive modelling	Good ORM practice
Independent ORM function	Y	Y
Board, senior management involvement	Y	Y
ORM integrated/documented	Y	Y
Capital allocation/incentives	Y	Y
Scenario analysis integrated	Y	
Regular ORM audits	Y	Y
External OR measurement validation	Y	Y

Source: Courtesy of Chase Cooper Limited

It can clearly be seen that most of the qualitative governance standards which are essential in inclusive modelling are also essential good operational risk practice. It is true that the depth of analysis may differ, for example, in the external operational risk measurement validation where it will be less detailed in good operational risk practice than in inclusive modelling. The capital allocation and incentives for good risk management will also be to a different depth and rigour. However, the only major item which stands separately in inclusive modelling is integrated scenario analysis. It is arguable that any well-run firm will include this in its business practices anyway.

Table 9.5

Quantitative governance standards

Governance standard	Inclusive modelling	Good ORM practice
Economic capital @, say, 99.9% one-year holding period	Y	
Comprehensive loss data gathering	Y	(Y)
Loss data assigning	Y	(Y)
External loss data use – integrated/documented	Y	
Methodology/data periodic review	Y	Y
Judgement overrides documented/reviewed	Y	(Y)
Sufficient volume of data	Y	
Parameter/risk estimates: validated/documented/reviewed	Y	(Y)

Source: Courtesy of Chase Cooper Limited

A comparison of the quantitative governance standards, as shown in Table 9.5, is equally informative. Clearly the need to calculate economic capital at, say, the 99.9 centile for a one-year holding period, to integrate and document the use of external loss data and to hold a sufficient volume of loss data are specific to the inclusive modelling approach. However, the other governance essentials are covered (albeit to a lesser depth) by good operational risk practice. It is also true that a number of these are implicit within good operational risk governance (reflected in Table 9.5 by a (Y)) rather than explicit. A firm practising good operational risk governance should take account of implicit as well as explicit needs.

The final, and important, factor about modelling governance is to ask whether the board understands the modelling approach and whether it can trust the results. On the first point, there is really no excuse for board members not understanding the assumptions and principles on which the models are based, including the basis of the mathematics. On the second, there should be a robust and independent system of model validation. This can be undertaken through peer review by modelling experts and business managers within the firm, supported by effective and independent assurance from internal audit. This will help to make sure that models are consistent and also help to eradicate any bias in the process. If independent experts are not available, they will have to be brought in from outside. Whichever approach is taken, models should be thoroughly validated to provide comfort to the board who will use them for business decisions.

DISTRIBUTIONS AND CORRELATIONS

Many distributions can be used for modelling operational risk. Clearly, continuous distributions are relevant for impact or severity, whereas discrete distributions are relevant for frequency or likelihood. Typical impact distributions are lognormal, Gumbel, Pareto and Weibull, and typical discrete distributions used are Poisson, uniform, binomial and negative binomial.

Mathematicians involved in operational risk modelling have their favourite distributions. However, the choice of distribution has a smaller effect on the capital requirement, whether economic or regulatory, than the quality of the primary data, such as the relevance of the loss to the firm, the accuracy of the risk assessment score and the accuracy of the control assessment score. This further underlines the importance of the quality and completeness of the primary data.

Similarly, there is much debate about the correlations of different risks and risk categories in operational risk. Again, the correlations are less relevant than the accuracy of the primary data. However, most risk managers have a favourite pairing of risks (such as staff turnover and internal fraud) with correlations which should be incorporated into any probabilistic analysis. It should be noted that a perceived set of correlations will often lead to a non-positive matrix (which can be confirmed if a Cholesky decomposition is used to test the data) and therefore the resulting correlations will be mathematically invalid. Such correlation matrices often become positive-definite (i.e. mathematically valid) if the correlation is reduced to 0.2 or 0.15. However, at these low levels of correlation it is questionable whether the time and effort spent on correlations is worthwhile.

PRACTICAL PROBLEMS IN COMBINING INTERNAL AND EXTERNAL DATA

Gaps

There are often gaps in the internal loss data. It is very common, for instance, in banking for there to be a significant quantity of loss data in the loss event type 'Execution, delivery and process management' for all firms and, for retail banking institutions, in the loss event type 'External fraud'. This may be because senior management gets to know about fraud losses or because they come directly from the general ledger. Either of these reasons means that fraud loss reporting is not reliant on individual staff reporting the loss. However, some loss event types such as 'Damage to physical assets' have a historically low data count. In order for data to be significant, there must be sufficient data points for reliable statistical modelling. For these purposes, at least 30 independent sets of data are required.

Scaling

Such gaps can be partially filled by external loss data. However, there is considerable debate around how to scale external data for a particular firm. For example, what scaling factor should be used in order to adjust the loss suffered by a Barings or BCCI to a particular firm's risk profile? A number of commentators have suggested metrics such as number of staff, gross revenues or the number of trading tickets processed. However, there is no evidence to show that losses can be scaled using such metrics. The answer, as we saw in the section on Scaling in Chapter 6, Events and losses, is that precise scaling is not possible, but an assessment can be made by identifying common factors between the loss-suffering firm and your own and extrapolating an answer on that basis.

Data cleansing

It is very clear that models using external data are particularly sensitive to the data, as its principal impact will be on the extreme right-hand end of the curve from which a capital figure is taken. As such, cleansing of external loss data is vitally important when it is used for modelling. The term 'cleansing' denotes the process of checking that the losses are relevant to the firm and determining an appropriate size of the loss with respect to the firm.

Whilst the appropriate size can be determined through some form of scaling, as discussed above and in Chapter 6, the relevance of the loss to the firm is the first step in the process, as there is no point scaling a loss which is not relevant. To understand the relevance, it is important to have a narrative in the external data which comments on the cause of the loss. A full and accurate description is therefore required.

It is of course clear that, for a financial services firm, a trading loss made through a 'fat finger' error by a competitor is relevant, at some size, to another trading firm. Equally, this loss is unlikely to be relevant to a small retail financial services firm. However, a loss suffered by a retail bank through mortgage fraud may be conceptually relevant to a trading firm if the loss was caused through poor documentation standards. Such standards are equally applicable to a trading and sales firm and are particularly relevant if the trading and sales firm conducts, for instance, over-the-counter derivatives.

Additionally, there may be losses made by firms outside the financial services sector which are directly relevant to a financial services firm. For example, the British Airways and Gate Gourmet outsourcing case (mentioned in Chapter 14, Outsourcing) is directly relevant to almost all financial services firms, as outsourcing is significant in their industry.

It is therefore important for external data to be carefully challenged, both in terms of relevance and size, before putting such data into a model. This challenge does not have to be carried out every time the model is run, although it is appropriate to review previous challenges on a periodic basis, such as an annual review. Similarly, it is also appropriate to challenge internal data when the firm's business model changes, when there are significant changes in the marketplace and as it degrades over time and may become only partially relevant.

Weighting the cells

In the IMA, each cell is given an exposure indicator which effectively gives a weighting to that cell. It may be appropriate for the model to have a weighting factor, depending on the exposure of the firm to that particular loss event type/business line combination. The weighting may be occasioned by a particular downturn in the markets relevant to a business line or by the firm deliberately decreasing or increasing its exposure to a business line, either in a discrete fashion through, for example, hiring a trading team or in a slow continuous fashion by, for example, a measured withdrawal from that market.

Taking insurance into account

One challenge for modellers is how to take insurance into account. Often a manual adjustment is made to the relevant cells following the calculation of the gross capital. Alternatively, a very sophisticated model may allow the entering of insurance details such as the deductible and the claims limit so that these can be automatically taken into account. However, this means that each insurance contract must be mapped to a firm's loss event types and business lines and those of any regulator to which it has to report. This is a challenging exercise because of the number of potential overlaps between policies, causes of losses and loss event types (see Mapping in Chapter 12, Insurance).

Fat tails

The term 'fat tails' is sometimes used, often somewhat disparagingly, during a discussion about modelling operational risk events and losses. This refers to the higher quantiles in a distribution and to the seeming paradox that a considerable number of high-quantile events have occurred within the last 15 to 20 years.

Mathematically, very large events are supposed to happen only once in many lifetimes. Yet any operational risk manager can name at least half a dozen very large events they have experienced or been aware of, without even touching the events of the financial crisis of 2007–9. To have a very large number happening in such a relatively short timescale means that at least one of the assumptions underlying modelling must be incorrect. The most obvious assumption to challenge is that the shape of the curve is correct. The response of many mathematicians involved in operational risk has been to increase the size of the tail above that which is demanded by the standard shape for a distribution (see Figure 9.2). This inevitably increases the size of the capital required, but it makes the model appear more in touch with reality, as higher losses demand more capital.

However, it is also possible that another distribution exists in the higher quantiles which is largely separate from the distribution which covers expected losses in the high-frequency/low-to-medium impact part of the curve. The challenge for modellers is to model a bimodal distribution with one mode in the expected losses area and a second in the low-frequency/high-impact area (see Figure 9.3). Resolving this challenge is a significant mathematical exercise and is beyond the scope of this book.

Lognormal distribution and 'fattened' tail

Figure 9.2

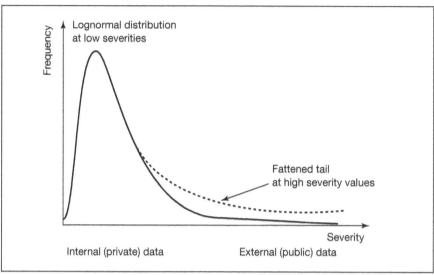

Source: Courtesy of Chase Cooper Limited

Lognormal and bimodal distributions

Figure 9.3

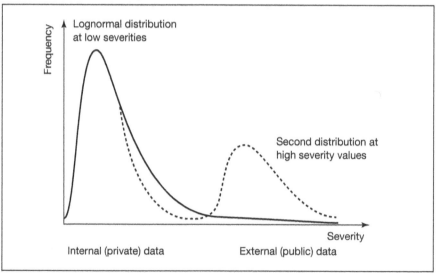

Source: Courtesy of Chase Cooper Limited

CONFIDENCE LEVELS AND RATINGS

If a firm is not bound by specific regulatory requirements, it has a choice of confidence levels from which to choose. As a guide, the European insurance industry uses a confidence level of 99.5%, whereas the Basel Committee's advanced operational risk approach uses 99.9%. It is interesting, however, that regulators generally also choose a multiplier on top of the confidence level. A multiplier may move a capital requirement from 3 to 7 standard deviations and give a higher level of capital, as well as a greater level of confidence that the capital requirement will not be exceeded.

Whatever confidence level is used, it is simply a guide to the capital required. For example, a confidence level of 99.9% for a holding period of one year means that *on average* the capital required will not exceed that level except for a 1 in a 1000 event occurring. This therefore requires many years (if not thousands!) to pass before the average capital required can be stated with some degree of certainty. Clearly this can only be an approximation in our lifetimes, as has been amply demonstrated during the 2007–9 financial crisis.

OBTAINING BUSINESS BENEFITS FROM CAPITAL MODELLING

In a report from any capital model using a cell approach there will be many cells containing valuable business data which can be used to give information on the quality of the firm's controls and the capital needed to support each of the businesses.

In Figure 9.4, the capital requirement of approximately £283m can be seen in the bottom right-hand cell. However, this output can yield significant business information. For example, in the 'Employment Practices & Workplace Safety' column it can be seen that Corporate Finance has a capital requirement of approximately £16m whereas 'Trading & Sales' has a requirement of approximately £2m for the same Basel loss event type. Both Corporate Finance and Trading & Sales are regarded by Basel as higher-risk business lines and both attract a weighting of 18% under the Standardised Approach to capital calculation. If both businesses have a similar number of staff and a similar culture within the firm whose output is represented in Figure 9.4, it is likely that the capital required for risks under the 'Employment Practices & Workplace Safety' heading will also be similar. Why then are the capital requirements so different?

There are at least three possible explanations:

■ Corporate Finance has been through a very difficult period in terms of staff relations and has had to make a number of out-of-court settlements. If this is the reason, clearly some senior management work is necessary in order to improve staff relations in Corporate Finance.

■ Corporate Finance has been assiduously submitting its losses and events to the Operational Risk Department whereas Trading & Sales has inadvertently or otherwise not disclosed all of its events. If this is the reason, clearly some work is necessary with senior staff in Trading & Sales in order to encourage them to disclose all of their events.

- Trading & Sales has very good controls which have both prevented losses from occurring and, when they have occurred, the losses have been detected quickly and the control failures have been corrected without delay. If this is the reason, management should determine whether the good-quality controls in Trading & Sales can be replicated in Corporate Finance (and in other high-capital requirement areas such as Retail Banking and Retail Brokerage). Such replication will significantly reduce the amount of capital required to run the firm.

Model output example: capital requirement **Figure 9.4**

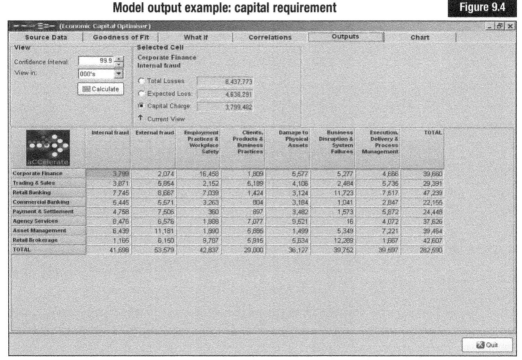

Source: Courtesy of Chase Cooper Limited

Similarly, in the 'Business Disruption & System Failures' column there is a very small capital requirement against Agency Services. Either very good controls (perhaps a hot standby computer system) exist in Agency Services for Business Disruption & System Failures or Agency Services is very dilatory in reporting events and losses and also has assessed its business and internal control environment as excellent (i.e. its risks are very low and its controls are very good). If good controls exist then it will be worthwhile investigating whether these controls can be replicated in, for instance, Retail Banking or Retail Brokerage where a substantial reduction in capital could be achieved.

Linking model data and reports

It can also be helpful to look at the number of losses reported and to link these with the value of capital required. Figure 9.5 gives the numbers of internal losses recorded relating to the capital figures given in Figure 9.4.

Figure 9.5 **Model input example: number of internal losses (part of the data used to generate the output in Figure 9.4)**

	Source Data	Goodness of Fit	What If	Correlations	Outputs	Chart	

Source
- ● LDA Internal
- ○ LDA External
- ○ CRSA

View in: full

Selected Cell
Corporate Finance
Internal fraud
- ● Number of Loss Events: 44
- ○ Mean Severity of Losses: 80,658
- ○ Std Deviation of Losses: 104,540
- ↑ Current View

	Internal fraud	External fraud	Employment Practices & Workplace Safety	Clients, Products & Business Practices	Damage to Physical Assets	Business Disruption & System Failures	Execution, Delivery & Process Management	TOTAL
Corporate Finance	44	12	95	22	77	44	63	357
Trading & Sales	24	12	39	11	74	30	10	200
Retail Banking	22	79	21	46	38	10	14	230
Commercial Banking	35	10	35	10	18	36	3	146
Payment & Settlement	26	59	89	32	35	9	47	296
Agency Services	41	54	46	36	94	1	94	366
Asset Management	20	72	85	77	56	77	85	472
Retail Brokerage	56	16	27	98	55	97	46	395
TOTAL	267	314	437	332	447	303	362	2,462

Quit

Source: Courtesy of Chase Cooper Limited

Linking the number of losses in the 'Employment Practices & Workplace Safety' column for Corporate Finance and Trading & Sales to the capital requirements in Figure 9.4 gives a clearer picture of which of the three possibilities above are more likely. Given that Trading & Sales has only reported 39 events against Corporate Finance's 95 events, it would appear that the second possibility is more likely, i.e. Trading & Sales has not reported all of its events and losses, whereas Corporate Finance has been very diligent. However, the third possibility remains feasible and clearly the next step is a short investigation of Trading & Sales to see which of these two remaining possibilities has actually occurred.

In much the same way, Agency Services having only one event reported requires further investigation. In both cases, the firm will benefit from either better reporting of losses and therefore better data on which to manage the businesses or from good controls in one business being developed and implemented in other businesses. Either way the firm's operational risk profile will be better managed and potentially significantly reduced.

Preventative control testing

Even a brief glance at the two screens shows that there are many other challenges which can be made which are of business benefit. As the number of events reported relates directly to the quality of the preventative controls, an examination of Figure 9.5 will yield data about the quality of the preventative controls. For example, in 'Clients, Products & Business Practices' Trading & Sales and Commercial Banking both have relatively low numbers of events and therefore possibly very good preventative controls.

However, by also looking at Figure 9.4, it can be seen that Trading & Sales has a much higher capital requirement than Commercial Banking for this loss event type. This implies that when Trading & Sales has a loss in 'Clients, Products & Business Practices' it is a much larger loss on average than Commercial Banking. Clearly, assuming the transaction size and business practices of these two businesses are similar, Commercial Banking is able to minimise the size of its losses at the same time as minimising the number of its losses. Any business practices which can be copied from Commercial Banking into Trading & Sales, Retail Brokerage and/or Asset Management will again substantially reduce the capital required by the firm.

Detective and corrective control testing

The ability to minimise the size of losses speaks directly to the quality of the detective and corrective controls operated by the business line. Good detective controls will reduce the possibility of the loss growing through lack of detection. Good corrective controls will rapidly return the firm to the position that it was in (or better) and thereby also minimise the size of the loss. Modelling can show areas where the firm has good detective and corrective controls through the average size of the loss and, more particularly, through the standard deviation (SD) of the size of the loss. (The standard deviation of a set of numbers can be obtained through the standard formulae in Excel.)

A large standard deviation indicates that the detective and corrective controls are poor as the impact of a risk has a wide number of values. In contrast, a small standard deviation indicates that the controls contain the impact of the risk event to a relatively small range of values around the average. Figure 9.6 shows this in graphical terms.

A standard deviation of a set of losses, typically represented by the losses relating to a single cell in the 56-cell matrix, is a common input to or output from a model. Examination of the standard deviations will yield conceptually similar challenges and business benefits to those noted above in the examinations of capital requirements and numbers of losses.

Figure 9.6

Small, medium and large standard deviations

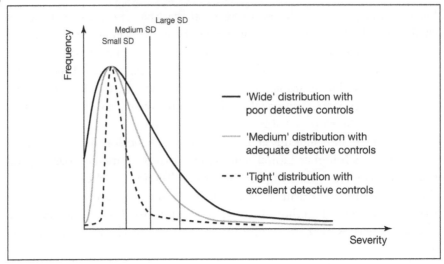

Source: Courtesy of Chase Cooper Limited

MODELLING QUALITATIVE DATA

Whilst any firm that is considering modelling operational risk naturally thinks about modelling quantitative data (that is internal and external events and losses), few think about also modelling the qualitative data that they all have. This is a surprising denial of the forward-looking data that have been gathered largely through discussions with subject matter experts within the firm. In the financial services industry, some data is described as business environment and internal control factor data. Just because qualitative data is difficult to model does not mean that it should not be modelled. Indeed, actuaries often model using qualitative data when harder quantitative data is either not available or not available in sufficient number.

What qualitative data do we have?

Qualitative data is, of course, the risk data and control data that is generated through risk and control assessments (see Chapter 5, Risk and control assessment). The data is almost always available and very often refers to the risks to the business objectives and mitigating controls to those risks. Also included is data on the risk owners and control owners and the assessment of risks and controls at both gross and net levels. This is precisely the data that a firm should be modelling in order to assess the capital required by the business from a risk management perspective. In addition, further qualitative data can be obtained through scenario analysis and stress testing (see Chapter 10, Stress tests and scenarios).

Why isn't qualitative data modelled?

The first objection to modelling qualitative data is generally that it is soft and therefore changeable. That reflects reality. The nature of the data simply needs to be borne in mind when analysing the results. Secondly, risk and control assessment data is mainly management's view of the future. This objection was addressed earlier in this chapter (see discussion on Scorecard approach).

The third objection that is often raised is the fact that a number of banks misjudged their strategic risks before and during the financial crisis of 2007–9. Although this is true, it is easy to refute by referring to the many thousands of firms that survived the financial crisis. The sins of the few should not be visited on the many.

A fourth objection to qualitative data is that it is only good for broad adjustments as it is inherently unstable. However, although management's view of the future does change it tends to be remarkably consistent given a stable environment. Internal and external losses (that is the so-called hard quantitative data) will also change to reflect changes in the business environment.

Some of the general problems with modelling are also equally applicable to the modelling of qualitative data. For example, an entirely incredulous look can be achieved by telling a board member that 2 + 2 does not equal 4 but is equal to somewhere between 3.9 and 4.1 approximately 95% of the time. This is of course simply a lack of understanding of the difference between probabilistic modelling and deterministic mathematics. Senior management should be looking for a range of results, and not a single figure. However, the true casualty in modelling is that the many assumptions underlying modelling are either forgotten or conveniently ignored.

Challenging the input

As well as challenging the assumptions, the qualitative data to be used in modelling should be challenged in exactly the same way. Experts differ in their opinion of risk impact scores and they should be challenged and revised. Likelihood scores are also subject to bias (see Chapter 10, Stress tests and scenarios, Recognising and mitigating natural biases). Control assessments too are also subject to bias, with control owners tending to overestimate the effectiveness of controls and risk owners tending to underestimate them. All the data should be challenged and reviewed prior to use in modelling (just as quantitative data should also be conditioned).

OBTAINING BUSINESS BENEFITS FROM QUALITATIVE MODELLING

Significant business benefit can be obtained from modelling risk and control assessments by themselves. This means that the business benefits of modelling can be achieved by firms much more quickly than waiting for significant volumes of internal loss data to accumulate. In particular, simulations can be done for any parameter such as gross risk, net risk, control benefit, owners, or any risk category. Comparison can be made with deterministic values, and the confidence level at which the deterministic value has been set can be challenged. Lastly, control changes can be tested without running the risk of jeopardising the firm.

Risks

Risk and control assessment data can be modelled through using standard Monte Carlo simulation techniques. An output example for risks is shown in Figure 9.7. A risk and control assessment model will take the risk and control scores assigned during an assessment and model these through simulating the potential losses using a given distribution.

| Figure 9.7 | Risk and control assessment model output example: potential gross and net losses |

CFM - Chase Cooper Internal (V 1.2)   Printed on: 5-Jun-13 at 4:18 pm   Page: 1

Risk Results [MOR(1,147) - Session: RTRA Risk Profile demo(459) - Quantile: 99.90%]
Time Frame Factor: 1 - Iterations: 50,000 - Seed: 1
Created on 6/5/2013 4:18:31PM

Risk	Risk Owner	Gross Loss (M)	Control Benefit (M)	Net Loss (M)
R01 Failure to attract, recruit and retain key staff	SG	19.047	7.753	11.894
R02 Poor staff communication	SG	8.214	2.029	6.185
R03 Failure to understand the law and/or regulations	FT	12.023	3.144	8.880
R04 Failure to capture market opportunities	RB	2.725	0.741	1.984
R05 Poor detection of money laundering	JC	2.713	1.070	1.543
R06 Inadequate or insufficient IT infrastructure	JR	0.535	0.431	0.104
R07 Weakness in information systems security	JR	5.990	1.107	4.883
R08 Poor employee incentives	SG	3.363	1.366	1.998
R09 Increasing external fraud activity	JC	2.715	0.727	1.988
R10 Failure to grow staff competences	FT	2.225	0.974	1.251
R11 Misaligned employee goals	FT	0.607	0.083	0.524
R12 Failure to detect and eliminate internal fraud	JC	3.366	3.366	0.000
R13 Unfit or inappropriate new products launched	RB	10.156	1.605	8.550
R14 Poor strategic decision making	RB	1.636	0.921	0.715
R15 Inaccessible premises	JR	4.463	2.946	1.518
		80.378	28.261	52.117

Source: Courtesy of Chase Cooper Limited

As can be seen from the histogram in Figure 9.7 there are several risks, in particular R01, R03 and R13, which have significant modelled net losses (pale bars). Their net values of approximately £12m, £9m and £9m respectively can be read from the detailed spreadsheet below the histogram.

It is not surprising that most risks have a net loss as the data has been modelled at a confidence level of 99.9%. What is surprising is that one risk, R12, Failure to detect and eliminate internal fraud, still has zero net risk even at the 99.9 quantile. It is most unlikely, although possible, that the controls mitigating this risk are so good that they are still operating perfectly at the average of the worst year in 1000 years. It is far more likely that:

- the quality of the controls has been overstated
- the number of controls mitigating the risk has been overstated, or
- the independence of the mitigating controls has been overstated.

Clearly, if the controls are all scored with a top score for both design and performance they are most unlikely to fail together and cause a net loss, particularly if there are two or three controls all with maximum scores. Equally, if there are a number of controls, perhaps six or seven, it is very unlikely that sufficient will fail in order to generate a net loss, even if some are rated below maximum. The positive effect of having many controls can be compounded if the controls identified are not independent. One of the fundamental assumptions underpinning all operational risk models which use control scoring is that the controls are independent. If this is not the case, the model will overstate the mitigating effect of the controls.

Controls

An alternative way to look at a risk and control assessment is through the controls. Rather than have the model aggregate results by risks it is also of business benefit to have the model aggregate results by controls, particularly as one control may mitigate several risks.

Figure 9.8 gives the reduction in risk exposure achieved by each control and, taking into account the cost of each control, gives the net benefit of the control. This enables a firm to see the net reduction that a control gives in risk exposure. It can be seen at the top of Figure 9.8 that Retention packages for key staff and long-term incentive plans give high values of control benefit after cost with Group Survey (remuneration) giving the highest benefit. It is interesting that 'Retention packages for key staff' gives the highest control benefit but only the second-highest benefit after taking costs into account.

Figure 9.8	Risk and control assessment model output example: potential control benefits

CFM - Chase Cooper Internal (V1.2)   Printed on: 5-Jun-13 at 4:21pm   Page: 1

Results for All Controls [MOR(1,147) - Session: RTRA Risk Profile demo(459) - Quantile: 99.90%]
Time Frame Factor: 1 - Iterations: 50,000 - Seed: 1
Created on 6/5/2013 4:18:31PM

Control		Control Owner	Cost of Control (M)	Control Benefit (M)	Control Benefit after Cost(M)
C01	Group survey (remuneration)	SG	0.200	2.445	2.245
C02	Training and mentoring schemes	SO	1.000	1.029	0.029
C03	Retention packages for key staff	SG	1.000	2.649	1.649
C04	Long term incentive plan	SO	0.500	1.630	1.130
C05	Clearly defined communication channels exist	SG	0.300	0.913	0.613
C06	Shared P&L	SG	5.000	0.461	-4.539
C07	Shared bonus pool	SG	10.000	0.655	-9.345
C08	Technical knowledge of the document	FT	0.100	0.547	0.447
C09	Regular updates from various sources	FT	0.100	0.769	0.669
C10	External training courses	FT	1.000	1.827	0.827
C11	Competitor monitoring	RB	0.010	0.407	0.397
C12	Staff innovation	RB	0.100	0.334	0.234
C13	AML annual training	JC	0.100	0.310	0.210
C14	Circulation of BBA awareness circulars	JC	0.010	0.184	0.174
C15	KYC	JC	0.010	0.576	0.566
C16	Business/strategic planning	JR	0.400	0.145	-0.255
C17	IT system performance and capacity monitoring	JR	0.010	0.145	0.135
C18	Employment contract/confidentiality agreements	JR	0.100	0.476	0.376
C19	Fire-proof cabinets for Personnel and confidential data	JR	0.010	0.271	0.261
C20	Record retention	JR	0.010	0.361	0.351
C21	Salary survey	SG	0.100	0.427	0.327
C22	Reward linked to performance	SO	0.100	0.534	0.434
C23	Incentive plan	SG	3.000	0.405	-2.595
C24	Reconciliation of Personnel accounts	JC	0.010	0.378	0.368
C25	Staff movements	JC	0.100	0.349	0.249
C26	Staff training	FT	0.100	0.364	0.264
C27	Documented procedures and processes	FT	0.010	0.121	0.111
C28	Appraisals	FT	0.010	0.230	0.220
C29	Department heads to identify training requirements	FT	0.100	0.259	0.159
C30	Ombudsperson scheme	FT	0.100	0.044	-0.056
C31	Corporate governance	FT	0.500	0.039	-0.461
C32	Criminal background check	JC	1.000	0.468	-0.532
C33	Corporate security	JC	1.000	0.561	-0.439
C34	Segregation of duties	JC	0.100	0.468	0.368
C35	Disciplinary process	JC	0.010	0.374	0.364
C36	Staff training	JC	0.100	0.561	0.461

Source: Courtesy of Chase Cooper Limited

At the other end of the scale, shared P&L and shared bonus pool are both controls which cost considerably more than the value that they bring to reducing the risk profile. The business question to be asked now is whether these two controls can be operated at a lower cost, whilst still achieving an acceptable mitigation of risk. In other words, is the firm willing to spend that level of money in order to achieve a relatively small reduction in risk profile? In some cases such a spend may be acceptable for controls related to, for example, a regulatory risk which has to be mitigated in order to comply with regulations. In other cases the choice will be much more up to management to determine whether or not the reduction in risk justifies the spend.

Risk owners

Figure 9.9 shows a comparison between the risk owners who were captured during the risk and control assessment for gross loss, control benefit and net loss. It is interesting to note that the highest net loss is risk owner SG, followed by risk owner FT. It is to be expected that SG is the CEO of the firm and that FT is one of the senior business heads. If this is not the case the firm should ask itself whether it wants someone other than the CEO to be the largest risk owner by value. It is also worth noting that risk owner JC has the lowest gross loss exposure and also the lowest net loss, i.e. the controls for JC's risks mitigate the highest value risks in the firm. Is, perhaps, JC being over-optimistic in his/her control assessment and risk assessment? And, therefore, is the firm more exposed to JC's risks than it has previously thought?

Risk and control assessment model output example: risk owner results   **Figure 9.9**

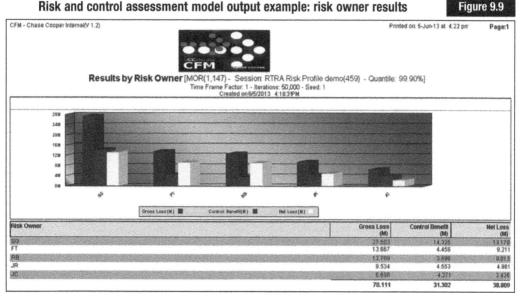

Source: Courtesy of Chase Cooper Limited

Ranking risks and controls

With the basic simulations complete on risks and controls it is possible to extract further business benefit by ranking them. For example a report showing the 10 highest residual risks will give the firm the opportunity to challenge whether, for example in Figure 9.10, Failure to attract, recruit and retain key staff is the risk in which the firm wishes to have its highest residual exposure. If this is the case, modelling has validated the firm's risk appetite. If this is not the case, modelling of the risk and control assessment has given the firm the opportunity to challenge and improve the controls around this risk.

Such a report is particularly helpful when a firm has carried out a considerable number of risk and control assessments and is wondering how to prioritise its control enhancements. There will inevitably be a considerable number of action plans, all of which will be vying for scarce resources and money. An explicit statement of the monetary value of the potential net loss relating to each of the risks is invaluable in assisting the prioritisation thought process.

Just as ranking risks can be very helpful to the firm, so too can be ranking of controls, as shown in Figure 9.11. The obvious question for the firm to ask

Figure 9.10 Risk and control assessment model output example: highest potential residual risks

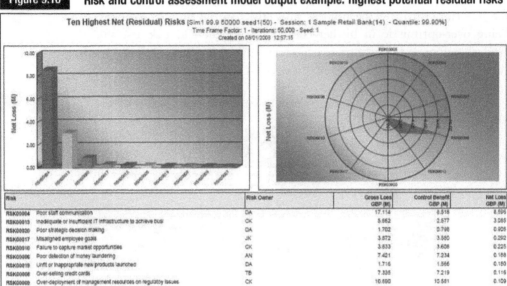

Risk		Risk Owner	Gross Loss GBP (M)	Control Benefit GBP (M)	Net Loss GBP (M)
RSK00004	Poor staff communication	DA	17.114	8.518	8.596
RSK00013	Inadequate or insufficient IT infrastructure to achieve busi	CK	5.662	2.577	3.085
RSK00020	Poor strategic decision making	DA	1.702	0.796	0.905
RSK00017	Misaligned employee goals	JK	3.872	3.580	0.292
RSK00010	Failure to capture market opportunities	CK	3.833	3.608	0.225
RSK00006	Poor detection of money laundering	AN	7.421	7.234	0.188
RSK00019	Unfit or inappropriate new products launched	DA	1.716	1.566	0.150
RSK00008	Over-selling credit cards	TB	7.335	7.219	0.116
RSK00009	Over-deployment of management resources on regulatory issues	CK	10.690	10.581	0.109
RSK00007	Insufficient funds/deposits to cater for lending activities	TB	7.416	7.322	0.093
End of Ten Highest Net (Residual) Risks			66.76	53.00	13.76

Source: Courtesy of Chase Cooper Limited

Figure 9.11 Risk and control assessment model output example: best and worst controls

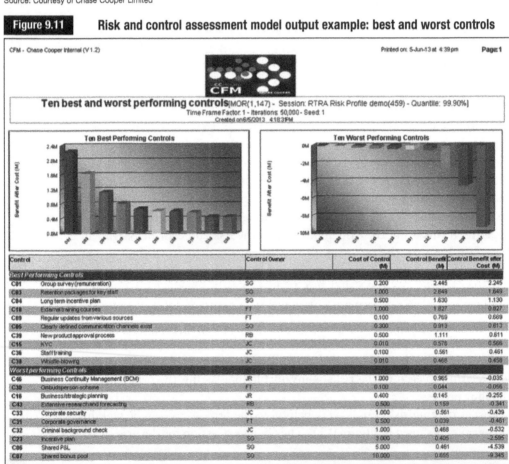

Control		Control Owner	Cost of Control (M)	Control Benefit (M)	Control Benefit after Cost (M)
Best Performing Controls					
C01	Group survey (remuneration)	SG	0.200	2.445	2.245
C03	Retention packages for key staff	SG	1.000	2.649	1.649
C04	Long term incentive plan	SG	0.500	1.630	1.130
C18	External training courses	FT	1.000	1.827	0.827
C09	Regular updates from various sources	FT	0.100	0.769	0.669
C05	Clearly defined communication channels exist	SG	0.300	0.913	0.613
C39	New product approval process	RB	0.500	1.111	0.611
C15	KYC	JC	0.010	0.576	0.566
C36	Staff training	JC	0.100	0.561	0.461
C38	Whistle-blowing	JC	0.010	0.468	0.458
Worst performing Controls					
C46	Business Continuity Management (BCM)	JR	1.000	0.965	-0.035
C30	Ombudsperson scheme	FT	0.100	0.044	-0.056
C16	Business/strategic planning	JR	0.400	0.145	-0.255
C43	Extensive research and forecasting	RB	0.500	0.159	-0.341
C33	Corporate security	JC	1.000	0.561	-0.439
C21	Corporate governance	FT	0.500	0.039	-0.461
C32	Criminal background check	JC	1.000	0.468	-0.532
C23	Incentive plan	SG	3.000	0.405	-2.595
C06	Shared P&L	SG	5.000	0.461	-4.539
C07	Shared bonus pool	SG	10.000	0.655	-9.345

Source: Courtesy of Chase Cooper Limited

itself is: 'Do we want this set of controls to be our best performing controls and this other set to be our worst performing controls?' In particular, and looking at Figure 9.11, the firm's board of directors and senior management should be asking: 'Are we happy that KYC Corporate is only the eighth most effective control and are we also happy that "Physical security" is in the list of our 10 worst performing controls?'

Clearly these questions are dependent on management having faith in the risk and control assessments, although the questions will inevitably challenge the scores in those assessments. This has the effect of a virtuous circle where scoring, modelling and challenging generate real business benefit through modifying the risk and control environment to fit the risk appetite of the firm.

SUMMARY

Modelling operational risk can be, but should not be, an abstruse 'black box' approach accessible only, literally, to rocket scientists. It can and should be rooted in the core operational risk framework processes of risk and control assessments, loss events and indicators, as we have shown in this chapter. And its assumptions and principles should be understood by the board and senior management. Since it is used for capital modelling it can have a direct impact on reports on both product and business line performance.

Within operational risk, as with most things, there is no one methodology, let alone a limited set of distributions which can be applied. As was said in the early days of operational risk, 'let a thousand models bloom'. But even if the assumptions are understood and the methodology is thoroughly and independently validated, the nature of operational risk means that its modelling should be hedged with health warnings. The greatest danger is to take the number at a particular point and not the range of possibilities.

10

Stress tests and scenarios

INTRODUCTION

Stress testing and scenario analysis are essential tools for a firm's planning and operational risk management processes. They are rooted in the firm's business and strategic objectives and should form part of the process of identifying those objectives. They alert the firm's management to adverse unexpected outcomes, beyond those which have been identified in risk and control assessments (RCAs) or modelling, and supplement other operational risk management approaches and measures. Stress tests and scenarios are not forecasts of what is likely to happen; they are deliberately designed to provide severe, but plausible, possible outcomes. They are necessarily forward-looking and therefore involve an element of judgement. Finally, they are invaluable during periods of expansion, by providing a useful basis for decisions when none is available from other sources.

Stress testing and scenario analysis interact with the three fundamental processes of operational risk (see Figure 10.1) and are also a natural part of modelling. As we have seen, events and indicators can be used to develop scenarios, which are then applied to risk and control assessments.

| Figure 10.1 | Typical operational risk framework, showing position of stress tests and scenarios |

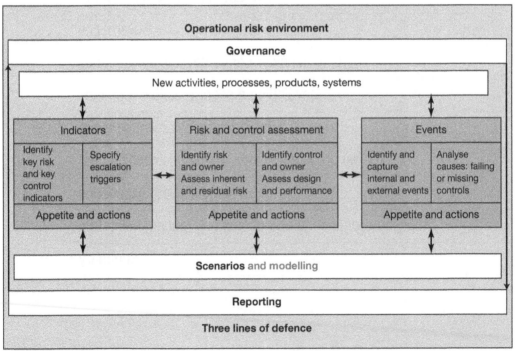

Source: Courtesy of Chase Cooper Limited

WHAT ARE THEY AND WHAT'S THE DIFFERENCE BETWEEN THEM?

A typical description of stress testing and scenario analysis is the identification and analysis of the potential vulnerability of a firm to exceptional but plausible events. Other descriptions mention events, or combinations of events, which have a low probability of occurrence, but are realistic.

Stress testing is generally described as the *shifting of a single parameter* (often involving a number of standard deviation movements). In an operational risk context, this can be taken to refer to either the occurrence of a single risk, such as internal fraud or a system failure, or to the movement of a factor which may affect or does affect the firm as a whole, such as a significant increase in interest rates or a significant equity market downturn.

By contrast, scenario analysis is about simultaneously *moving a number of parameters* by a predetermined amount, based on statistical results, expert knowledge and/or historically observed events. Alternatively, scenarios can be described as multiple stress tests occurring within a reasonable period of time.

In reality, firms use both approaches in order to ensure a comprehensive analysis (see Figure 10.2). For the sake of brevity, the term scenario will be used in this chapter to cover both stress testing and scenario analysis. As has been shown, stress testing is simply a special case of scenario analysis, in which only one parameter changes.

Combining stress testing and scenario analysis **Figure 10.2**

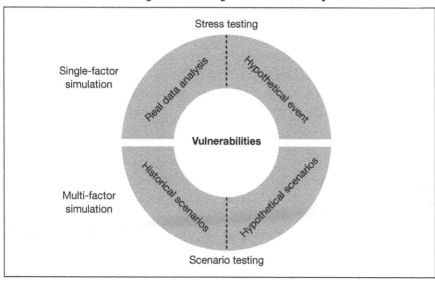

Source: Courtesy of Chase Cooper Limited

WHY USE SCENARIOS?

Scenarios are particularly important in operational risk because the only other subjective and forward-looking information is available from risk and control assessments. Scenarios usefully supplement and provide challenge to the equally subjective risk and control assessments. By having two sets of data challenging each other, both of which have been derived subjectively, better clarity is achieved and a firmer base is available from which to create action plans to enhance risk management, perhaps through improving controls or implementing further controls. Trends in key risk indicators can also be forward-looking, based on actual current and past data. As such, the trends form a useful input when creating scenarios.

Scenarios also help overcome some of the limitations of models and other historic data described in the previous chapter. All models, including operational risk models, are constructed on the basis of a number of assumptions, such as correlations, but which are often lost in the mists of time or enthusiasm, are forgotten or are simply ignored. For instance IT systems failure may be correlated with the business continuity plan. However, if the IT system does break down, it may turn out that there is no need to invoke the business continuity plan. The correlation is not as certain as had been thought. Challenging the models through extreme but plausible scenarios tends to uncover where some of these assumptions break down when an extreme event occurs. In addition, there is often a lack of appropriate loss data in operational risk. Constructing hypothetical yet realistic additional data points can shed useful light on rare events.

By giving transparency to management thinking about the firm's exposure to operational risk, scenarios support both internal and external communication. They can enable staff to understand more fully the board's and senior management's approach to operational risk. And if they are reported in the annual report and accounts, they can assist investors to monitor their investment and to hold the board accountable. They can also demonstrate the quality of the firm's risk management.

Scenarios, of course, also feed into capital and liquidity planning. They provide useful stretch and challenge to the assumptions underlying the firm's financial planning and enable the board and senior management to understand better the sensitivities of the firm to its risk exposures. Similarly, indicator thresholds and risk appetite gaps are exposed, so that management can better identify where additional controls may be necessary or where a higher risk appetite may be appropriate.

Finally, contingency planning (see Chapter 11, Business continuity), risk appetite (see Chapter 4, Operational risk appetite) and strategic planning are all supported by scenarios through the challenge which they provide. Contingency planning is quite naturally about exceptional events, although only a few limited events are usually contemplated. Scenarios enable a wider variety of situations to be considered for which contingency planning may be a valuable and practical solution. Risk appetite too is assisted by the use of scenarios in that a firm can better understand the limits of its risk appetite and how far beyond those limits extreme but plausible events take the firm.

Despite all the above points, scenarios should not be considered as the salvation to all risk management weaknesses and problems. They are an important tool in the operational risk manager's tool kit, but only one amongst a number.

PROBLEMS WITH SCENARIOS …

The financial crisis of 2007–9, the kind of event for which scenarios might have been thought to have been designed, exposed a number of issues. This was partly because, with few exceptions, there is no agreed scenario methodology. One exception is Lloyd's of London, which publishes realistic disaster scenarios to establish a common basis for estimating underwriting risk to a 99.5% degree of confidence and has also published examples of operational risk scenarios.[1]

Too short a timeframe

After the financial crisis, it emerged that a number of scenarios used by firms related to relatively normal events such as might happen every 1 in 10 or 1 in 20 years. This is probably unsurprising, since it is much easier to focus on events of which you are aware or which may occur within a career lifetime. This is known as *availability bias* and is considered later in this chapter in Recognising and mitigating natural biases.

Another flaw was to assume that scenarios have short durations, affecting no more than, say, one quarter's earnings. Whilst this may be true of a relatively benign scenario, it is highly unlikely to be true of an extreme scenario.

Outcomes too modest

Another issue is that scenarios often do not produce sufficiently large enough loss numbers. They usually produce large numbers, but availability bias – the experience of those devising and running the scenarios – means that they often fail to produce sufficiently large ones. Before the attack on the World Trade Center in September 2001, it would generally have been thought that a fall in equities of 40% could not have occurred at the same time as interest rates falling to a 50 year low, let alone happening at the same time as two world-class buildings being destroyed. But they did. Indeed, it is reported that six months before the attack the CIA had rejected the scenario of the twin towers being destroyed, let alone the other events occurring. As we have said before, scenarios demand a fertile imagination.

Another reason for the failure to accept sufficiently extreme outcomes is that they may suffer from motivational bias – the wish not to contemplate seriously adverse outcomes. Or very large outcomes are not believed to be credible by the business. This is, of course, easily managed by involving senior management in their development.

In the experience of the authors, whilst scenarios generally do produce large loss numbers they can also, counter-intuitively, produce relatively small numbers. This happens when certain controls are assumed to have failed during a scenario, but more vital and key controls are given fuller and more comprehensive attention (see a worked example later in this chapter). This may well lead to a lower than expected level of loss, if the key controls are then assumed to operate at their most effective and efficient level.

Not involving the business

Scenarios often tend to be performed as a mainly isolated exercise by risk management, in the misguided belief that senior management is too busy and will not be interested in them. Even in firms where scenarios are used as part of the firm's normal management process, they are frequently undertaken within business lines and are not part of an overarching programme covering the whole firm.

If scenarios are linked to the business objectives of the firm, through for example the risk and control assessment, senior management often willingly gets involved in them, because the scenarios can help them understand the sensitivities to what are often their personal objectives set during their performance appraisals.

Mechanical, point-of-time

Scenarios have also often been conducted as a mechanical and point-of-time exercise, with little thought for the reaction of the board or senior management to the unfolding scenario. In reality, as scenarios unfold, management takes action over a period of time (which could be as long as 18 months) to mitigate the effect of the scenario on the firm. This point is often overlooked. Additionally, a mechanical and point-of-time approach does not tend to take account of changing business conditions or incorporate qualitative judgements from different areas of the firm.

Failure to re-assess historic data

Firms which use historical events for scenario development and generation assume that very little change is required to the details of the historical event in order to forecast future risks. The rapid downward and upward equity market movements of 2008 and 2009 are a good illustration that the movements of the 1920s and 1930s, which were thought to be an overly extreme base against which to test scenario assumptions, required updating for the very different communication capabilities and investor skills and practices which exist in the world today.

It's too severe

How to get to severe (but not too severe) scenarios can also be a challenge. For example, if three separate 1 in 20 year events are considered and combined into a single scenario, in theory, there is a 1 in 8000 year chance of that scenario occurring. However, this ignores the fact that dependencies often exist in scenarios.

Consider, for example, the three operational risk stress tests of loss of the building, loss of the IT system and internal fraud. Each of these may be given, say, a 1 in 20 year chance of happening, which results in the scenario of all three happening being 1 in 8000 years. But the loss of the IT system (given the loss of the building) is likely to be much lower than the 1 in 20 times independent event. So, if the loss of the building independently is 1 in 20 years, then the loss of the IT system (given the loss of the building) will be much more likely, and may be as frequent as one in three times.

Similarly, the frequency of internal fraud (given the loss of the building and the loss of the IT system) is likely to be much higher, i.e. it will occur far more frequently than an independent internal fraud event. Many of the controls to prevent (and detect) internal fraud will not be working if the building and the IT system have both been lost. So again, an event which may be considered to be a 1 in 20 year event may only be one in four times when incorporated into a scenario. Given the above values, the likelihood now of a scenario where the building has been lost followed by the loss of the IT system, and then internal fraud becomes 1 in 20 multiplied by 1 in 3 multiplied by 1 in 4, or 1 in 240 years (rather than 1 in 8000 years).

Reputation risk ignored

Finally, many firms did not consider or capture reputational risk. This is despite the fact that many scenarios will inevitably contain a significant amount of reputational damage and that loss of reputation can be life-threatening (see Chapter 16, Reputation risk).

... AND HOW TO DO THEM BETTER

Scenarios should be reviewed frequently so that they can be adapted to changing market and economic conditions, as well as the changing risk profile of the firm. As new products, especially complex ones, are launched, the scenarios should be reviewed in order to identify potential risks and to incorporate the new products within the scenarios. The new products may even require additional scenarios to be developed, for example if a new product is launched in a country in which the firm has not previously operated.

The identification of risks which correlate, for example supply risk and production risk, or equity risk and interest rate risk, should be enhanced and how those risks aggregate should be considered. In addition, correlations between risks are often underestimated. It is either forgotten or ignored that correlations frequently break down under stress, and that different, probably unforeseen, correlations emerge.

Feedback effects across industries or markets, whether positive or negative, should also be considered, as should appropriate time horizons, rather than simply looking at the one-off effect of a scenario. For instance, the failure of Lehman Brothers, which could have been treated simply as the failure of a major counterparty, led to a significant feedback effect across the liquidity markets.

GOVERNANCE

As with any operational risk methodology or procedure, it is vital to ensure that the governance relating to the methodology is documented and understood. Good governance will enable the board and senior management to guide and direct the operational risk scenario strategy and to review its effectiveness. From a practical perspective, this will involve setting the scenario objectives; defining the scenarios; discussing and promoting the discussion of the results of the scenarios; assessing potential actions and making clear decisions based on the results; fostering internal debate on the results of the stress tests and scenarios programme as a whole; and challenging prior assumptions such as cost, risk and speed for raising new capital or hedging/ selling positions. All of these governance points may be taken up by the board in its meetings or may be delegated to a board scenario sub-committee which reports back to the full board.

An example of scenario governance came in a paper from the Basel Committee in May 2009. The headline principles are shown in the example below. Although they were written for banks, they apply equally to any industry.

Principles for sound stress-testing and scenario governance   ▐ Example

Stress-testing should:

1. form an integral part of governance;
2. promote risk identification and control;
3. take account of views from across the firm;
4. have written policies and procedures;
5. have a robust infrastructure which is also sufficiently flexible to be capable of;
6. be speedily re-run as circumstances are rapidly changing;
7. regularly maintain and update the scenarios framework; regularly and independently;
8. assess the effectiveness of the scenarios programme;
9. cover a range of risks/business areas, including firm-wide;
10. cover a range of scenarios;
11. feature a range of severities, including ones which could challenge the viability of the bank;
12. take account of simultaneous pressures in different markets;
13. systematically challenge the effectiveness of risk mitigation techniques;
14. explicitly cover complex and bespoke products;
15. cover pipeline (supply) and warehousing (product) risks;
16. capture the effect of reputational risk;
17. consider highly leveraged counterparties and the firm's vulnerability to them.

Source: Basel Committee, *Principles for sound stress-testing and supervision*, May 2009

On the face of it, principles 15 and 17 can be said to be not applicable to operational risk. However it is easily arguable that pipeline and warehousing risks and the firm's vulnerability to highly leveraged counterparties include a significant element of operational risk and therefore should be included in any operational risk exposure review such as scenarios.

Operational risk scenarios should enable a firm to understand the sensitivities of all of the elements of the firm's operational risk exposure, as set out in the operational risk framework we have described in this book. This includes:

- clarifying interactions and causal relationships between risks and controls
- acting as a challenge to the subjective nature of risk and control assessments

- compensating for the lack of internal loss data
- allowing adjustments to the likelihood and impact assumptions in risk assessments
- allowing adjustments to the design and performance assumptions in control assessments.

POINTS TO CONSIDER BEFORE DEVELOPING SCENARIOS

The crisis management team

When management focuses on a major event, there is a loss of focus on other controls so that the firm is much more likely to experience another major event. A typical mitigant is the firm's crisis management team, which should preferably exclude the CEO, and allow essential business line management to continue focusing on the business, confident in the knowledge that other members of the senior management team are sorting out the crisis.

Combinations of events over a period of time

When developing a set of scenarios it is important to consider more than one major event happening over the period of the scenario. Scenarios do not involve a combination of events at one point of time, but should be generated on the much more realistic assumption that one major event may be followed by another within a matter of months. Indeed, a survey of S&P 500 firms some years ago showed that five out of six firms which suffer one major event suffer another one within 12 months.

Recognising and mitigating natural biases

In a very helpful working paper[2] published in September 2007, the Australian Prudential Regulation Authority (APRA) notes that there are conscious or subconscious discrepancies between a participant's response when developing a scenario and an accurate description of their underlying knowledge. There are many biases, but they probably resolve themselves down to two generic types:

- availability bias
- motivational bias.

Availability bias refers to the ease or otherwise with which relevant information is recalled. A sub-set of it is overconfidence bias, where undue weight is given to a very small set of perceived events. Interestingly, it can be overcome by using two other forms of availability bias, partition dependence and anchoring. Partition dependence arises when respondents' responses are affected by the choices they are asked to make, or the buckets into which their answers have to be put. Anchoring is the bias towards information presented in background materials to survey questions or within the questions themselves. The APRA paper gives an example of this in a question about the population of Turkey. One group is asked:

1. Is the population of Turkey greater than 30 million?

2. What is the population of Turkey?

The other group is asked:

1. Is the population of Turkey greater than 100 million?

2. What is the population of Turkey?

The answer is around 70 million, but the first group will give answers near to 30 million and the second will give answers near to 100 million. Try it at your next party and amaze your guests!

The use of external loss data can help in inspiring scenarios which might otherwise have been overlooked and can therefore mitigate availability bias. However, availability bias can also affect the frequency assessments. The likelihood or frequency of an event may be overstated if the relevant event has occurred recently or if it has been personal experience. Conversely, the likelihood may be underestimated if the event has not been previously experienced. For example, someone who has previously been involved in a fire is more likely to overestimate the risk of a fire. On the other hand, firms often significantly underestimate the frequency of internal fraud since relatively few internal frauds are actually detected. It is therefore important to bear in mind availability bias and, if necessary, adjust for it, especially when using external loss data. Taking in this data may give a false sense of having covered most eventualities.

Motivational bias arises when a participant has an interest in influencing the result. It can lead to the understatement of frequency and impact, the understatement of the effectiveness of controls, and the understatement of the uncertainty surrounding the assessment made. It is very common, for example, for control owners to overstate the efficiency and effectiveness of the controls for which they are responsible. When a control assessment is presented to the risk owner and business line manager, a very different view of the capability of the controls mitigating that risk often emerges. There is also, of course, an incentive to understate potential losses in order to reduce the capital required to run the business line or the firm; or simply to provide a rosier view of the riskiness of the business line to the firm. Making scenarios subject to peer review, in addition to the formal challenge process carried out by risk management, is a good way to reduce the influence of motivational bias.

The influences of these biases can be seen in likelihood assessments. Estimates for likelihood can be particularly difficult when considering rare events. It is, for instance, difficult to distinguish between a 1 in 1000 chance in one year for the event, and a 1 in 10,000 chance. Both events are beyond most people's comprehension. Availability bias is almost inevitable in these circumstances, particularly when using external likelihood data, of which there will be relatively little. Examples of how likelihood and impact can be assessed are shown in Tables 10.1 and 10.2.

Impact assessments of scenarios are also prone to problems as most people find it difficult to think in terms of probability distributions. Ideally, several impact values for the scenario will be helpful at specified percentiles along the distribution. This is known as the percentile approach.

From a practical perspective, the assessment quantile for the scenario is likely to be agreed as the 95th, 99th, 99.9th or 'worst case' (which is often subsequently defined as one of the extreme quantiles). This will give one impact estimate, say £5m, linked with a single likelihood of occurrence, say 1 in 100 chance, and is known as the individual approach. However, the single value estimate it produces can introduce a spurious accuracy.

Table 10.1   **Alternative likelihood terms and possible weaknesses**

Labels	Low	Med-low	Med-high	High	Subjective; judgemental
Phrases/ categories	Impossible	Possible	Probable	Very likely	
Odds	1:100	1:30	1:10	1:2	Spurious accuracy
Percentages	1%	3.3%	10%	50%	
Decimals	0.01	0.033	0.10	0.50	
Chance	1 in 100	1 in 30	1 in 10	1 in 2	
Ranges	<1%	1–5%	5–15%	50% or greater	Artificial; may not reflect the true range

Source: Adapted from Information Paper: Applying a Structured Approach to Operational Risk Scenario Analysis in Australia, APRA, copyright Commonwealth of Australia, reproduced by permission

Table 10.2   **Alternative impact terms and possible weaknesses**

Labels	Low	Med-low	Med-high	High	Subjective; judgemental
Phrases/ categories	Negligible	Minor	Moderate	Severe	
Values	£20,000	£100,000	£500,000	£2,000,000	Spurious accuracy
Ranges	<£50,000	£50,000– £250,000	£250,000– £1,000,000	£1,000,000– £5,000,000	Artificial; may not reflect the true range

An alternative but more difficult approach is the interval approach, which consists of frequency estimates for a series of distinct impact ranges. This is conceptually similar to a risk and control assessment approach, although obviously different in detail.

Assumptions

Scenarios will be used in conjunction with the other techniques used by the firm such as risk and control assessments, forecasting and strategic analysis, resource allocation and business planning. As a result, the assumptions which form the base case for the scenarios should be consistent with the assumptions in the other techniques and should broadly reflect events envisaged in the long-term plans made by the firm.

Environment

Scenarios should also take account of the broader business environment. Political, financial/economic, social, technological, environmental and legal factors will inevitably affect the scenarios over the period they cover. The scenarios should be challenged by each of these factors to ensure they have been fully incorporated.

Historic or hypothetical data

Scenarios can be developed using either historical real data or hypothetical data. When using historical data, care must be taken to reflect changes to the internal and external environment within which the scenario is planned. A good starting point is to use the factors mentioned in the paragraph above. When using a hypothetical approach, care must be taken to devise a scenario which is sufficiently extreme but still plausible. Either way, the scenarios must be consistent with the firm's risk and control profile as there is no value in analysing stresses which will not apply to the firm.

DEVELOPING A SET OF PRACTICAL SCENARIOS

Using risk and control assessments

The scenarios above are a helpful starting point for developing relevant scenarios for financial services firms. But it is equally possible to develop scenarios by considering the key risks to the firm and assuming that several of the key risks occur either simultaneously or within appropriate timescales. This has the advantage of clearly being relevant to the firm, as the key risks have already been identified through risk and control assessment. However, this method of development, if used as the only method, has the disadvantage that extreme risks not identified during the assessment will not be used. Ideally, scenarios should be developed independently of the risk and control assessment and then challenged back to it.

Random words

At the other end of the scenario development spectrum lies the random word methodology. Using random words is a surprisingly powerful way of generating scenarios. It consists of taking a number of scenario-related words or phrases which may apply to the firm (such as fire, flood, utility failure, outsourcer failure, money laundering, internal fraud, terrorist attack) and choosing two or three at random. A scenario is then constructed around the chosen words or phrases which is relevant to the firm. It can be surprising how randomly chosen words are a powerful and imaginative way to construct credible and relevant scenarios.

Using industry information

Scenarios obviously need to be tailored to your particular business activity, but generic, yet relevant, operational risk scenarios can be found in industry-based information. We have already mentioned the Lloyd's scenarios. Another example comes from the Basel Committee's 2008 Loss Data Collection Exercise for operational risk, published in July 2009.[3] A number of scenarios from a wide cross-section of banks were analysed. Typical scenarios used were:

- embezzlement
- fraudulent transfer of funds
- loan fraud
- occupational accident
- employment discrimination
- regulatory breach
- IT system failure.

These were used by a wide variety of business lines within the banks concerned. As a comparison, the most common scenarios used by retail banks were:

- cyber crime
- cheque fraud
- theft of information/data

- regulatory breach
- mis-selling practices.

The retail banking scenarios are clearly more focused on a particular line of business, whilst the broader, more general, scenarios are just that.

Using news stories

The key to good scenarios is imagination. Perhaps the 'unknown unknowns' are not really so unknown, but simply reflect a lack of imagination in people's thinking. So the first thing is to be imaginative. With that in mind, a good place to start when developing a set of practical scenarios is to look at recent news stories.

These may be events with no obvious link to a particular firm or to your industry so they should enable a more diverse and innovative way of thinking. An example of using news stories concerned a wind farm which was proposed near a military airforce base. At first glance this should not be a problem. However, the military objected on the grounds that the turbines would interfere with its radar. Clearly during the feasibility study for the wind farm, this outcome had not been considered. When developing scenarios you need to consider the wider impact on others.

Another example is the significant earthquake experienced by the UK in 2008. It was the biggest in the UK for nearly 25 years. This brought into focus the fact that the UK has suffered a number of earthquakes (albeit only moderate to significant) and is situated at the boundaries of minor plates. Even moderate to significant earthquakes can cause damage, in particular to sensitive electronic equipment. However, it is very unusual for UK firms to include an earthquake within their scenarios.

Common scenario outcomes

However the scenarios are generated, a number of common themes emerge in the outcomes. These are often:

- failure of the firm to meet its objectives (whether these are profit, market share, staff retention or some other objective)
- funding difficulties
- exposure to fraud
- inability to maintain business volume
- lack of building access
- impact on ratings
- reputational damage

- adverse environmental impact
- supply chain disruption
- major competitor win.

PREPARING FOR THE EXTREME EVENT

Once common themes have been identified, a firm can prepare itself by adopting a variety of defensive approaches. Many of these are good risk management and should already exist. However, scenarios test risk assessments and risk appetite and it is vital that the defensive approaches are also tested. These defensive approaches should be in place and used during normal times so that they are part of the normal way of doing business. They will be essential during a period of stress.

Strong risk culture

A strong corporate culture of business risk awareness is an important part of risk governance. It is particularly important in times of stress and market extremes. In their report in March 2008 on the financial market problems of late 2007,[4] the Senior Supervisors Group noted that firms which performed better not only had good risk management structures but also a culture that gave risk management views appropriate weight at the highest levels.

Integrated risk management

The benefits of an integrated risk management approach also come to the fore during times of stress. Whilst it is always helpful for senior management and the board to be aware of the firm's overall risk profile, it is particularly important when the firm is suffering extreme events. Linking together market risk, credit risk, liquidity risk and operational risk in a scenario will enable a firm to be more effective in its defensive manoeuvrings.

Informed decision making

An emphasis on informed management decision making and good information flow is almost too obvious to state. However, particularly during times of stress, decisions can be made 'on the hoof' and without full information. If a culture of informed decision making and robust communication up and down the firm is embedded in everyday business practices, it is more likely to continue during times of stress.

Risk appetite

Knowing and understanding the firm's risk appetite and its thresholds may also help the firm reduce the impact of a stress event. Although it is very likely that the firm's risk appetite will be exceeded during a period of stress, there is more likely to be a defined escalation procedure and understanding of the sensitivities of the firm's risk profile if consideration is given to the risk appetite.

If a firm does have a developed risk appetite, it is more likely that it will have a full set of risk and control assessments and a realistic view of the risk and control profile of the firm. Challenges to the assessments and the resulting profile need to be made during normal times for this particular defensive approach to be valuable. If such challenges form a routine part of the firm's governance, the resulting information is much more likely to have the confidence of senior management and therefore to be used in a period of stress.

Business process improvement

Continuous business process improvement can also be an effective defensive structure to protect the firm against difficult times. A corporate mindset which is flexible is essential at such times. By continuously seeking to challenge the firm's business processes, its control environment will have been subject to significant testing and should therefore be in good shape.

TYPICAL PROBLEMS FOLLOWING SCENARIO DEVELOPMENT

Balancing effort and understanding

Scenarios should be kept as far as possible at the strategic level. They should only be as detailed as they need to be. Scenarios which go down to the nth degree of detail require much more analysis of risks and controls in order to generate meaningful results and a tested risk profile. Similarly, a scenario may touch on a wide variety of events and also therefore require considerable analysis. Either way significant effort is required to provide a suitable level of analysis for an extreme (although plausible) event. On the other hand, a scenario must be developed in sufficient detail that it can be seen to be directly relevant and appropriate for the firm. A two-word scenario, 'internal fraud', is neither useful nor helpful. The answer is to maintain a balance between effort and understanding.

Rejection of the technique

If too much detail is available, it is much easier to find ambiguities and irrelevancies in the scenario. This leads to a rejection of the overall technique. It is, of course, important to focus on the principle that various extreme but plausible events should be analysed in order to determine the sensitivity of the firm's risk profile to those events. Don't let that principle be swamped in the detail.

Paralysis

Sometimes the scenario result is so awful that the conclusion is drawn that little can be done to prepare for it. Even in the event of the scenario showing that the firm would be liquidated, action can always be taken, including drawing up a 'living will', similar to the recent proposals for internationally active banks discussed in the next section.

THE NEAR DEATH EXPERIENCE

Reverse stress tests

Reverse stress tests were previously known as testing to destruction. They start with a known outcome, for instance that the current business model of the firm is no longer viable, rather than a normal scenario for which the outcome is unknown at the start. The scenarios most likely to cause the failure of the firm are then reviewed. It should be borne in mind, incidentally, that a firm's business-as-usual model can fail before its regulatory capital or its liquidity provisions have been breached. This will probably be because there is a complete lack of confidence in the marketplace about the firm.

As with normal scenarios, senior management should be involved in the design of the reverse stress tests and in the actions which the firm decides are appropriate as responses to the reverse stress tests. A good place to start the development of reverse stress tests is to take severe scenarios and then stress these through the inclusion of a reputation event. Such events may be a natural consequence of the media discovering that an extreme but plausible series of events have happened to a firm, or reputation damage may occur to the firm through another stress event (unconnected with the original scenario).

Recovery plans

Reverse stress tests look at the stage shortly before collapse. Recovery plans are designed to be activated when that point has been reached and will be triggered when certain pre-defined events occur or criteria are met. The recovery plan will specify in some detail how the firm will downsize and completely restructure its business; allow itself to be acquired or its business to be transferred; or wind itself down in an orderly fashion over a relatively short period of time.

In short, the recovery plan is the firm's set of options for addressing extreme financial stress impacting its business. This stress may be caused either by problems unique to the firm, or by wider economic problems (or both). The recovery plan will address options for recovering from liquidity and capital difficulties as well as the practical points relating to the challenges and inter-dependencies which the firm may foresee in implementing the recovery plan.

Governance

As with all other operational risk matters, it is important to have appropriate internal governance relating to recovery plans. The board of directors (or another senior governance committee) should review and approve the recovery plan, including the firm's assessment of the probable success of each option considered in the recovery plan. The key executives and managers of the firm who will be involved in each recovery action should know the roles that they will play.

One frequent challenge around the recovery plan is the collection of sufficient (but not too much) information to enable the plan to be judged relevant and appropriate. The information required will include detailed information on the various types of assets held by the firm and its various liabilities. This will include contingent, as well as actual, assets and liabilities. A firm must know, at a minimum, when and how it can realise its assets and under what conditions its liabilities become payable.

Triggers

As well as specifying the detail of how the recovery plan works, it is equally important to decide on realistic trigger(s) for activating it. If a trigger point is not realistic, there is the danger that the point will be reached, and management will refuse to acknowledge reality and hope that something may turn up. It is, however, difficult to develop triggers that strike an appropriate balance between triggering a recovery plan too early or too late. There are a number of elements to effective triggers, which include:

- it should be clear when the triggers have been breached
- the triggers should be capable of being easily monitored
- the triggers should be effective for both firm specific as well as wider economic disruption
- the triggers will contain a combination of qualitative, as well as quantitative, indicators.

Whilst some of the triggers will inevitably measure the adequacy of the firm's financial resources, others will relate to items such as an unexpected drop in the firm's credit rating or negative market sentiment or perception towards the firm. Triggers should also be predictive or forward-looking (see Chapter 7, Indicators, Identifying the leading and lagging indicators) to enable an early start to discussions within the firm on pre-emptive actions to reduce the impact of the event on the firm.

Communication plan

A communication plan is another important part of the overall recovery plan. The communication plan will address both internal and external issues. The intention of the plan is to prevent doubts on the viability of the firm and to preserve the confidence of the markets and all other stakeholders (see also Chapter 16, Reputation risk).

Resolution plan

In certain industries (most notably the financial services industry), firms are also expected to contribute to a resolution plan. This is prepared by the authorities and provides a strategy and detailed roadmap to resolve a failed firm in a manner that minimises the impact on financial stability without needing to resort to public sector solvency support. However, for the resolution plan to be effective, it obviously requires the provision of up-to-date information on the firm's operations, structures and critical economic functions. This sort of analysis is best prepared by the firm itself.

APPLYING SCENARIOS TO OPERATIONAL RISK MANAGEMENT DATA

There are two main approaches to applying scenarios to operational risk management data:

- A deterministic approach, which uses a simple and straightforward approach although it is sometimes difficult to relate to reality. It is far less rigorous and relies on assumptions to a much greater extent.
- A probabilistic approach, which uses a statistical methodology for modelling risks and controls although it is sometimes difficult to understand due to the underlying complex mathematics.

Deterministic approach

This takes the scenarios which have been developed and tests the relevant risk and control assessment with the scenario outcomes. The testing is carried out through the analysis of which controls have failed for the scenario to occur and therefore which risks have happened and what is the impact of those risks.

Useful guidance is given in terms of the size of the likely impacts through the impact ranges which were developed during the risk and control assessment process. These impact ranges, though, should be considered as guidance only and should not be slavishly adhered to. For example, some controls which mitigate a particular risk may still exist and be operable during a scenario and therefore the impact may be significantly less than is given by the risk's impact range. However, the upper value of the range should only be exceeded after significant debate, as this will have already been considered and discussed during the risk and control assessments.

Having assessed the impacts of the risk events which occur during a scenario, it is possible to calculate (through simple addition) the extra impact of the scenario on the firm's risk profile. Action can then be taken in terms of a cost–benefit analysis of the controls which were affected by the scenario. This is combined with a review of the firm's risk appetite in order to determine whether or not control enhancement is required. Additionally, the application of the scenario and tests may uncover controls which were previously thought to be adequate and which now require action.

Probabilistic approach

This approach transforms qualitative and subjective risk assessment to monetary values through probabilistic modelling. It uses the same initial step as the deterministic approach, that is the existing risk and control assessment is tested with the scenario outcomes in order to determine which controls have failed. The revised, scenario-adjusted risk and control assessment is then subjected to risk event occurrence through control failure simulation (as we saw in Chapter 9, Modelling, Obtaining business benefits from qualitative modelling).

The advantages of this approach are:

- a more focused cost–benefit analysis of controls, as the monetary reduction of the risk profile is explicit
- a clearer view of risk appetite, again as the monetary value of risks and controls is explicit
- the ability to see the monetary impact of the scenario at different explicit confidence levels, rather than simply at one (unarticulated and implicit) level as in the deterministic approach
- the sensitivities of different risks are more apparent as their monetary values are available at different confidence levels
- analyses from different risk perspectives following the scenario (such as the risk owner, the risk category, the top residual risk and the worst and best performing controls) can be more easily extracted

■ access to different confidence levels allows reverse stress testing to be better understood as any scenario can be extended to a level at which the firm is no longer viable.

A worked example

A firm develops a scenario which involves internal fraud (due to an employee having gambling debts) occurring at the same time as IT system failure. The firm's current risk and control assessment contains, inter alia, the risks, controls and assessments shown in Figure 10.3.

Figure 10.3				Extract from current risk and control assessment		
ID	**Risks**	**I**	**L**	**Controls**	**D**	**P**
1	Failure to attract, recruit and retain key staff	4	4	Criminal background check	3	2
				Salary surveys	2	2
				Training and mentoring schemes	3	2
				Retention packages for key staff	4	4
12	Inadequate or insufficient IT infrastructure to achieve business objectives	2	4	Business/strategic planning	3	4
				IT system performance and capability monitoring	4	3
				Manual workarounds	2	2
16	Failure to sense and eliminate internal fraud	3	2	Criminal background check	3	2
				Segregation of duties	2	3
				Training and mentoring schemes	3	2
				Fraud monitoring	4	4
				Whistle blowing	3	3

Source: Courtesy of Chase Cooper Limited

The first step is to review the controls and identify those which are assumed to have failed for the purposes of the scenario, as the firm is then exposed to the risks which were mitigated by the failed controls. These are identified in Figure 10.4:

■ criminal background check, which did not identify the fraudster

■ training and mentoring schemes, which have not identified that the employee was at risk

■ business/strategic planning, which has failed to provide enough focus on an appropriate IT system

■ IT system performance and capability monitoring, which has not detected that the system was about to fail

■ segregation of duties, which has failed to prevent fraud

■ training and mentoring schemes, which have also failed to prevent fraud.

Consideration is then given to improving these controls to ensure that the firm's operational risk exposure is maintained within its risk appetite.

Fraud monitoring is a detective control and will not prevent this risk from occurring, but it will detect it when it does occur. For the sake of completeness, the controls which are unaffected by the scenario, although they are still relevant to the risks that have occurred, are salary surveys, retention packages for key staff, manual workarounds and whistle blowing.

The deterministic approach

The deterministic approach involves simply estimating the average loss for each risk using the risk and control assessment data. For the scenario above, we have three risks which occur:

1. failure to attract, recruit and retain key staff (Staff)
12. inadequate or insufficient IT infrastructure to achieve business object-ives (IT)
16. failure to sense and eliminate internal fraud (Fraud).

Extract from risk and control assessment, showing failed controls and subsequent improved controls with new assessment scores **Figure 10.4**

ID	Risks	I	L	Controls	D	P	Fail	Improve	D	P
1	Failure to attract, recruit and retain key staff	4	4	Criminal background check	3	2	Yes	Yes	3	4
				Salary surveys	2	2		Yes	2	3
				Training and mentoring schemes	3	2	Yes	Yes	3	3
				Retention packages for key staff	4	4			4	4
12	Inadequate or insufficient IT infrastructure to achieve business objectives	2	4	Business/strategic planning	3	4	Yes		3	4
				IT system performance and capability monitoring	4	3	Yes	Yes	4	4
				Manual workarounds	2	2			2	2
16	Failure to sense and eliminate internal fraud	3	2	Criminal background check	3	2	Yes	Yes	3	4
				Segregation of duties	2	3	Yes		2	3
				Training and mentoring schemes	3	2	Yes	Yes	3	4
				Fraud monitoring	4	4			4	4
				Whistle blowing	3	3			3	3

Source: Courtesy of Chase Cooper Limited

These are scored 4, 2 and 3 respectively for impact. We now assume that all the controls have worked as previously scored in the baseline risk and control assessment, but that the controls named on the previous page have failed in the scenario.

The methodology for calculating the baseline, scenario and adjusted baseline risk and control assessments is as follows:

Step 1 Start with the original baseline risk and control assessment and derive a gross loss figure, i.e. before the interaction of controls

The gross loss figure is simply given by the mid-point of the range or the maximum impact for each risk which occurs in the scenario. (The mid-point can be considered to be the deterministic equivalent of the 50th centile; the maximum impact can be considered to be the worst case, i.e. either the 95th centile or the 99.9th centile.)

In this case we have three risks, listed above, with impacts in bands 4, 2 and 3. We can assume that with no controls these will be at the mid-point or at the top of their respective bands, therefore the gross impact for the scenario will be equal to the mid-point or to the maximum of band 4 plus the equivalents of bands 2 and 3.

As you can see from the impact scale above, the mid-points give £(12.5m + 0.625m + 3m) or £16.125m and the maximum for band 4 is £20m, for band 2 is £1m and for band 3 is £5m, giving a total maximum gross loss of £26m.

Step 2 Calculate the strength of the control environment

We can assume that a full-strength control environment will fully mitigate the risk, i.e. reduce the net risk to zero. So, if a risk is fully mitigated, the impact amount will be £0m.

The control environment strength is found by the proportion of the control effectiveness score as a fraction of the maximum potential. Using the example above, in which controls are scored on a 1 to 4 basis for design and performance, the maximum possible score for a control is 16 (4×4).

To find the effectiveness score, we multiply the design and performance scores together, sum them and then divide by the maximum, which would be $16 \times$ [number of controls]. Working through Risk 1, at the baseline level we have four controls scored 3–2, 2–2, 3–2 and 4–4 for design and performance. Multiplying and summing the pairs gives $6 + 4 + 6 + 16 = 32$. The maximum potential score is $4 \times 16 = 64$. Therefore the effectiveness score is $32/64 = 0.5$. For Risk 12 the score is 0.583 and for Risk 16 the score is 0.5375.

Step 3 Use control effectiveness to calculate a net loss

The gross loss is positioned at the mid-point or the top of the relevant impact range, and a fully mitigated risk will have a net loss of zero. It follows that if a risk is fully mitigated its controls are scored at the maximum, and if the controls have an average of 50% effectiveness this will mitigate 50% of the impact (either at the mid-point or at the top of the range).

Applying this to Risk 1 again, we have a gross loss of £12.5m or £20m, a control effectiveness score of 50% and therefore a net impact of £6.25m or £10m.

Mathematically this is expressed as:

Net impact = Gross impact – (Control factor $\times$ Gross impact)

Substituting the relevant numbers for Risk 1 gives:

Net maximum impact (Risk 1) = £20m − [(3 × 2 + 2 × 2 + 3 × 2
+ 4 × 4)/(4 × 16)] × £20m

= £10m

Or

Net mid-point impact (Risk 1) = £12.5m − [(3 × 2 + 2 × 2 + 3 × 2
+ 4 × 4)/(4 × 16)] × £12.5m

= £6.25m

So we have values for the maximum and mid-point gross and net losses from Risk 1 in the scenario. We now duplicate this method with Risks 12 and 16, to find that in these cases:

Net maximum impact (Risk 12) = £1m − [(3 × 4 + 4 × 3 + 2 × 2)/
(3 × 16)] × £1m

= £417k

and

Net maximum impact (Risk 16) = £5m − [(3 × 2 + 2 × 3 + 3 × 2
+ 4 × 4 + 3 × 3)/(5 × 16)] × £5m

= £2.313m

The mid-points are similarly calculated.

Step 4 Deriving a total value for the net baseline risk and control assessment

The net impact of this scenario at the baseline level is therefore found by summing the net components of all the relevant risks, in the maximum case £10.000m + £417k + £2.313m = £12.730m. In the mid-point case £6.250m + £260k + £1.387m = £7.897m.

Step 5 Assessing control failures for the scenario risk and control assessment

The first thing to do is analyse the scenario to work out which controls have failed in order to allow this scenario to occur. In this case, and as shown in Figure 10.4, we have assessed that 7 of the 12 controls over the three relevant risks have failed. This judgement is subjective so you must consider which aspects of the risk and controls are relevant. Any control which is either not relevant or could not allow the scenario to occur if working correctly must be assumed not to be mitigating the scenario or to have failed.

The scenario gross loss is the same as the baseline gross loss, as the risk assessment should not change between the two, only the control assessment (which affects only the net loss).

Step 6 Calculate the new control effectiveness factor

Now we must calculate the new effectiveness factor after certain controls have failed. Any control failing has a contribution of zero to the effectiveness. So, revisiting Risk 1 and its four controls, if we thought that the first and third controls failed but the second and fourth worked in this scenario, we discount the scores for 1 and 3 (though they are still counted in the maximum potential). Therefore the new effectiveness score is $(0 + 4 + 0 + 16)/(4 \times 16) = 20 \div 64 = 0.3125$.

We must now calculate the net loss for the scenario using the same method as in the baseline and the new effectiveness score. In this case, the new net maximum loss for Risk 1 is

$$£20m - (0.3125 \times £20m) = £13.750m$$

We then calculate the same for the other risk components of the scenario and, as before, sum them to find a total net loss.

Step 7 The adjusted baseline scenario

The scenario has indicated where our control weaknesses lie, and as a result we can make some direct improvements to the weaker controls. After doing this, we reassess the control scores (as shown in Figure 10.3) to give the improved controls (as shown in Figure 10.4) and compute the adjusted baseline score using these new control scores.

A summary of these values is as follows:

	Baseline result £m		Scenario result £m		Adjusted baseline result £m	
	Gross	Net	Gross	Net	Gross	Net
Maximum	26.000	12.700	26.000	18.100	26.000	8.500
Mid-point	16.125	7.900	16.125	11.200	16.125	5.200

The probabilistic approach

As noted above, we can probabilistically model the scenario using a Monte Carlo simulation engine. This takes the risk and control assessment data along with the assigned distributions for impact and frequency, and uses the Monte Carlo method to derive a value for each impact at differing confidence levels. Using the same data as used for the deterministic approach above, the following results are obtained:

	Baseline result £m		Scenario result £m		Adjusted baseline result £m	
	Gross	Net	Gross	Net	Gross	Net
50% confidence level	13.400	0	13.400	13.200	13.400	0
95% confidence level	16.900	5.100	16.900	16.600	16.900	1.800
99.9% confidence level	22.200	10.600	22.200	21.700	22.200	9.200

It can be seen that the maximum deterministic values are at a similar level to the modelled 99.9% confidence level.

SUMMARY

Scenarios are all about imagination and not being afraid to think the unthinkable. Indeed, they are totally concerned with the unthinkable. They are not a mathematical exercise but a practical one, aimed at identifying events or, more precisely, combinations of events which could threaten a firm's objectives and even its existence. As a practical exercise, they are the glue which binds the other elements of the framework together and test whether the operational risk framework is robust and fit for purpose. However they do contemplate threats to the existence of the firm. If those threats appear, the immediate remedy is a well thought out and fully tested business continuity plan, which we shall consider in the next chapter.

Notes

1   www.lloyds.com
2   Australian Prudential Regulation Authority, *Applying a structured approach to operational risk scenario analysis in Australia*, September 2007; www.apra.gov.au
3   www.bis.org/publ/bcbs160.htm
4   Senior Supervisors Group, *Observations on risk management practices during the recent market turbulence*, March 2008; www.financialstabilityboard.org

MITIGATION AND ASSURANCE

Part

4

11

Business continuity

ENSURING SURVIVAL

It is a fact of life that 'stuff happens'. Dealing with it is much of what operational risk management is all about. Many operational risks can be managed and mitigated down to acceptable levels, as this book has shown. Some things, however, cannot be prevented. The best we can do is to have in place contingency plans which will mitigate the effects as best we can.

To that extent operational risk is rather like politics. When Harold Macmillan, British Prime Minister from 1957 to 1963, was asked by a journalist what was most likely to blow a government off course, he is alleged to have replied, 'Events, dear boy, events'. Business continuity is about coping with the unforeseen events, some of them apparently undramatic, which nevertheless threaten a business's survival. Attitudes such as 'It won't happen to us', 'We will cope – we always do', 'We're not a terrorist target' are unrealistic and, from a business point of view, life-threatening.

After an event, firms fall into two categories – 'recoverers' and 'non-recoverers'. Research regularly shows that firms which successfully deal with a crisis see their share value increase. Similarly, firms which invest and budget most on risk, business continuity and governance are the most profitable in their sector. Business continuity planning is an investment, not a cost.[1] Another survey has shown that each year nearly one in five businesses suffers from a major disruption and that, through lack of an adequate business continuity plan, 80% of them close within 18 months.[2]

Many people questioned the huge amounts of money and resource which went into coping with the potential disaster of the Millennium Bug (Y2K). The effort and investment repaid itself many times over when the planes hit the Twin Towers of the World Trade Center, New York on 11 September 2001. The enormous amount of work which had gone into cleaning up the spaghetti of systems which firms were running, understanding infrastructure dependencies and developing and testing comprehensive business continuity plans, prevented the 9/11 attack from being much more disastrous. Despite the tragic and horrendous loss of life and disruption, it was business as usual after a brief four days, including a weekend. Perhaps business continuity's finest hour.

In his foreword, as Director-General, to a CBI publication on business continuity, Digby Jones (later Lord Jones of Birmingham) wrote: 'A reliance on piecemeal procedures adopted and adapted over time will not suffice. Business availability is a strategic issue which covers the whole organisation and as such requires a comprehensive solution.'[3] If the business isn't available, there is no business. Strategic issues don't come more critical than that.

BUSINESS CONTINUITY AND RISK MANAGEMENT

Business continuity is obviously a vital part of overall risk management. However, Table 11.1 shows the differences between risk and business continuity management and also what gives business continuity its particular flavour.

Differences between risk management and business continuity management   **Table 11.1**

	Risk management	Business management continuity
Key method	Risk analysis	Business impact assessment
Key parameters	Impact and probability	Impact and time
Type of incident	All types of events – though usually segmented	Events causing significant disruption
Size of events	All sizes/costs – though usually segmented	Strategy deals with survival-threatening incidents, but can be applied to any size
Scope	Focus mainly on management of risks to core business objectives	Focus mainly on incident management, generally outside the core competencies of the business
Intensity	All, from gradual to sudden	Generally sudden or rapid events, though a creeping incident may become severe

Source: The Business Continuity Institute, *Good Practice Guidelines 2008*, Section 1, p.7

Business continuity deals with the management of incidents which will cause significant disruption to the business. It deals with low-likelihood events but is mainly dealing with their impact. The impact of an incident, as well as recovery from it, is measured primarily by time so that disruption to customers and suppliers is kept to a minimum and business as usual is restored as quickly as possible. To ensure that happens, firms need to develop and test business continuity plans, working their way through the business continuity life cycle. In practical terms this means:

- policy and governance
- business impact analysis
- threat and risk assessment
- the business continuity strategy and plan

- testing the plan
- maintenance and continuous improvement.

all of which we shall look at in the rest of this chapter.

POLICY AND GOVERNANCE

Policy and governance form the cornerstone of business continuity management. Without the right governance arrangements, the best plans in the world are useless.

Policy statement

The policy statement is the benchmark against which all business continuity activity should be continually checked. Since confusion is often the major obstacle to an effective response to an operational disruption, the policy statement should clearly set out the level of business continuity the firm sets out to achieve.

It should include:

- the firm's operational framework for business continuity management
  - board-level sponsorship
  - the roles and responsibilities of senior management and others, including the crisis management team or teams
  - authorities to act
  - business continuity steering committee (which oversees the development and implementation of the business continuity methodology and procedures)
- the firm's business continuity principles and priorities (e.g. staff welfare and key customer services)
- business critical activities, their resource needs and their time-criticality
- minimum standards for planning documentation, recovery times, service disruption, etc.

Ideally, the key points should be capable of being summarised on a sheet of A4 paper which can be distributed to everyone. This clear statement of the firm's priorities following an incident, with enough indication of recovery expectations, will provide a framework and context for the rest of business continuity activity.

Keep it brief – and achievable. Unrealistic policy statements such as 'zero downtime' render the whole document meaningless. What is a *realistic* recovery time? Which activities genuinely *need* to be prioritised? What are the short-term workarounds?

Governance

Business continuity is not an IT issue. Like operational risk, it concerns the whole business and threats to its existence. It therefore needs to be owned by all parts of the firm, with a central point of accountability on the board. That director will sponsor the 'project' and be responsible for ensuring that adequate plans are in place and are regularly tested and reviewed.

Developing, reviewing and invoking the business continuity plan will involve a steering committee which should be chaired by the board sponsor. This should include senior stakeholders from business, risk, IT and other support management. Joining the group should mean a serious time commitment. Apart from the time which is needed to develop a business continuity plan, which is rarely trivial, members should be prepared to meet regularly during the development and implementation phases of the project.

Both the plan and any testing of it should be independently reviewed and audited, perhaps by the internal or external auditor. Whoever does it, reports should go to the board, who are ultimately accountable for the project and, more importantly, for business availability.

BUSINESS IMPACT ANALYSIS

The business impact analysis provides the basis from which business continuity strategies and plans can be developed. It is the point in the process where recovery priorities are established, together with the minimum resources needed to maintain their availability.

The business impact analysis looks at the impact of given events on business activities *over time*. With business continuity, 'If in doubt, prepare for the worst'. It should therefore look at worst case scenarios, such as where a department or service line is completely stopped. This will identify the realistic, as well as essential, recovery time objective – the time by which critical systems and business processes must be up and running after the occurrence of an incident.

Understanding what we do and how we do it

The first step in the business impact analysis is to establish what activities the firm carries out and how, including how the various activities work together. The information gathered should include as a minimum:

- a complete list of products or services
- critical processes which support the most important products/services (with time-critical details)
- key staff who support the critical processes
- key systems (including Excel spreadsheets and Word documents), paper records and equipment which support the critical processes
- reliance on internal departments or external suppliers to carry out the critical processes
- reliance on specific premises to carry out critical processes
- key customers and stakeholders who would be affected by the loss of products/services.

A key element of the data gathering process is to identify interdependencies, not just within the firm but without it as well. Terrorist attacks such as 9/11 or the London bombings in 2005, and the global financial crisis, have highlighted systemic risks and dependencies on common infrastructure utilities and systems.

This phase is a good time also to gather other details such as call trees (essential people networks to spread information) and existing recovery arrangements.

What is business critical?

The test of criticality is what value is lost *over time*. For some activities, value lost will increase, perhaps exponentially, as time goes by. For others, the impact may not be felt until perhaps a week later.

It can be difficult to assess costs over time. One way is to use financial targets or budgets and divide the relevant weekly or monthly target into agreed time periods – hourly, daily, etc. In doing this, remember to split out revenue expected from existing and new business. New business is likely to be lost during a disruption.

Finally, don't forget indirect costs such as regulatory fines or client and intermediary compensation. Added together with direct losses, they will give an estimate of the worst case financial impact – *over time*.

At this point you should have identified your business critical activities, recovery priorities and the resources needed to maintain them, itemised over time – now, day 1, 2–6 days, week 1, 2, 3 and so on.

The next step is to think about what might happen and the effect on the business critical activities.

THREAT AND RISK ASSESSMENT

Threats

Before they actually happen, incidents are threats. The risk lies in the likelihood of their becoming incidents and the potential impact if they do.

The incidents which are likely to trigger invocation of the plan are often external threats or causes and largely outside your control. Where controls can make a difference, the incident is likely to happen when those controls have failed.

Each organisation will need to determine the threats which it believes have both sufficient impact and are likely to occur at some point as to be worth considering. The list needs to be reviewed regularly to check the current assessment of likelihood and to add newly identified threats. For example, a few years ago only a handful of organisations in the USA or EU would have been worried about infectious diseases or pandemics as a business continuity event. Then came SARS in 2003, avian flu (the H5N1 virus) in 2004 and H1N1 flu (swine flu) in 2009 so that pandemics have risen to the top of everybody's list of threats.

Impact assessment

Essentially, the method of assessment is the same as that used for building and evaluating scenarios in the previous chapter, with the proviso that, with business continuity, time is the critical measure of impact – how *long* will an interruption have to last to be intolerable, if not catastrophic?

In risk assessment terms, the threats should be at the extreme end of the spectrum in the low-likelihood, very-high-impact section, as measured against a firm's risk appetite. If the likelihood of a high (residual or net) impact event occurring is considered to be greater than 'low' then it is not a suitable case for business continuity. It needs to be dealt with now by a review of controls and probably the introduction of new ones to reduce both its likelihood (if possible) and its impact.

Response triggers

When a threat turns into an incident, it will generate a response. The business continuity plan formulates those responses. Response triggers usually come down to half a dozen or so, that are typically variations on loss of premises, staff, equipment, systems, a production line, key suppliers or outsourced activity.

One of the lessons of the London bombings in July 2005 was that the firms which were able to respond best had concentrated their business recovery on impacts and decision making, rather than the nature of a disruption and its possible causes. As a result, following a more generic-based approach, they had the flexibility to respond to a broad range of potential scenarios. The key point about scenarios is not to get into too much detail with them. As with much of business continuity planning – keep it simple.

Threats should be continually reassessed and reviewed. Whenever a new threat is identified, it should be checked against existing response triggers. If necessary, a new one can be added. The importance of each trigger is a mix of the results of the business impact assessment and the sum of the likelihood of the threats associated with it.

THE BUSINESS CONTINUITY STRATEGY AND PLAN

How to choose the best response

Having identified the incidents which will trigger a business continuity response, it is time to look at how to identify the best one, which will then form the basis for the business continuity strategy. Business continuity is a firm-wide project. In addition, many people will probably have their own ideas about suitable recovery strategies. It is therefore best to undertake this phase by way of workshops, or a similar approach which ensures that all the ramifications of a strategy are understood and that you have buy-in from everybody concerned. Gathering everybody together will also help to ensure that strategies and countermeasures do not conflict, so that the solution for one part of the business does not create a new issue for another part of the business or expose it to unmeasured risk.

Two tips:

- Make sure everybody understands the primary objectives – what needs to be achieved must be fully understood. Be pragmatic.
- The biggest risk is generated by doing things differently. Stick as closely as possible to normal practice.

Once you have agreed your approach and got everybody together, the next step is to list the response options that are currently available and then consider for each trigger which ones are suitable, and whether there is a risk of failure of the countermeasures you may wish to use.

In thinking about the options it is important to consider whether each one – people, place or systems – will be available, given a particular trigger. That's where you need to think about threats. A bomb or transport strike may not just make *your* building unusable, but also your alternative site.

It is probably helpful to consider the options under headings, such as those in the example below:

- business activity levels
- staffing
- locations
- communications
- infrastructure – power
- infrastructure – data and systems
- infrastructure – utilities.

Examples are provided of the kind of questions you need to ask when assessing the options.

Thinking about the response options Example

Business activity levels

What levels of business activity are acceptable, for what periods of time? Use a series of levels starting with 'business as usual', through one or more 'emergency levels' down to 'no business'.

Staffing

Business continuity critically involves human issues (including families of staff). In considering your strategy, always remember that human safety is paramount.

Will there be sufficient staffing in the event of a pandemic, when significant numbers may be quarantined? Will there be sufficient staff in the event of no transport or very limited communications, such as mobile phones? Does everybody know and understand their role in the event of an incident? Are sufficient staff trained to carry out critical functions?

The SARS pandemic and 9/11 have emphasised the importance of planning on the basis of there being no people available in a location. Are succession plans adequate?

Locations

What alternative locations are there? These could range from a mirrored site for immediate use with minimum downtime to working from home. For most, it will probably involve relocating to a different site, often a syndicated site. If you have chosen syndicated backup facilities, will they be available for all the people who might need them in the event of a 'wide-area' event? How many times has each seat been contracted out in the event of an emergency? How does the provider assess priorities? Is there an exclusion zone in the contract that means that you are the only user of the syndicated facilities within, say, 400 metres?

▶

For each kind of alternative site the important thing is for it to be outside the risk zone of the primary site, and with separate sources of critical supplies of telecommunications, power and water. However, if it is too far outside the risk zone, significant travel by large numbers of staff may be required. The expense of this travel (and possibly accommodation) can lead to a potentially fatal delay in invoking the plan.

Communications

Another lesson from major, wide-area incidents such as 9/11 is that mobile phone networks cannot handle the concentrated traffic. That means considering the whole range of alternatives: digital and analogue land line telephones, mobile phones (with a reserve of spare batteries), satellite phones, websites, etc.

Where can phone lines be diverted to? What other switchboard/reception facilities could be used? Importantly, how will you communicate with staff away from the main site – whether at the alternative site or at home? Or with key stakeholders such as suppliers, customers, service providers or, if appropriate, regulators?

And, probably more importantly, how will the crisis management team keep themselves up to date? It became apparent at the time of the London bombings in 2005 that the best news of what was happening was coming from satellite news channels. However, crisis management teams were in locations without access to them, so that at times staff at the front desk were better informed than they were.

Infrastructure – power

Will there be sufficient backup power? That problem was highlighted during the major power grid failures in the NE United States and eastern Canada in 2003. The American Stock Exchange appeared to have sufficient backup electrical power. However, the utility provided steam power which worked the air conditioning system which began to fail as a result of the general lack of electrical power, by which time there was insufficient time to relocate to an alternative site. In the end, a backup steam generation boiler was installed, with the avoidable loss of nearly a day's trading.

Infrastructure – data and systems

How will we ensure systems and up-to-date data will be in place and available for use? What backup data centres exist? Which systems have fallbacks in remote sites? Which systems have backups offsite? How often are the backups sent offsite?

Infrastructure – utilities

In the event of an incident will we be able to rely on utilities such as power, transport and telecommunications? Are there alternatives? If we depend on them, have we tested the availability of supporting infrastructure such as clearing or money transmission facilities, whether we're a bank or not?

Choosing the strategy

The results of the exercise should enable you to identify a preferred strategy for each response trigger and assess the effectiveness both of the strategies and of the controls you have in place for mitigating an incident. It should also highlight any gaps (i.e. where there is no recovery strategy for a response trigger) and those strategies which are inadequate. From this you can identify the priority action areas where you need to focus attention.

Budget and business case

Having identified the preferred strategy you are ready to write the plan. Before you do that, though, you need to obtain a budget. Just because your strategy has a clear relationship with the underlying business risks does not guarantee there is a good business case to justify it. You need to cross-check back to the value that the particular business area brings to the overall organisation, and then calculate how much it would cost to deliver the proposed business continuity strategy – including filling any gaps you have identified.

From strategy to plan

The 'strategy' segment is the key thinking point in the business continuity life cycle. The planning stage is the practical 'how to' phase that follows.

The best way to develop the plan is to sit down with staff and walk through the various activities, asking 'why?' as well as 'how?' When the plan is invoked, it is quite possible that different people will have to put it into action from those you speak to at this stage. However, if you've asked the simple questions you will end up with a plan which is relatively jargon-free and easy to implement when it is needed.

Take time over this so that you and your interlocutors have gone through everything in detail. The aim must be to get it right first time. There is always the chance that an incident will occur and the plan will have to be invoked before it has been fully tested and reviewed.

Documenting the plan

As a minimum, the plan will detail:

- background and scope
- primary objectives and priorities
- members of the various crisis management teams (assuming there are different ones for different generic crises)
- arrangements for testing, training and awareness
- assumptions – at a plan level: these will change over time and must be constantly reviewed to ensure the plan continues to protect the right aspects of the business
- recovery sites
- comprehensive emergency communication protocols and procedures – internally; externally with market/industry; regulatory or other statutory authorities; utilities; security; the public and other stakeholders.

And, of course, the recovery procedures which will ensure continuing business availability as soon as possible. For each of these you will need:

- a detailed description of the recovery procedures
- an individual owner who is responsible for implementation
- a trigger for invocation
- an authority level for invocation (e.g. board, CEO, head of IT)
- assumptions – at an activity level, so that any changes to these can be easily identified during subsequent reviews and appropriate action taken.

One word about the crisis management team before we move on to documentation. They are the people who will have management responsibility when the plan is invoked or tested. The team will have representatives from all relevant functions, depending on the type of incident impact being considered. As was pointed out in the previous chapter, unless the firm is so small that it is unavoidable, it should not have the CEO as a member. In the event of a crisis, the CEO continues to run the business. The crisis management team runs the crisis.

However you document – Word file, iPad or sophisticated software tool – make sure that it is manageable and readily accessible for all those who will need it. Not everybody needs the whole plan. Work on a 'need to know' basis and plan at all levels, from enterprise-wide to individual departments, so that staff have what they need at their level and understand their role in the event of an incident. There is no definitive list of the types of information which a department may find useful during a crisis, but remember that the more that is included, the more work will be needed to keep it up to date.

When a department has an alternative location to relocate to, it can usually store whatever it may need there in the way of specialised equipment and paper documentation. This is often referred to as a contingency box (or battle-box). A list of its contents, together with the last time they were checked or updated is a vital part of the plan.

TESTING THE PLAN

Why test?

As the military often say, no plan survives contact with the enemy.[4] Having said that, thorough planning and training will give you a better chance of succeeding and your business surviving and being available as soon as possible for business as usual.

As a result of the Hanshin-Awaji earthquake which struck Kobe and the surrounding area in January 1995, Japan, including its financial system, spent considerable effort refining business continuity plans in the light of the lessons learnt from the earthquake. When the Niigata Chūetsu earthquake, 6.8 on the Richter scale, struck the Chūetsu region in October 2004, there was minimal disruption to financial services, despite the considerable structural damage. Frequent lightning strikes in the region had also led to resilient plans to cope with loss of telecommunications, power, water and transport.

Rather than endure an emergency, it is essential to test the plan – or exercise it, as business continuity professionals prefer to say, echoing the military – and learn the lessons. The point of a test is to practise and to learn. The more you test, the more you can continuously improve.

It is often said that a business continuity plan is like a fire extinguisher – it sits inert, possibly for years, but must be there and working when needed. And as a plan must work under all circumstances, not just ideal ones which, by definition, will not exist at the time, it needs to be tested as fully as possible – to the limit in critical areas.

Testing what, and how often?

Fundamentally, it's up to you. You can do the classical annual event, working the crisis management team, relocating staff to the recovery site and making sure systems and backups work within a reasonable timeframe, keeping your fingers crossed that staff successfully make their way to the site and can log in to the systems. Not great, but the bare minimum. Alternatively, you can identify specific needs and run one of a number of tests, depending on how far you wish to go. These can range from a desktop walk-through, to a simple call tree cascade or notification test, role playing through the relocation test just mentioned, and on to:

■ a backup and restoration test – the process and timeframe for backing up data and restoring it onto contingency servers
■ a connectivity test – reconnecting sites after a tele- or data failure
■ a full technology restoration test

and all the way to a

■ full enterprise-wide test in which a firm relocates to its recovery site for one or two days carrying out business as usual.

You should also seriously consider testing with critical industry participants, as well as local authorities, utilities and other organisations on which your business may depend. It's the only way of finding out whether your plan will in fact work, since it will inevitably be dependent on these organisations.

The choice is yours, but whatever you choose, the key will be good planning.

Planning the test

The key to planning the test is to understand the objectives of the test, which in turn will determine its extent. Before you try something too ambitious, it's worth asking if the firm is ready for the level of the planned exercise, or if you should be building up to it in more gradual test steps. And one final check on your ambition – how disruptive will the test be? Will it be sufficiently practical and achievable and not endanger the organisation?

Once you've agreed the objectives and scope of the exercise, it's time to establish:

■ a date
■ who will be involved
■ that your test will be based on a plan which is up to date
■ that facilities will be available
■ a system of independent review and evaluation before, during and after the test.

The review before the test could be vital in ensuring that all dependencies have been allowed for.

Finally, build in sufficient contingency time to restore systems back to the real-world environment after the test is concluded. This is often underestimated so that there is real disruption to business-as-usual, which is not the point of the exercise and simply brings the business continuity effort into disrepute.

The test

The idea is to validate a process and identify weaknesses or errors in the plan. It's a learning experience. The key to a good test – and a good plan – is documentation. Good documentation should be kept before, during and after the test to form a basis for reviews and for the next test.

During the test, have an independent observer (or more than one, depending on the scale of the test and resources available) to provide objective feedback on how the test works, including the effectiveness of communication between staff, the crisis team and others – and to note where things went well.

After the test

If possible, grab staff before they slip away from the test to get their initial feedback on things which went well and things which didn't, whilst they're still fresh in the mind. You will probably organise more formal feedback by way of questionnaire or interview. The key is getting the feedback and then analysing it.

- Were the test objectives met?
- Was the test completed on time?
- Did the test participants and resources perform as expected?
- Was the testing approach considered appropriate?
- Which parts of the plan were inadequate or out of date?

The lessons learned from testing must be applied to the plan and steps agreed to remedy any deficiencies. At the same time, the assumptions on which the plan was based should be reviewed in the light of the test results, including assumptions made about external dependencies. It may mean that the business continuity strategy has to be re-evaluated or even changed. That's why we test.

And keep the report readily available for next time. Otherwise, all those valuable lessons will be lost and the next exercise will just repeat the mistakes of the past.

MAINTENANCE AND CONTINUOUS IMPROVEMENT

Testing is a practical way to review the plan and the assumptions on which it is based. But all risks, assumptions and critical recovery requirements should be regularly reviewed to ensure that they are up to date and appropriate for changing business circumstances. Such reviews are key components of the planning timetable.

Another element which ensures the firm will be prepared for any eventuality is training. It is essential to ensure that staff are familiar with the plan. Training, in addition to testing, is an effective way of ensuring cooperation between recovery team members. It needs to be reviewed, because staff frequently change, as do intra-business relationships.

In the end, it will all be down to communication (which training is designed to enhance) and documentation, without which the whole exercise will be undertaken in an atmosphere of ignorant bliss. Documentation at every stage means that lessons can be learnt and that the process will be capable of being audited and properly reviewed by business line management.

So the final tips are:

Communicate, communicate, communicate.

Document, document, document.

and

Keep it simple.

The simpler it is, the easier it will be to follow in a crisis and the sooner business availability will be restored.

Notes

1 See Knight, RF and Pretty, DJ, *The Impact of Catastrophes on Shareholder Value*, (Oxford: Metrica 1996), and www.thebci.org
2 Source, Coventry City Council 2006; www.bsigroup.com
3 *Business as Usual*, CBI Business Guide (London: Caspian Publishing), 2002.
4 As frequently adapted from the statement of German Field Marshal Helmuth, Graf von Moltke (1800–91) that 'No plan of operations extends with certainty beyond the first encounter with the enemy's main strength' (*Militarische Werke*. vol. 2, part 2, 1892).

Insurance

OPERATIONAL RISK AND INSURANCE

For some operational risks it's simple – or at least fairly simple. There's a fire, you put in a claim, you get the money. The same happens with a burglary, or if an employee is critically ill. Subject to appropriate proof, the insurer pays under the policy. For many operational risks, however, it might be fairer to say that paying the insurance policy premium is akin to taking out an option on a court case, a view policy-holders have been holding since at least 1384. Here is an extract from a letter written by Francesco di Marco Datini, merchant of Prato, to his wife:

> For when they insure, it is sweet to them to take the monies; but when disaster comes it is otherwise and each man draws his rump back, and strives not to pay.[1]

And, of course, some operational risks are simply uninsurable, either because it is illegal, impossible or morally hazardous to insure the particular risk, or because of the financial limits of insurance available. In fact, it has been estimated that when allowance is made for uninsurable risks and the levels of deductibles and limits in insurance policies, only 30% of operational risks in financial services are probably eligible to be insured. However, even at 30%, it is the most direct way of mitigating operational risk losses and, if approached properly, a cost-effective way of reducing risk exposure.

It can also mitigate reputation risk when, for instance, there has been a major robbery. And insurers can bring their claims expertise to reducing an operational risk loss. But essentially insurance acts as an operational risk transfer mechanism – to the insurer – at a price.

INSURANCE SPEAKS TO CAUSE

Insurance is a contract of fortuity. In other words, it depends on something happening which is not foreseen and over which the insured ostensibly has no control, such as the examples at the beginning of this chapter. If it were the same as a guarantee it would simply respond to the event having occurred and pay. It is not like a guarantee because whether an insurance policy will respond goes back to cause.

In Chapter 1 we talked about the chain of causality:

$$\text{CAUSE} \quad \rightarrow \quad \text{EVENT} \quad \rightarrow \quad \text{EFFECT}$$

In the context of operational risk and insurance this translates into:

Operational risk often (perhaps too often) concerns itself with identifying and measuring events. Insurance is also triggered by an event, but it then looks to why the event occurred. A fire policy will pay for the damage caused by a fire, but not if it is shown that the cause was arson on the part of the policyholder; or if a sprinkler system on which the insurance was conditional had not been installed. Insurance will pay for a theft, but possibly not if the alarm system had knowingly been allowed to remain inactive for a period of time, or security controls had lapsed.

The reason why will also determine which kind of policy will respond to an event. Take fraud, for instance. In the case of a bank, it may be covered under a Bankers' Blanket Bond, assuming it was caused by employee dishonesty. Non-banks will have similar policies covering employee dishonesty. However, if it involved computer crime by somebody outside the firm, then a specialist Electronic and Computer Crime policy might come in to play. A Professional Indemnity policy's fraud extension might be relevant if a third party is harmed or suffers loss. And finally, in a case like Enron, it could be that the company and non-negligent directors will seek to claim under the company's own Directors' and Officers' policy. In all of these, *cause* is the critical issue.

BUYING INSURANCE

The insurance buyer

To buy insurance effectively you need a clear understanding of your firm's risk exposure and also the effectiveness of controls already in place to mitigate that risk. Given the costs involved, the analysis required and the fact that the whole point of insurance is to be a mitigant to the residual risks a firm faces, it is extraordinary how very often, in firms which have a risk function, there is little or no contact between the insurance buyer and the risk department.

Too often risk buying comes out of procurement or premises management – presumably on the basis that it is seen as having to do with property and cars – or at best finds itself parked (possibly with the management of the car fleet) in the company secretary's office. So first make sure insurance buying is either part of the operational risk function, which is where the relevant risk reports are being captured, or at least has close contact with it.

Buying centrally also helps to ensure that cover is consistent and not duplicated. Too often insurance buying is undertaken in the silos of the various business units, wasting resource and money and probably not getting the best insurance coverage.

Coverage and the asymmetry of information

The next step is to understand what the insurance actually covers, by reading the policies, and then to attempt to map that to the firm's risk profile. Aligning the policy to your risks is not easy and must be frequently reappraised because your business and risk profile will inevitably be in a state of constant change.

There will inevitably be exclusions to the policy. Sometimes they simply state what would be expected good practice, such as the sprinkler system example mentioned earlier. Insurers assume that people will take sensible precautions to protect themselves and their property. In other cases, exclusions clarify intent and make sure that a risk (or peril) is placed in the right kind of policy. In the Enron case, should the claim go against a crime or liability class of policy? The policy makes sure there is no confusion.

In the case of emerging risks, such as cyber-terrorism or terrorism generally, they could affect a number of classes of insurance and render historic pricing models obsolete. Similar considerations apply to historic operational risk data which can become less relevant or degrade if the internal or external risk and control environment changes. When new risks emerge, insurers often introduce an exclusion initially from the standard policies, but then design a new product specifically to deal with the risk, which is what has happened in the case of terrorism.

However, insurers have learnt painfully over the years about the times when the risk–reward ratio goes against them across the cycle and why. Premiums are as much market driven as risk driven. Price is not entirely elastic, so insurers' real protection, especially if market rates are soft, is to restrict coverage.

Risk-pricing depends on information. In the case of an insurance buyer and seller, the asymmetry of information is hugely biased in favour of the buyer. Insurers will often rely primarily on fairly simple parameters such as number of employees, size of assets and where they are based, as well as splits by business type. And of course on historical claims data, where at least they have industry-wide experience to go on. Surprisingly, they often do not ask for details of risk and audit assessments or of losses which fall below the level of the deductible in a policy, the amount which the policy-holder has to bear. Having said that, the intelligent insurance buyer will provide operational risk information which will encourage insurers to improve their offer. There should be a dialogue, so that each side understands where the other is coming from and gets the best deal it can.

So the good risk manager should be armed with detailed information with which to assess the value of the insurance offered. Historical data and/ or modelling should point to a reasonable level of deductible, especially for attritional losses which are effectively 'the cost of doing business'. In the same way, using historic data and resulting estimates of severity, the risk manager should be able to work out a suitable limit or cap to the amount of cover he or she wishes to buy. Figure 12.1 shows this in diagrammatic form.

Using the loss distribution curve for insurance buying: lognormal curve showing insurance portion   Figure 12.1

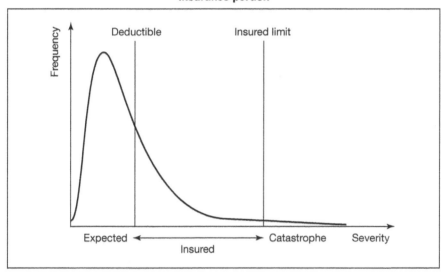

Mapping

In order to evaluate whether it is worth buying insurance, you must first assess how far it covers the risks you have identified. That's not too difficult where the class of insurance maps neatly onto your loss event type, such as with fire and property damage. But that's a minority of operational loss events.

With operational risk, a number of causes can lead to a particular type of loss event and a particular cause can trigger a number of different types of loss event. In the same way, as we saw above with the internal fraud example, different types of policy will respond to a particular loss event, depending on the cause, and a particular class of policy may respond to a range of loss events. The Bankers' Blanket Bond, which is essentially a crime policy, will cover fraud and theft, for instance, two major classes of operational risk. But other policies such as Electronic and Computer Crime, Directors' and Officers' liability and Professional Indemnity policies may also respond. Similarly, with theft from banks, the Bankers' Blanket Bond covers theft of physical property such as computers, cash or artwork, but does not cover theft of intellectual property. For that, again depending on cause, you may have to turn to a Fidelity Guarantee policy (covering your own loss) or a Professional Indemnity policy if a third party has suffered loss and the firm was unaware of the theft.

Where simple direct mapping from a risk category such as fire is not possible to help assess the value of insurance, the best answer is to use scenarios (see Chapter 10, Stress tests and scenarios). That is what the insurance industry does, not only to understand its own underwriting risk exposure, but also to evaluate its operational risk, as was noted in Chapter 10. If you use scenarios to assess your operational risk exposure, use them to test your insurance coverage. Whether you are assessing insurance or operational risk exposures, a severe enough scenario is generally produced by considering a number of serious events happening over an appropriate time. In assessing insurance coverage, an appropriate time could be the 12 month term of most insurance policies.

Evaluating the cost

The first thing to remember is that a non-life insurance policy has no intrinsic value. Policies taken out by different firms may have the same monetary limits, but the value of the policy to each insured will be different. It will depend on the ability of the insurer to pay a claim and on the precise wording of the policy, the deductibles, exclusions and, most importantly, an individual firm's risk profile. Each policy is different and each insured has a different risk profile.

Evaluating the scenarios will lead to an estimate of loss which can then be matched against the relevant coverage and insurance premiums being offered. By tweaking deductibles, limits and exclusions, from the information you have and the assumptions you make in modelling your scenarios, you can find out how that would affect premiums.

After that, it is a question of comparing the cost of capital to support the relevant operational risk against the premium you are being asked to pay. If the operational risk capital multiplied by the internal cost of capital is greater than the premium asked, it sounds like you have a good deal. In many ways, the sums should add up because the basis of insurance is to spread the risk and so be able to charge a competitive premium. Signor Datini worked that out in the fourteenth century and so gathered his merchant colleagues into a form of mutual insurance. And, of course, the same principle applied to those who met in Edward Lloyd's Coffee House in the City of London in the seventeenth century. By pooling their risks, they were able to spread the cost.

This is perhaps the point to remember that insurance is not about capital replacement – at least not in the short term – even if its value can be assessed against the cost of capital. Cause has to be established before an insurance claim can be progressed. An event may happen in 2001 which gives rise to, say, a claim of negligence. Whilst you will notify your insurer of the possibility of a claim, it may take years before negligence is ascribed to you, the insured. Once it is, you can go to your insurance company and provide proof of loss. But that, too, may lead to further time being spent whilst it is determined that the specific circumstances are covered by your policy, or whether and to what extent you may have contributed to the loss. Once everything is agreed, the insurer will pay. But that can be years after the operational risk event occurred.

That points also to the importance of having data which enables you to assess the net present value of the amount which is finally paid, allowing for the time value of money – the time between an event occurring and the amount and timing of an insurance settlement.

Types of policy

In this connection it is worth remembering that there are broadly three types of policy: losses occurring, claims made and losses discovered (or discovery based).

With a losses occurring policy, the loss must occur during the period covered by the policy. These are the types of policy with which most of us are familiar in our private lives – property, motor and so on.

With a claims made policy, the insured must notify a circumstance, accepted by the insurer, during the term of the policy, even though the event may have taken place before that period. Into this category fall the various liability policies such as Directors' and Officers' or Professional Indemnity.

With a discovery-based policy, the policy responds to an event discovered during the policy period, again even though the event itself happened some years before. A good example would be an Unauthorised Trading policy. As a class of insurance it was not available until some time after the Barings case in 1995, but it would have covered the Allfirst Financial case in 2001, where the deceptions practised by trader John Rusnak went back over four years before they finally came to light.

Table 12.1 gives some idea of the range of policies which a firm might consider buying and how the policies fit in to the three broad categories of policy.

Table 12.1

Types of insurance cover

Policy coverage	Type of cover
Business Interruption policy	Losses occurring
Computer Crime policy	Losses discovered
Commercial General Liability policy	Claims made
Directors' and Officers' Liability policy	Claims made
Employment Practices Liability policy	Claims made
Environmental policy	Claims made
Key Man policy	Losses occurring
Kidnap and Ransom policy	Losses occurring
Motor Fleet policy	Losses occurring
Pension Trustee Liability policy	Claims made
Property Insurance policy	Losses occurring
Professional Indemnity (Civil Liability) policy	Claims made
Reputation (PR Costs) policy	Claims made
Terrorism policy	Losses occurring
Unauthorised Trading policy	Losses discovered

THE INSURANCE CARRIER

The capitalisation of the general insurance market worldwide is probably less than the capitalisation of HSBC, or a similar global corporation, alone. That, and events such as the collapse and rescue of the giant AIG in September 2008, show the importance of assessing the creditworthiness, or more specifically claims-paying ability, of the insurer. Another criterion, if you are an international business, is to look for a carrier with the same geographic spread as your own.

Naturally, insurers are rated just like every other corporate, but it is a difficult decision to accept that you are paying for protection from a firm which is less creditworthy than you are. Indeed, it makes little sense, unless the mere transfer of risk is so attractive or the coverage is based on reducing reputation risk, as described earlier in the chapter.

So evaluating the security of the insurer is important, whatever size of company you or they are, and it may be prudent, depending on the importance of insurance to the firm, to have a system of credit limits in place as a check against over-reliance on one particular insurer. Of course, one way of reducing exposure is to take a leaf out of the insurer's book and spread the credit risk through co-insurance with a number of insurers. But that's a discussion for you and your insurance broker.

ALTERNATIVE RISK TRANSFER MECHANISMS

Most insurance needs relating to operational risk are satisfied by the conventional insurance market. However, for some risks there may be no cover available in the conventional market, either because of the nature of the risks or the size of cover required. Hugely increased coverage has been demanded by industries such as energy, space or even mass air transport. New types of claim, such as latent disease, pollution and terrorism, have emerged. Greater awareness and knowledge of insurance by better informed insurance buyers has also led to a questioning of traditional insurance methods, pricing and distribution. As a result, a new generation of alternative risk transfer mechanisms has been developed by both the insurance and capital markets.[2]

Captive insurance companies ('captives')

A 'captive' is an insurance company formed to insure or reinsure the risks of its (generally non-insurance) parent or associated third parties. Whilst most are wholly owned subsidiaries which insure the risks of their parent, over 10% have been formed by trade associations, industry bodies or specific groups of companies to share their members' risks and address their specific insurance needs.

Captives can be an efficient way of obtaining insurance cover. For a traditional insurer, up to 35% of its premium cost may have to be charged to cover expenses whereas, for a captive, the charge can come down to 5%. This is driven in part by the growth of captive management companies, which enable the parent to benefit from not having to staff a fully functioning insurance company.

Other benefits of forming a captive include:

- it may be the only way in which a parent can obtain cover for certain risks, or at least cover at a reasonable price
- being able to take a share of the more attractive layers of an insurance programme
- premiums paid to a captive, as well as its reserves, are available for investment – until they are needed to pay for claims
- reasonable premiums paid to a captive are tax deductible, whereas reserves maintained to cover losses in the form of self-insurance are not

- reinsurers may quote lower premiums to a captive due to the fact that the parent is financially involved with its own risk: however, reinsurance requirements can also be different from a traditional insurer, since risk will be much less diversified

- direct access to the reinsurance market should also mean lower premiums since the costs have been avoided of going to the direct insurance market.

It is not uncommon for some captive structures to use a 'fronting' insurance company, with the captive taking on the role of reinsurer.

Whether to use a captive or not depends on: a clear understanding of the parent group's risks and risk management; the true cost savings involved; and the effect on earnings volatility of replacing the range of external insurances with a substantial degree of self-financing, just as with self-insurance considered below.

However, for specialist needs, captives can be a more stable source of insurance for a firm than traditional carriers – provided effective reinsurance can be obtained.

Mutual insurance companies ('mutuals')

The section on captives mentioned that they were sometimes set up by industry bodies to protect their members' risks. That concept lies at the heart of mutual insurance companies, which typically differ from captives that are generally owned by a single entity.

Mutuals also have a long history. Examples are:

- marine mutuals, formed by ship-owners to protect their fleets in a particular port

- fire mutuals, formed by property-owners to protect property in a particular town or region

- the factory mutual system, originally formed by New England mill-owners who could not get fire insurance

- trade mutuals formed by companies in a particular industry.

Perhaps the best-known mutuals today are the marine P&I (protection and indemnity) clubs. Protection covers liabilities relating to crew, passengers, ports and docks. Indemnity covers cargo liability.

The advantage of mutuals is that they are non-profit making and so can produce better returns or lower premium rates than other insurers. They may also have specialist knowledge of the risks being underwritten, and so can produce better underwriting results and secure better reinsurance cover and terms. They are particularly useful as a concept for mitigating operational risk, since they can enable industries to free themselves from the general market when that market has either closed the door to them or is only offering penal rates and conditions. The disadvantage is that members face the possibility of a call in the event of a serious claim made by any one of them.

Capital markets

For a number of years, capital markets and insurance professionals have been working to see if a capital market instrument could be devised which would protect against a firm's overall level of operational risk. If so, it could mean that investors outside the insurance market could be brought in and so increase capacity for protection.

Such thoughts were prompted by the success of catastrophe bonds and other instruments. Catastrophe bonds were developed following Hurricane Andrew in 1992 which, at a cost of around US$30bn, was the most expensive hurricane in US history, until it was surpassed by Hurricane Katrina in 2005. The market really began in earnest in 1997 when over US$500m of bonds were issued, rising steadily to US$2bn in 2005 and then rapidly to US$7bn in 2007.[3]

Catastrophe bonds are issued by an insurer or other organisation. They are neither insurance nor reinsurance but are structured as investments. There is no requirement for an insurable interest. They provide for normal redemption at term, but in the event of a catastrophe within predetermined limits of geography, type and size of loss, the investors in the bonds contribute to the loss by forfeiting their interest and/or principal. A typical example of a qualifying event would be an earthquake occurring of a particular size on the Richter scale and within a certain radius of a predetermined point, such as the centre of Tokyo.

Catastrophe bonds generally relate to property damage caused by a catastrophic natural or man-made event. They are particularly attractive to investors in the hardening market which follows 'market-changing' events such as Hurricane Katrina and the attacks on the World Trade Center in September 2001, so that returns can be considerable if no further catastrophe occurs. And indeed by the end of 2007 they accounted for 12% of US and 8% of global property insurance limits.[3] However, they tend to lose their attraction when rates soften. After the record year of 2007, issuance has dropped to an annual figure of around US $4–5bn.[4]

It is perhaps no accident that these instruments cover specific events such as hurricanes or earthquakes in a particular geographic location, since there is a large body of historic data to support assessment of the frequency and severity of an event. Operational risk, however, is business-wide and, as we have shown repeatedly in this book, is difficult to assess to the level of confidence which could create a benchmark index which would sustain a deep and liquid capital trading market.

There is one area, though, where firms can protect themselves against the effects of a particular threat to their business – weather derivatives. Whilst general insurance (and catastrophe bonds) offer protection against low-probability catastrophic risks, firms can buy protection against higher-probability weather events. Weather derivatives were first traded on the Chicago Mercantile Exchange in 1999. They trade against an index of temperatures over a particular period at a particular location and pay if temperatures are so many degrees above or below the benchmark index – depending on the time of year. Principal users are energy-related companies, but agricultural businesses and those involved in transport and tourism are also beginning to protect themselves against above average hot summers or cold winters.

Capital markets are extending the alternatives available for mitigating certain operational risks, but we are still a long way from a capital market alternative to insurance to protect against the general range of operational risks.

Self-insurance

The one option which is available to everybody is self-insurance – or not buying insurance. Self-insurance is a perfectly reasonable choice, provided the risks have been fully assessed and managed. So the best form of self-insurance is good internal controls. Self-insurance can, of course, be inadvertent – or even deliberate, but badly thought out. For our purposes, let's assume rational behaviour and good operational risk management.

Insurance removes an element of financial uncertainty and replaces a possible unknown large loss by a series of smaller known premium payments. The rationale for self-insurance is that the cost of insurance in the form of premiums is removed, as is the loss of the time value of money between paying the premiums and receiving a claims payment. And of course the money saved is available for investment. However, these benefits are offset by the volatility of losses which may occur if insurable operational risk events occur.

If we return to the curve shown in Figure 12.1, it is highly likely that firms will self-insure for the attritional losses, the cost of doing business. Where the discussion becomes more interesting is the extent to which a firm is prepared to self-insure as it moves along the curve.

As with the cost evaluation described above, the fundamental rationale is to look at the cost of loss and the cost of controls which maintain losses at an acceptable level and then consider whether the cost of insurance shows a benefit. Once you get further along the curve either in relative or in absolute terms, the debate becomes more difficult. It will depend on the confidence you have in the firm's ability to assess and manage its risk exposure, as well as its risk culture and risk appetite.

In some cases, of course, a very large firm may be prepared to suffer individual losses of, say, US$500m and find that the cost of only buying insurance above this level is penal or even find that there is little or no market. To that extent the market may force firms to self-insure – or spend more on controls to offset the possible volatility in results which could follow a major loss.

CONCLUSION

Insurance is probably the commonest form of operational risk transfer. It is, however, one which is not well understood. If the right person is put in charge of buying it across the firm – somebody who knows how it works and who works closely with operational risk management to understand the firm's risk profile – then it can be a hugely business beneficial exercise. However, if you fully understand your operational risk profile and what insurance offers, you can also make an intelligent and informed decision to self-insure, which might be just as business beneficial.

Notes

1   Iris Origo, *The Merchant of Prato* (London: Jonathan Cape), 1957.
2   The section on alternative risk transfer mechanisms draws extensively on sections of *Alternative Risk Financing: Changing the face of insurance* (London: Jim Bannister Developments Limited), 1998, written by the inestimable insurance expert, Jim Bannister.
3   Guy Carpenter, *The catastrophe bond market at year-end 2007*; www.guycarp.com
4   www.thomsonreuters.com

Internal audit – the third line of defence

AUDIT AND THE THREE LINES OF DEFENCE

Independent assurance is the critical third line of defence shown in Figure 3.1. It has two complementary parts – internal and external audit. In respect of risk, internal audit provides independent assurance to the board on the effective operation of the risk management framework and validates the risk measurement process. External audit's role is to give an opinion on the financial statements. To enable it to do this, it has to assure itself of the quality of risk governance and of controls over such things as ethical values, management style and values, and human resource policies and practice. These factors do not form part of its assurance to the board, but do provide the auditor with assurance that information provided to it is likely to be reliable, transparent and comprehensive.

INDEPENDENT ASSURANCE

Independence

In order to fulfil its function, internal audit must be functionally independent from the activities it audits. Clearly it must be independent of the business lines. Whilst it may have a direct line to the CEO or CFO for pay or rations, they should not be its functional reports. Nor should the head of internal audit report to the CRO. Since internal audit is required to provide assurance on the risk management process, reporting to the CRO presents an obvious conflict of interest. That conflict is not resolved by dotted line reporting elsewhere. Dotted lines, like dual lines, are a fudge. Delete them.

Assuming there is an audit committee, it should report to the chair of that committee. If there is no audit committee, it should report to the non-executive chairman or senior non-executive director. The point of reporting to the non-executive directors is that internal audit must have a direct functional line to those who are there to oversee management and to assess the firm independently and objectively on behalf of shareholders.

The approach of an audit committee should be trust, with verification. Internal audit provides that independent verification. Reporting to the audit committee will protect internal audit's organisational independence and objectivity. If internal audit reports only to the CFO, or another senior executive, its independence is immediately called into question. In this chapter we shall assume that the function to which internal audit reports is the audit committee.

Maintaining independence is easier said than done, especially in the face of some regulatory demands. The Sarbanes–Oxley legislation in the USA, for instance, requires independent verification of information and for senior management sign-off. Ideally, an independent team should fulfil this function. There is a danger that if internal audit provides the independent verification of the information, it may be seen as effectively the 'owner' of the information rather than management.[1] That can present an immediate conflict with the need for internal audit to be independent of the design, inputs and outputs of the process and to provide appropriate assurance.

Assurance

From a risk perspective, internal auditors will normally provide assurance on:

- risk governance and the risk management processes from board level down, looking at their design and how well they are working
- the management and oversight process for risks, including the effectiveness of controls and other responses to them
- the accuracy and reliability of the components of the risk assessment and reporting process.

Whilst management, and especially those providing risk management oversight, will challenge the accuracy of risk assessments provided by the business, there needs to be an independent review to ensure the reliability and robustness of the assessment process, including data inputs, assumptions and outputs.

There is no single method, partly because the nature of assessment processes, especially with operational risk, is so various. Assurance concerns all aspects of the process. It tests processes to ensure that information is complete, accurate and valid. In this context, valid means that the information is genuine and not fictitious.

A good example is the auditing of scenarios and stress tests, which we discussed in Chapter 10. Scenarios rely on judgemental and expert decisions, so that independent review plays a key role in reviewing the process. Here are some of the qualitative questions that could be asked about the process:

- Were all the right people involved in the assessment?
- Challenge by risk managers and others is an important part of the process, but were the challenges consistent across the various scenarios?
- Since they involve a significant degree of subjective judgement, scenarios are notoriously open to human biases (as outlined in Chapter 10). Have these been adequately considered and mitigated?
- Have all the causes, events and consequences been included, and included appropriately?
- Has the process been adequately documented, so that it could be replicated in a consistent manner?

In summary, business line management creates the scenarios and assumptions; risk management challenges the assumptions made in the scenarios and the outcomes; internal audit provides assurance on the process and the process by which the assumptions are derived.

INTERNAL AND EXTERNAL AUDIT

Internal and external audit share a common agenda of providing assurance to the board that the risk and control processes are appropriate and effective. Both should function independently of management and report to the board. But there are differences in the roles they play.

Internal auditors are part of the organisation and, whilst they maintain their independence, their objectives are determined by the audit committee or, in its absence, the board. External auditors are, by definition, outside the organisation. Their objectives, whilst framed and signed off by the audit committee in their terms of engagement, are also driven partly by statutory and professional requirements. They are answerable for their professional standards to their professional bodies (as indeed should a good internal auditor also be) and can be answerable also to regulators who may have outsourced investigatory work to them.

One of the advantages of being inside the organisation is that internal audit can sense changes in culture creeping in, for instance slackness in operating controls or in recording events and losses. As the organisation's independent eyes and ears, internal audit can also spot breaches of the firm's ethical standards – or simply ethical creep – which could cause significant reputational damage. In an interview published in *Audit and Risk*, Lord Smith of Kelvin, who wrote the Smith Report on audit following the Enron scandal of 2002, suggested that internal auditors had work to do 'to get under the skin of a business and understand the leadership behaviour and cultural issues and incentives that drive its operations and functions'.[2] This role of internal audit as the 'canary in the mineshaft' when it comes to culture and behaviour can be formalised if the firm has clearly articulated behaviours against which staff performance is assessed (as we explain in Chapter 15, Culture and people risk).

Those are advantages which are unlikely to be enjoyed by a firm to which internal audit has been outsourced (assuming it works much of the time outside the firm) and are beyond the scope of an external audit. On the other hand, being outside the firm, the external auditor may spot conflicts or problems which are not seen by those involved in day-to-day management, including the internal auditor.

The external auditor also brings an outsider's view, informed by having seen many businesses in the same or similar industries. He or she should be a helpful provider of best practice and advise on new developments in risk management, corporate governance, financial accounting and controls. If the external auditor reports only on balance sheet issues and not on how the business is run, the firm is not getting best value.

Internal audit is continuously reviewing risk processes and controls. For their part, the external auditor's primary responsibility as regards risk management is to assure itself that appropriate governance standards are being maintained to enable it to sign off the financial reports, including statements made by the directors about risk. And of course, the external auditors make their assessment at a point in time rather than on a continuous basis. That assessment is fundamental to external audit's primary role, which is to establish whether the financial statements represent a true and fair reflection of the financial position of the organisation at that point in time.

The two auditors come together in two respects – their independence and their need to work closely together. We have commented on the independence of the internal auditor. As regards the external auditor, independence is critical. A board, or audit committee, should understand the auditor's processes for ensuring its independence and avoiding conflicts of interest. These may include auditor rotation, ensuring that secondments from the auditor to the firm do not make management decisions, and its policy on the overall level of fees for audit and non-audit services. In the end, the board or audit committee has to make a subjective judgement.

In the USA, the Sarbanes–Oxley legislation has specifically prohibited an external auditor from undertaking certain work including: book-keeping and related services, designing financial information systems, actuarial services, internal audit outsourcing services, management functions or human resources and expert services unrelated to the audit.[3] Other countries are considering their own approaches and whether to impose similar restrictions or requirements, including more active corporate governance and greater transparency regarding non-audit engagements.[4] Ultimately, though, the decision on whether the auditor's position has been compromised is for the board. Complying with legislation is a minimum, not the standard.

The board should also be able to agree with the following statements:[5]

Management respects the auditors as providers of an objective and challenging process.

You need an external auditor (and internal one for that matter) who is prepared to go on asking unpleasant questions if necessary and for management to accept and respect that.

The relationship with the audit firm is controlled by the audit committee (or the independent non-executive directors) and not by management.

External auditors must remain independent of management. The board needs assurance that they do not come too close, especially to the CFO who is often their prime point of contact in their day-to-day audit.

Finally, to enhance cooperation between the internal and external audit, personnel should meet periodically to discuss common interests. They are complementary parts of the audit process, the third line of defence, and support each other. Coordination of activities and mutual provision of reports and working papers will reduce disruption to the firm and will lead to improved efficiency and effectiveness in the overall audit process.

INTERNAL AUDIT AND RISK MANAGEMENT OVERSIGHT

In financial services the internal audit function is obligatory, whether in-house or outsourced. Elsewhere, it is increasingly prevalent, but that is a relatively recent phenomenon. The rise of internal audit in some ways mirrors the rise of the discipline of operational risk management and probably dates from the early 1990s when internal audit began to come out of the shadow of external audit, did more than provide process assurance and became involved in risk management.

Internal audit provides assurance to the board on the first and second lines of defence. Regarding the first line, it provides assurance that controls are working effectively and are appropriate to the risks of the organisation. As for the second line of defence, oversight functions such as risk management ensure consistent application of the risk management framework and provide a challenge to business operations. Internal audit provides assurance that the oversight functions are working effectively, picking up on adverse changes in the risk profile and that these are being reported. As can be seen from Figure 3.1, oversight covers both financial and non-financial controls, including the people risks overseen by HR (see Chapter 15, Culture and people risk) and regulatory and statutory compliance.

It is, of course, important that the second and third lines of defence work closely together, leveraging each other's expertise and experience. Whilst their activities are complementary, there needs to be clear demarcation so that their respective roles are understood both by themselves and by others in the firm. They also need to map sources of assurance over key risks and controls, so that there are no underlaps or overlaps. Internal audit is part of the risk management process but is not risk management. It should not set the risk appetite or in any other way have accountability for risk management. Its role is to review and give assurance on the process elements of the risk management framework.

Specifically, internal audit should not be responsible for operational risk management. In the late 1990s, when few firms had a structure for operational risk management, let alone designated operational risk managers, responsibility for operational risk often fell to internal audit on the basis that operational risk was all about internal processes, and internal auditors were the only people in the organisation who knew the processes and controls operating throughout the firm. Times have moved on. Operational risk is recognised as going beyond systems and process. Whilst auditors can and should provide guidance, responsibility for risk rests with business line management.

As an independent assurer, internal audit is, in fact, especially valuable and necessary in operational risk. Operational risk managers are usually intimately involved in the development of the operational risk framework within a central team, or work in business units where they can offer advice and guidance and are responsible for providing data inputs and resulting reports. That effectively places them in the first and second lines of defence, a confusing enough position. There therefore needs to be an independent assurance process of the information they are providing and the methodologies used.

Where there is no risk management function, the internal auditor may act as a facilitator in establishing a risk management strategy and framework. But it is important that they do not compromise their independence or confuse their role by taking risk decisions or being executive risk managers, however attractive that role may seem.

THE ROLE OF INTERNAL AUDIT

Policy

Internal audit should operate within a clear policy statement, approved by the firm's board and management, which outlines:

- its objectives and the scope of the internal audit function
- its status and position within the firm, including its relationship to the business lines and oversight functions
- its competencies, tasks and responsibilities.

The scope of possible responsibilities is wide. According to the Institute of Internal Auditors (IIA),

> Internal auditing is an independent, objective assurance and consulting activity designed to add value and improve an organisation's operations. It helps an organisation accomplish its objectives by bringing a systematic, disciplined approach to evaluate and improve the effectiveness of risk management, control, and governance processes.[6]

In addition, whether it is the audit committee or the board to whom internal audit reports, that body is not only responsible for financial reporting and the process relating to the company's financial risks and internal control, but their concerns will also include non-financial risks such as whistle blowing and 'speaking up' (see p. 304), remuneration policy (including the information on which remuneration may be based) and exposure to fraud, almost all of which require some degree of internal audit assurance.

To add to the mix, internal audit has an outward looking role. First, it should protect and safeguard the reputation of a firm by ensuring that ethical and other guidelines or codes are adhered to through assurance of the process. Second, it should be able and encouraged to take a broader view of the firm and its environment and not be bogged down in the detail of process, important though that is. The board needs to be clear from all of this exactly what it wants from internal audit, but also consider internal audit's ability to meet changing expectations.

Finally, it is important that the audit agenda is shaped by the needs of the business and not by internal audit's capabilities. If that is not the case, its resources and personnel will need to be changed.[7]

Planning and priorities

Having established its role, the head of internal audit can work with the board to develop and deliver the audit plan. This should be risk-based, using a form of the risk and control assessment process described in Chapter 5. To see what we mean by risk-based in the case of internal audit, let's look at the example of a risk and control assessment shown in Figure 5.6, which is reproduced in Figure 13.1.

The risk and control assessment should be one of the main inputs to the audit plan. That does not mean that internal audit's priority is to look at those risks which are seen as 'net' red or amber. Rather it should be to look at those risks which show a 'gross' red and a net 'green'. Here management is saying that they have put in place excellent controls to mitigate the risks of a 'red' event taking place. If they fail or are inadequate, the firm will be faced with the possibility of a very high risk materialising. That is where internal audit should concentrate its attention. If a risk is 'net' red, then it is assumed – but internal audit should obviously check – that management is taking appropriate action. Internal audit can then provide assurance that the controls which management has put in place are effective. Using the example given in Figure 13.1, internal audit's priorities will therefore be as shown in Table 13.1.

Of course, the audit cycle will also be influenced by such events as the arrival of a new unit head or launch of a new business process or product.

Generic risk and control assessment

Figure 13.1

ID	Risks	Owner(s) of the risk	I	L	S	Controls	Owner(s) of the control	D	P	E
1	Failure to attract, recruit and retain key staff	SR		4	4	16	Salary surveys	TJ	2	2	4
							Training and mentoring schemes	TB	3	2	6
							Retention packages for key staff	TJ	4	4	16
2	Financial advisers misinterpret/fail to understand the complexity of 'equity release' products	PL AB	4	4	16	Staff training	TB	4	4	16
							Learning gained from previous deals	KW & EL	4	4	16
							Review of individual needs in performance appraisal process	TB	3	2	6
							Procedure manuals for processes	EL	4	4	16
3	Poor staff communication	SR JK	4	4	16	Defined communication channels	ZK	4	3	12
							Documented procedures and processes	EL	3	2	6
4	Failure to understand the law and/or regulations	PL	4	3	12	Internal training courses	EL	4	4	16
							Regular updates from various sources	EL	4	1	4
							External training courses	TB & EL	4	3	12
5	Poor detection of money laundering	PL	4	3	12	AML annual training	TB & EL	3	2	6
							Circulation of BBA awareness circulars	EL & ZK	3	1	3
							KYC	ALL	4	3	12
6	Insufficient funds/deposits to cater for lending activities	CK	4	3	12	Liquidity risk policy	ZK	4	4	16
							Advertising	KW	4	3	12
							Economic forecasting	CK	3	3	9
7	Over-selling credit cards	CK	4	3	12	Staff training	TB	3	3	9
							Credit scoring	EL	4	4	16
							Forward business planning	ZK	3	3	9
8	Over-deployment of management resources on regulatory issues	RU CK	3	4	12	Monthly budget against actual review	TJ	3	4	12
							Corporate governance	CK	4	4	16
							Monthly head of compliance & CEO meetings	CK	2	2	4
9	Failure to capture market opportunities	AB	3	3	9	Competitor monitoring	TB	3	4	12
							Product development	TB	2	2	4
10	Over-dependency on outsourcing	CK	3	3	9	SLAs	CK & EL	4	4	16
							Outsourcing monitoring	CK & EL	4	4	16
							Due diligence	CK	4	3	12
							Policy	CK	3	4	12
11	Weakness in information security system	RU JK	4	2	8	Record retention	ZK	2	2	4
							Information security policy procedure and monitoring	ZK	3	2	6
							Staff training and certification	TB	3	3	9
							Client agreements/marketing	ZK & KW	2	1	2
12	Inadequate or insufficient IT infrastructure to achieve business objectives	JK	2	4	8	Business/strategic planning	ZA & KW	3	4	12
							IT systems performance and capability monitoring	ZK	4	3	12
13	External fraud activities	PL	3	2	6	Anti-fraud training	ZK	4	4	16
							Systems security	ZK	4	4	16
14	Failure to grow staff competencies	SR	3	2	6	Staff training	TB	4	3	12
							Hire of temporary staff	TB	2	2	4
							Appraisals	TB	2	3	6
15	Misaligned employee goals	SR CK	2	3	6	Appraisals	TB	2	3	6
							Corporate governance	ZA	4	4	16
16	Failure to sense and eliminate internal fraud	PL	3	2	6	Criminal background check	EL	3	2	6
							Segregation of duties	ZA	2	3	6
							Staff training	TB	3	2	6
							Fraud monitoring	EL	4	4	16
							Whistle blowing	ALL	3	3	9
17	Unfit or inappropriate new products launched	AB	4	1	4	Staff training	TB	3	2	6
							New products approval process	KW	3	2	6
18	Poor strategic decision making	CK AB	4	1	4	Monitoring of market data	KW	4	4	16
							Research and forecasting	KW	4	2	8
							Monthly Management Forum	ZA	4	3	12
							Marketing strategy review	ZA & KW	3	3	9
19	Inaccessible premises	RU	3	1	3	BCP/M	EL	4	3	12
							Security of floors (to enable loss to be better managed)	ZA	3	4	12
							Building and firm guards	ZA	4	4	16

Key: I = impact; L = likelihood; D = design; P = performance

Source: Courtesy of Chase Cooper Limited

But the fundamental approach should be to go back to the risk and control assessment and identify those risks for which management considers controls to have had the greatest effect. Since the risk and control assessment will also encompass strategic risks, it should mean that internal audit's plan will give equal weight to both the board's and management's risk assessments. The priorities of the board and internal audit should be aligned.

Table 13.1	**Internal audit priorities drawn from Figure 13.1**	
Risk	**Controls**	
Failure to attract, recruit and retain key staff	Retention packages for key staff	
Financial advisers misinterpret/fail to understand the complexities of 'equity release' products	Staff training Learning gained from previous deals Procedure manuals for processes	
Failure to understand the law and/or regulations	Internal training courses	
Insufficient funds/deposits to cater for lending activities	Liquidity risk policy	
Over-selling credit cards	Credit scoring	
Over-deployment of management resources on regulatory issues	Corporate governance	

Status and resourcing

Audit, the third line of defence, is a critical part of a firm's risk management framework, which should be accepted and recognised as such by everybody in the firm. That is achieved partly by the attitude of the board and partly by the behaviour of the internal auditors (see Effective internal audit below).

Internal audit must be free to obtain all the information it needs, when it needs it, and not find itself obstructed or ignored in any way. This will be less likely if it reports unequivocally to the chair of the audit committee or the senior non-executive director. If it does not, that may reflect its status within the organisation. The board, or its audit committee, must also ensure that audit has the right number and quality of staff, another issue which is dealt with in the section on Effective internal audit below.

Finally, a word about remuneration. As with those in an oversight role, remuneration should not present the possibility of a conflict. Those in the second and third lines of defence (oversight and independent assurance) should be remunerated on the basis of achieving their own objectives rather than have their remuneration based on the firm's financial performance.

Reporting to management and the board

Having established the plan and put it into action, it is internal audit's job to report its progress and significant issues to the board and to senior management for action. Auditors must be ready to report issues beyond the standard and agreed framework and, if they have something especially sensitive to report, there must be a clear line of communication from them to whoever is appropriate – the chairman, chair of the audit committee or senior independent non-executive director.

To be an effective part of the risk management process, audit reports should be prompt and concise, with issues prioritised according to their materiality and significance. Reporting is not a comprehensive exercise in blame avoidance, but a pointer for the board and management to take action. As with so much risk management activity, there is little point in doing it unless it results in action.

Once internal audit's recommendations are accepted as action points by management, it is then the role of internal audit and the board to monitor whether they are completed satisfactorily and to time. Speed and completeness of clearing audit queries is a powerful key risk indicator for testing that the risk of a poor risk culture is of minimal likelihood.

It is also a good plan for internal audit, apart from its regular reports to audit committee, to report to the board at least annually, not just with an overview of its activities and performance against objectives, but to provide a 'state of the union' message of its view of the state of the risk and control environment within the firm.

The internal auditor as consultant

The IIA definition quoted above states that internal audit, amongst other things, is a 'consulting activity designed to add value and improve an organisation's operations'. Risk management consulting is, of course, far sexier than ticking back-controls and procedures. That's understandable, but not if it means the fundamental job of checking processes is down-graded or, even more seriously, if it provides potential for conflicts of interest.

Having said that, consulting can be a legitimate activity for internal audit where there is no strong risk management function, but it requires careful control. Consulting can:

- make available to management the tools and techniques used in internal audit to analyse risks and controls
- support risk management by leveraging internal audit's expertise in risk management and controls, and its overall knowledge of the organisation (and indeed vice versa)

- support risk management by providing advice and promoting the development of a common language and understanding as part of embedding risk in the firm

- support managers as they work to identify the best way to mitigate their risks.[8]

However, whenever internal audit acts to help management to set up or to improve risk management processes, its plan of work should include a clear strategy and timeline for migrating the responsibility for these services as soon as possible to members of the management team. Advice and support is one thing; taking risk management decisions itself quite another. Even being involved in designing part of the process can lead to significant conflicts for later audits.

Where internal audit does become responsible for some aspect of risk management, it cannot then provide independent assurance for that aspect. This will have to be obtained from a suitably qualified independent third party.

If everybody is satisfied that internal audit's independence will not be compromised and it is asked to undertake work beyond its standard and agreed assurance activities, this should be recognised as a consulting engagement and appropriate terms of engagement agreed.

Investigations

Events continually occur which require investigation and assurance. If the request comes from the chairman of the audit committee or the non-executive directors, there is no risk of internal audit being conflicted.

If, however, the request comes from management, they should seriously consider using their own resources wherever possible, probably from those in an oversight role (i.e. the second line of defence), leaving audit to fulfil its proper role of independent reviewer and assurer.

AUDIT COMMITTEES

The audit committee, comprising as it does independent non-executive directors, performs a key oversight role for the board and should be the critical link between the board and both internal and external audit. In most financial sector firms, there will be a separate risk committee. That was also a key recommendation by Sir David Walker in his report in 2009 on corporate governance issues in UK banks, which was undertaken in response to the financial crisis.[9] However, in many firms, the audit committee fulfils both functions. It therefore acts as a catalyst for improving both oversight and risk management.

Audit committee and internal audit

As we said at the beginning of this chapter, the head of internal audit should report to the chair of the audit committee from a functional point of view (or failing that the senior independent non-executive director) even if, administratively, he or she reports to the CEO or CFO. Given the key role of the audit committee in the audit governance structure, its chairperson should be actively involved in the appointment of a new head of internal audit. The committee should also ensure that the review of the effectiveness of internal audit is truly independent.

It is for the audit committee to agree the internal audit plan and any changes to it. The committee may also wish to consider the extent to which it is able to call on internal audit to perform investigations on its behalf. In all of this, though, it must make sure that the board is kept fully advised of its activities.

For its part, internal audit needs to have a clear understanding of the responsibilities and operation of the audit committee and the expectations of both the committee and its chairperson. In summary, the board, audit committee and internal audit need to have a shared vision for internal audit.

Audit committee and external audit

Here, the audit committee's duties are clearer cut in that it is its job to appoint the external auditors and agree their terms of engagement and fees. Whilst the chairperson of the audit committee does not manage the relationship between the firm and its external auditors, he or she should be fully aware of plans for the audit, its progress and outcomes.

The external auditors' principal point of contact will be the CFO and the point has already been made that the audit committee should be satisfied that there is an appropriate relationship between the auditors and the CFO. It has a duty to ensure that management's processes deliver adequate disclosure, but it must also ensure that the finance function is adequately resourced to fulfil its functions.

An audit committee health check

A last word on oversight. Audit committees are not just about financial reporting and assessing internal controls. Their brief as independent assessors of the quality of risk management also takes them into non-financial risk assessments.

Table 13.2 offers a useful checklist of risks which audit committees should be continually considering in assessing the overall health and tone of the company they serve. Some are what might be termed 'soft' risks for which the indicator is effectively a binary 'yes' or 'no'. If there are more than a very few 'yes' answers, it is likely that the firm is dangerously exposed to risk. For some risks, however, firmer indicators can be established.

Table 13.2

Risks and risk indicators for audit committees

Soft risks	
• Inappropriate tone at the top	
• Autocratic management	
• Inexperienced management	
• Poor management oversight	
• Frequent senior management over-rides	
• Overly complex organisational structures or transactions	
• Lack of transparency in the business model and the purposes of transactions	
• (Late) surprises	
• Unrealistic earnings expectations	
• Exposure to rapid technological changes	
Hard risks	**Risk indicators**
• Unusually rapid growth	• Percentage growth in sales
• Frequent organisational changes	• Number
• High turnover of senior management	• Key staff lost
• Lack of succession plans	• Percentage of divisions/units completed
• Ongoing or prior investigations by regulators or others	• Number
• Untimely reporting and responses to audit committee enquiries	• Number of days
• Industry softness or downturns	• Industry growth/decline from industry reports

Source: Derived from: KPMG Audit Committee Institute, *Shaping the audit committee agenda*, May 2004

EFFECTIVE INTERNAL AUDIT

Given its key role in relation to internal audit, what are the qualities an audit committee chairperson might look for in a new head of internal audit? Given internal audit's position in the no man's land between the business and the non-executive directors, it's a role which requires both diplomacy and courage.

In an article in *Internal Auditing*, its editor, Neil Baker, suggested that the person specification would have at the top of the list:

- integrity: the highest moral and ethical standards

- challenge: at every level

- tenacity: 'stick to your guns' and stay focused

- pragmatism: an open mind and a corporate mind

- independence: strength of character; resilience

- good communicator and ambassador.[10]

Those qualities should, of course, apply equally to the members of the audit team as well as its head, and are probably also valid when appointing a new CRO.

There is an obvious need to be independent and to challenge and, if necessary, keep on challenging. Inevitably, the job involves difficult and contentious issues. Handling them with candour and frankness will generate confidence in the function.

Communication is two-way. It is as important for internal audit to communicate its views effectively, as it is for the business to report to audit its concerns and problems and not wait, in a destructive game, for audit to discover them.

Internal auditing is about continuous improvement, as is suggested in the IIA definition, not merely checking that controls are working. To achieve improvement you have to be a politician and understand both the culture of the organisation and the art of the possible. You need to understand how to gain acceptance for your recommendations – and not rely on some ill-defined threat of whistle blowing.

A key role of the head of internal audit is to build an effective audit team. Ideally, it will come from a diverse talent pool of relatively senior and experienced people. Often, though, that is not possible. Where individuals lack experience, they should be able to make up part of the deficiency through common sense and pragmatism. One of the problems for any audit team is that the people they rely on for information are also the people they are evaluating. They need the skill to ask the right questions and to develop a 'nose' for assessing the answers. Without those skills, the role becomes one of inquisitor rather than constructive critic.

Long outstanding audit queries are a good indicator of the poor quality of risk management in a firm and of its risk culture. They can also be an indicator of the level of respect for the internal audit function, and even of the quality of queries being raised. If it works well, internal audit will gain credibility and respect from the business, who will therefore listen and seek advice from the function, such as when a new project is being considered.

Much of the job is about building awareness of the value which internal audit can bring. The obvious way is in providing the board and management with objective assurance that the risk governance and risk management processes are being operated appropriately and that the internal control framework is operating effectively.

But internal audit can demonstrate its value in an active as well as a passive way. We have referred to internal audit as being a catalyst for continuous improvement within the firm. In addition, people need to be made aware of what it does and how it can help, perhaps through leaflets or the intranet, or simply by networking.

Two of the best ways for people to see the benefits of the function are:

- to second staff to it and
- to make sure that a term in internal audit is seen as a value-adding career move which is remunerated appropriately.

Secondments are particularly useful because, when they end, the secondee will go back into the mainstream operations. That way, audit's knowledge of the organisation is constantly refreshed and the quality of risk management and internal controls will be continuously improved.

That is an excellent way for a good internal audit function to add real value.

Notes

1 See Michael Power, *Organized Uncertainty* (Oxford: OUP), 2009, for further discussion on this point.
2 *Audit and Risk*, 1 September 2011.
3 Sarbanes–Oxley Act 2002, s 201.
4 See www.frc.org.uk/apb for details of the Auditing Practices Board consultation in the UK, October 2009.
5 Derived from *Checklist – Evaluating the external auditor*, KPMG Audit Committee Institute, 2008; www.kpmg.co.uk/aci
6 www.iia.org.uk
7 For further commentary, see *In control: Views of audit committee chairmen on the effectiveness of internal audit*, PricewaterhouseCoopers; www.pwc.co.uk
8 For further discussion, see IIA position paper on internal audit and ERM, January 2009, at www.iia.org
9 Sir David Walker, *A review of corporate governance in UK banks and other financial industry entities*, November 2009; www.hm-treasury.gov.uk
10 Neil Baker, 'Internal auditing and business risk', *Internal Auditing*, January 2006.

PRACTICAL OPERATIONAL RISK MANAGEMENT

Part 5

14

Outsourcing

WHAT IS OUTSOURCING?

Outsourcing is the transfer of selected projects, functions or services and the delegation of day-to-day management responsibility to third-party suppliers. It is not confined to IT, human resource functions or offshore outsourcing. It could involve the transparent transfer of part of the business to a third party, or the transfer of a service, by white-labelling, to a third party, including another member of the same group. It involves all agency arrangements and could be by way of a joint venture.

In all cases, if it is to work effectively, both parties will work as partners. Nearly all aspects of outsourcing risk management, as we shall see, revolve around the need to establish a balanced and fair partnership between the outsourcing client (or buyer) and the service provider.

Although this chapter deals specifically with outsourcing, the principles and management processes apply just as well to any major procurement or third-party dependency, such as the supply chain. Third-party dependency is, in fact, a useful generic term to describe the risk which we accept in any buyer–supplier relationship, of which outsourcing is but one.

OUTSOURCING – TRANSFORMING OPERATIONAL RISK

From the buyer's point of view, outsourcing transforms the risks of managing an activity into one of managing and relying on a third-party provider whose day-to-day actions are outside its direct control. It does not eliminate risk, but it should reduce the original risk by placing its management in the hands of somebody who can manage it better, somebody who can provide access to experienced skills at a reasonable cost.

Many firms are reluctant to relinquish control to a third party. They see that as an unacceptable risk. In part, they probably overestimate the extent to which they are in control of such elements as data security, or have quality IT skills to achieve high performance or to embrace new technology opportunities. However, to reduce risks arising from lack of direct control to acceptable levels, the buyer needs to understand fully the operational risks of the service provider and the effectiveness of their controls because, if things go wrong, the impact will be felt by the buyer and its customers. Whilst day-to-day management responsibility may be delegated to the provider, responsibility for quality and reputation remains firmly with the buyer. In the end, the buck stops there.

In August 2008, Barclays-owned credit card company Goldfish sent out the correct front sheets of monthly statements to its account holders, but enclosed backup sheets relating to other customers. In the same month RBS and NatWest customer data was found being sold on e-Bay. Everybody has heard of the problems at Goldfish and RBS. Few, if any, know the names of the firm which printed the Goldfish statements, or the company which operated RBS's archive centre.

So you cannot outsource responsibility, nor can you outsource reputation risk. If the change you are making through outsourcing is likely to have an effect on your customers, especially during the transition period, you need to have an effective media and employee communications strategy in place, from the time when the decision to outsource is made to when it has been successfully implemented. Effective communication is the best mitigant to reputation risk and also, as we shall see, to ensuring a successfully managed outsourcing project.

In this chapter we shall go through the outsourcing process, identify the key risks at each stage and discuss the actions or controls which need to be in place to reduce them.

DECIDING TO OUTSOURCE

Benefits of outsourcing

When people are asked in surveys what makes a successful outsourcing deal, it is noticeable that cost savings come a long way behind features such as:

- concentrating management on core activities
- achieving higher activity levels
- improving customer service(s) and
- improving financial control.

All of these help to improve the buyer's competitive advantage, something which should be a fundamental test of whether to outsource or not.

Outsourcing makes business sense by improving both the speed and quality of customer service. A service provider may, for instance, be able to handle a variety of resource-consuming compliance tasks more cost-effectively, and free the buyer's staff to concentrate on a major systems project.

In the best deals, where there is a true partnership, the buyer passes on expertise derived from its strengths and the supplier is proactive in coming to the buyer with innovative ideas. New products can come to market more quickly.

At a higher level, outsourcing can be a force for cultural change if it is part of the transformation to a differently shaped and focused organisation. It can also help in a merger, when it is often difficult to combine two infrastructure cultures. Basing the future infrastructure on a third-party provider can remove the problem and take it outside the politics. Outsourcing can thus be a major force for changing and transforming the operational risk environment.

It's not about cutting costs

So the decision to outsource should be made on good business grounds, looking at the overall value outsourcing can bring, and not solely, or even primarily, on grounds of saving costs or improving return on investment. In 2007, Compass published a survey of 240 large IT outsourcing deals which showed that 65% unravelled before their term because they did not deliver anticipated cost savings.[1] That was often because of the unrealistic pressure by clients on providers to deliver a service at prices which were unsustainable in the long term.[2]

There should, of course, be appreciable cashflow benefits in outsourcing, but if cost-cutting is the primary driver for deciding to outsource, the chances are that the outsourcing project will be a failure. Cost reduction on its own brings little sustainable business advantage. In any case, the cost savings can often be seductively more apparent than real. The Compass survey also showed that although outsourcing providers were pricing contracts at a level which showed immediate cost savings of up to 18% on the in-house operation being replaced, costs then increased to an average of 30% above the original in-house cost by year three of the contract. What is cheap is usually dear.

One of the biggest risks in deciding whether to outsource or not is to fail to assess the true costs of the activity as it is currently run, and the costs, both financial and non-financial, when it is outsourced. Without proper information on costs, you run the serious risk of making the wrong decision in principle and of not assessing potential service providers against a robust benchmark.

When considering outsourcing, ask yourself whether you have allowed fully at the outset for the costs of:

- the activity in-house, including premises and supporting infrastructure
- start-up and the transition to the service provider
- ongoing management and monitoring of the contract, especially if the outsource provider is offshore
- contingency plans if something should go wrong
- maintaining sufficient resource in staff and infrastructure to enable you to take the activity back in-house should the contract be terminated.

If cost reduction is the priority, it tends to build short-term relationships that cannot stand the test of time. You may have got a good deal at the outset, but that could be because you squeezed your provider unduly, and you will suffer when things go wrong at their end. They will feel little commitment to helping you with what is your problem as much as theirs.

But there are positive aspects to outsourcing and cashflow. For instance, outsourcing should mean that future costs are more certain, which will help with planning and pricing. Outsourcing can also bring flexibility, by turning fixed costs into variable costs and freeing up capital which would otherwise have to be invested in non-core activities or large investment projects. The service provider has already invested in the necessary process and can provide the benefits of infrastructure and economies of scale. Even more positively, on the question of cash, outsourcing may bring a cash infusion, if the provider buys assets such as hardware or software, or increased opportunities for revenue generation.

Cash benefits such as these are positive reasons to outsource. Cash benefits based on cost-cutting are not.

High-level principles and policy for outsourcing

A fundamental part of outsourcing risk governance is for the board, as with any other major risk or control issue, to agree the principles and policy which will govern outsourcing within the firm. The board, after all, retains responsibility for the policy, and ultimate responsibility for activities undertaken under that policy. The policy should also outline:

- the principles to be followed in deciding whether to outsource and the internal approval process
- how outsourcing projects are to be managed, including requirements for defining aims and objectives, risk assessments, the assessment and selection process, reliance on and dealings with sub-contractors, contractual terms and conditions, change management protocols and ongoing service monitoring
- the governance arrangements which should apply.

Deciding what to outsource

Once the policy and process are established, you can consider possible functions or activities as candidates for outsourcing. The best approach is to work on the basis that the company you outsource to will do it better than you can or that they can do something which you cannot do.

At the level of a small firm, that may, for instance, mean outsourcing areas which are subject to changing legislation, such as tax or accounting, because that is what the outsourcing firm is expert at. In this way the firm can reduce its risks and save the costs of somebody internally who is probably not able to keep as up to date as a professional firm whose reputation depends on having that knowledge. Another example for a small firm is where it is able to share state of the art technology which it could not otherwise afford, so that outsourcing brings competitive advantage as well as a saving in costs.

Whatever activity is outsourced, there are three golden rules:

- Don't try to outsource a problem. The outsourcer can't sort out your mess. Only you can do that.

- Talk to the business. It's the business's needs which are paramount, not those of procurement.

- Never outsource whatever gives you competitive advantage, i.e. the function which is so core to your business that you need to control it directly to ensure your continuing competitiveness.

Leaving aside the cynics who say that 'core' is the part of the business you can't sell, what is 'core' will vary from firm to firm. Does 'core' mean 'strategic'? If so, what is truly 'strategic'?

In 1996, British Airways, which has always been an aggressive outsourcer, was highly successful in outsourcing its customer correspondence function from the UK to India. Some 2000 jobs were outsourced but only two redundancies resulted in the UK as staff were redeployed to higher-value, less mundane, jobs. What is more, the function was more efficiently handled in India and customer satisfaction rose.[3] Following this, in 2001, the company declared its intention to be a 'virtual' company, with its aircraft leasing, maintenance, ground handling, ticketing, IT, website, in-flight staff and even its pilot staffing being outsourced. That just about left only the brand.

Similarly, Coca-Cola does not make Coke. It markets it and looks after advertising and strategy, but most of the product is produced under licence by bottling companies around the world. And Virgin merely badges the financial services and mobile phone activities which bear its name. Perhaps managing the brand and reputation is the real core activity, along with managing the outsourcing contracts, which replace the previous core activity for these firms of managing a large number of people.

But it is not just activities which are core. Some *risks* are so 'core' that they also should not be outsourced. The Potters Bar rail crash, just north of London, was a salutary lesson.

Case study   **Railtrack – the Potters Bar train crash (2002)**

Railtrack, the group of companies which owned the track, signalling and stations of the British railway system, was privatised in 1996. After two serious crashes in 1999 and 2000 it failed to raise necessary funding of £700m and was placed into administration in October 2001. It was sold in October 2002 to Network Rail, a not-for-dividend company.

In May 2002, 7 people were killed and 70 injured when a faulty track caused a passenger train to be de-railed. Railtrack, which was responsible for the line, had outsourced its maintenance to Jarvis. Shortly before the crash, Jarvis employees had passed the track as meeting relevant safety standards. Railtrack had therefore outsourced safety which, given its history, might have been assumed to be one of its key risks and core activities.

In May 2011, Network Rail was fined £3m after admitting breaches of safety regulations and being criminally guilty under the Health and Safety at Work Act.

THE OUTSOURCING PROJECT – GETTING IT RIGHT AT THE START

Two of the biggest risks in outsourcing projects are:

- not having clearly defined goals and objectives; and
- not planning properly.

Since risks are threats to objectives, it is difficult to identify risks to the project if clear objectives have not been set. Failing to set clear goals and objectives is therefore a major risk in itself.

Too often projects go wrong because unrealistic timelines have been set at each stage of the project. Or there is poor planning on the timing of the transition to the service provider and, importantly, on the effect the outsourcing arrangement will have on employees and processes in other parts of the organisation, and on areas of risk, including environmental and regulatory factors.

Once the decision has been made to outsource, the key to minimising failure is preparation:

- set objectives for the project
- understand the scope of what is to be outsourced
- be clear about the benefits you are trying to obtain
- appoint a project team who will have day-to-day responsibility to run the process and deliver a workable outsourcing solution
- use your risk management system to manage the process and re-assess the risks at every stage.

If you have agreed principles on how to manage the outsourcing process, you will manage the outsourcing risks effectively.

RISK ASSESSMENT

Once you have decided to outsource and have established a project team, the next stage is to undertake a full risk assessment and identify the threats to successful implementation. Initially, you need to undertake three risk assessments:

1. as you are today
2. the project itself
3. where you want to be.

Risk assessments 2 and 3 will help to frame the request for proposal (RFP), the criteria for selecting the provider and, most importantly, the service level agreement (SLA).

Risk assessments 2 and 3 will then be reviewed at each critical stage of the project. When the SLA is signed, the provider should provide its own risk assessment (4) and agree indicators by which risks are to be monitored. During the transition period, a further assessment should be undertaken (5), but this time jointly with the provider. It is at this point that real knowledge transfer can take place in both directions.

To put it diagrammatically:

	Goals ➔	RFI ➔	RFP ➔	Shortlist ➔	Site visits ➔	Selection ➔	SLA signing ➔	Transition
1								
2								
3								
4								
5								

Source: Courtesy of Chase Cooper Limited

To make sure the risk assessment process for the project (2 and 3) is as comprehensive as possible, involve everybody who may be affected. That will include HR, legal, PR, finance, procurement, those whose functions are being considered for outsourcing, and those who will interact with the function once it is outsourced – and of course, risk management. If you have previous experience of outsourcing, draw on it. If this is the first time, remember that fact when you consider the risks you will face. Outsourcing will produce new risks at each stage of the project, especially when the project has gone live and you have little day-to-day control. Here are a few:

■ service delivery falls below expectation
■ confidentiality and security are not respected
■ contract is too rigid to accommodate change
■ failure to devote enough time and energy to managing the relationship
■ failure to provide sufficient resources in-house to safeguard the outsourced business processes
■ inadequate contingency planning by the provider

- management changes at the outsourcing company – a frequent problem which affects both performance and communication
- the outsourcing company goes out of business.

As you consider these new risks, remember that a key mitigant is communication, both with the service provider and especially with your employees. Communicate openly with them at every stage. Not only will this mean that you get the best out of the outsourcing project, but you will understand and be able to document the consequences for those who will be affected – a fundamental part of the decision to outsource.

SOME TIPS ON THE REQUEST FOR PROPOSAL

The first step towards the RFP is the request for information (RFI). This should go out to as wide a field as possible, not just to the usual suspects and one or two others whom you have picked up through anecdote or hearsay. You are trying to narrow the field from as many of the available candidates as possible.

The goals and objectives which led you to outsource will point to your outsourcing needs and form the basis of your selection criteria. Those objectives and needs should have been agreed with the business rather than procurement. It is the need, not the document, which matters. Remember golden rule 2 – talk to the business. That also means that you should be careful not to prescribe the solution and make the RFP too tight. If a benefit of outsourcing is to bring in expertise which you lack, get the most out of the relationship and be open-minded about how your needs can best be met.

The risk assessment of the activity to be outsourced will guide you to what is required in the RFP. The RFP will deal with the specifics which go into the service level agreement (see Some tips on service level agreements below), but it will also provide the information with which to identify:

- the management capability and resources of the provider
- how the provider handles relationship management
- processes for reporting and quality monitoring
- training requirements – on both sides
- technology requirements – and future scalability
- the transition timetable and resources needed during this period
- governance issues, to establish that the service provider shares your values.

The RFP establishes expectations and further qualifies providers on the shortlist. Because clarity is essential, use quantitative rather than qualitative criteria wherever possible. And don't underestimate the work which will still be undertaken in your firm. The RFP should lead to as clear a matrix of risk and other responsibilities as between you and the provider.

If the RFP has been framed well, it should ensure that you are able to narrow the selection down to a small, manageable number of genuine and acceptable candidates.

SELECTING THE PROVIDER

The worst risk of all in outsourcing is to choose the wrong partner. The approach must be commercial rather than personal. The risks of poor selection will be enhanced if you do not put enough resource into it, including having a variety of perspectives and the appropriate skills to manage the process effectively.

Assessment and evaluation

Just as the decision to outsource should not be based on cost saving, so the selection of a provider should not be based on whoever provides the cheapest deal. To ensure that the process is objective and properly competitive, you need to put together an evaluation scorecard based on your goals and objectives in choosing to outsource. The scoring need not be hugely sophisticated. It could be as simple as first looking at your requirements and assessing them as being:

- vital
- necessary
- nice to have.

and then scoring the providers on the basis of:

- does not meet requirements
- meets requirements
- exceeds requirements.

In many ways, it is relatively easy to assess the 'hard' criteria, such as the financial, legal, contractual, performance and even regulatory risks. What is more difficult is assessing the 'soft' criteria, the ones which are fundamental to successful outsourcing – cultural fit, leadership, people, communication and innovation.

The RFP should have provided much of the information. But it needs to be tested by using channels such as the Web, trade press and expert advice, as well as the customer references which will have been provided. How well is the provider recognised within its industry? What are its strengths? How good is it at dealing with problems? What is its track record of service commitment?

Above all, visit each potential provider on the shortlist. You are in it for the long term, so don't skimp on your due diligence. Person-to-person is the only sensible way of assessing the critical 'soft' criteria. At a practical level, use your subject experts, not your sourcing or procurement executives, to check IT systems and equipment, management processes or quality assurance procedures. If the provider is overseas and it is difficult to visit them at this stage, meet and take references from existing users in your own country. But that should be a last resort.

Statements made by the provider have got to be tested and verified. What is the detailed breakdown of staff retention and turnover? Precisely how do they track customer satisfaction? How will they make sure you have the right resource when you want it? How do their sales people talk to their delivery people?

Providers often quote data such as revenue earned from top clients or utilisation rates (staff efficiency). But these are almost impossible to verify, without perhaps hiring an independent investigator, something which the Satyam case brought home in January 2009.

Satyam Computer Services (2009) — Case study

Satyam was India's fourth largest software group and one of its biggest outsourcing companies, counting more than one-third of Fortune 500 companies amongst its clients. In January 2009, following disclosures in a public letter from its founder and chairman Ramalinga Raju, it emerged that it had overstated its financial results by more than $1bn over several years. In addition, it had inflated the number of employees by more than 25% (from 40,000 to 53,000) and siphoned off their salaries to companies over which Raju had control. Together with other fraudulent activities which had allegedly benefited the chairman and others, the Indian Central Bureau of Investigation estimated in November 2009 that the fraud amounted to more than US$2.6bn.

In April 2011, the company and its auditors, affiliates of PricewaterhouseCooper (PwC) India, accepted fines totalling $1.6m from the SEC. The PwC affiliates also agreed to pay penalites of $1.5m to PCAOB. A criminal trial is under way in India.

Source: Based on 'Scale of Satyam fraud escalates ahead of trial' by Rhys Blakely, *The Times*, 27 November 2009, p. 77; *SEC digest*, 5 April 2011.

Commenting in the *Financial Times* on the Satyam case, Ashutosh Gupta, a Vice President of research firm Evalueserve, said: 'Smart companies are already hiring investigative companies to poke around and ask difficult questions and we'll see more doing so.'[4]

Capability and competence

It is assumed that the provider can deliver functionality, otherwise how did they get on the shortlist? The important thing is the quality of service provided – *how* they will do the job, not *whether* they can handle a specified number of transactions in a particular time-frame.

In most outsourcing contracts, quality – and therefore risk – depends not on systems capability but on the people who are managing the process and the people who interface with your customers. Management change at the outsourcing company is a frequent problem which affects both performance and communication. It may be that certain individuals are critical to the process or interface. If so, one control can be to insist that they are retained in their role and that you, as client, have the right to approve substitutes if they have to be moved or are absent. Consistency of the quality of service delivery is critical to your reputation.

Pricing

Pricing is another key risk. Is there sufficient transparency in the supplier's pricing structure to ensure that you obtain the best value for money? Is there absolute clarity about fixed, upgrade and ongoing costs and their basis? Have price escalators or volume-related costs been fully factored in? They may be differently priced from the base standard. What about training costs and pass-through items? We noted earlier (see It's not about cutting costs) how final costs can far outstrip those imagined when the contract is awarded.

If an outsourcing arrangement is not set up well and managed carefully, it is not uncommon to find that incremental add-ons can increase the original costs by as much as 50%. So do the analysis thoroughly and then stretch the results through various activity scenarios. That should point you to the true costs – and the true cost savings.

Data security

One risk which looms large in financial services, but also in other sectors such as healthcare, is that confidentiality and security is not respected. What guarantees can the provider give about data security and information relating to your customers? What security measures do they have? Do they subscribe to and are audited against industry and, if appropriate, international standards? Consider whether you need to run checks on their staff. That may be where independent investigators reappear.

The chain of dependency

And just as they are going to be a third-party dependency risk for you, on whom do they depend? Will they be doing everything themselves, be in a partnership or rely on other suppliers?

The Gate Gourmet case at Heathrow in August 2005 provided a further slant on the question of dependency.

British Airways and Gate Gourmet (2005)

Case study

In August 2005, Gate Gourmet, to whom British Airways had outsourced its in-flight catering in 1997, sacked 650 staff who had stopped work to hold a canteen meeting in protest at a restructuring. With that, 1000 British Airways staff at Heathrow, including baggage handlers and other ground staff, came out on strike in sympathy. It then transpired that many of them, as well as being in the same trade union, were related to the Gate Gourmet workers. The strike forced BA to ground all its aircraft at Heathrow for over 24 hours. As a result it lost 700 flights and over £30m.

BA had failed to understand and make allowance for the links between Gate Gourmet staff and their baggage handlers.

If there is going to be any sub-contracting, the same checks and requirements apply as were applied to the primary provider. Any significant or material sub-contractor should be subject to approval by the buyer – on the assumption that the definitions of 'significant' or 'material' have been clearly documented.

Compatibility and culture

Above all, you need to establish that your chosen provider shares your values and buys in to your vision and beliefs. They are partners, as much as they are providers, and only common values can build a sustainable relationship. Trust is critical. You do not want to be exposed to a service provider which may behave opportunistically and steal IP or provide fewer staff than required or staff without the requisite skills. That is one of the reasons why site visits, involving your experts, are so important. Apart from anything else, if you don't make a site visit – or several – you won't meet the people with whom you are going to be dealing, only the people negotiating the contract.

You need to know that you can work together as a team; that your people, at each level, will get on with theirs. Are they open, sincere and positive? Do they fully understand your needs? Are they focused on continuous improvement and willing to share with you the outcome of their efforts? Since one of your risks is probably the danger of falling behind the curve of industry innovation, it may be worth negotiating incentives for the provider to allow you to access improvements in service delivery.

The process also has to fit. That applies as much to decision processes and management structures as to the points of interaction between the two firms; the frequency of formal interactions; the process for escalating performance or problem issues. One of the lessons of the Gate Gourmet case was that the unofficial employee power structures rendered Gate Gourmet's management powerless and impotent.

Overall, assessing compatibility is an intuitive, rather than an analytical process, but a scorecard approach, based on your strategic and risk assessments, will be a great help. The risk is that judgements, which are inevitably subjective, become clouded by personal feelings. As a result, whilst compatibility is fundamental to selection, you may be wary of assigning it too high a percentage of the overall score, probably no more than 30%.

To reduce the risk that emotion and dominant personalities have too great a bearing on the final choice, it is best if each member of the assessment team makes their assessment independently. Then the various scores are added together, rather than allowing one dominant member to exert undue influence.

One final risk consideration – size matters. How important are you to them? Unless you are a big player, the 80–20 rule will apply and it is likely that you represent only a relatively small fraction of the provider's income and therefore attention. If you are the smaller party you must be prepared to be aggressive in getting top-table attention to make sure your needs are not relegated in the priority stakes. On the other hand, you do not want to be in a position where they depend on you. If you are, you run the risk of relying on a provider which has an inherently unstable business model. The trick is to be big enough in the provider's eyes, but not too big. All of this needs to be explored during your due diligence. And of course, the situation is dynamic. You need to monitor their take-up of new clients and regularly re-assess your relative position with the provider during the term of the contract.

Commercial soundness and sustainability

This is a long-term relationship which is going to have a major impact on your reputation. We have already mentioned the provider's functional capability to provide a service over time, especially if your requirements grow. Considering whether the provider will be there in the long term is an important part of the overall assessment.

One element of that is, of course, the financial due diligence you will have undertaken on the providers you are considering. Since outsourcing is very often driven initially by an investment funding or cost need, the provider must have the strength of a sustainable cash flow to offer the required performance over time and the ability to provide the investment required to meet present and future needs. It is therefore important to ask about competing resource needs and how the provider might handle future needs, if they are successful.

This can be part of a strategic visioning session with prospective service providers looking at where you each expect to be in three or five years' time. It also provides an opportunity to consider whether their processes are scalable to the level you have in mind – and beyond. Sustainability is not just about cash but about intangibles, such as position in the market and the ability of the provider to change with changing market requirements. The visioning sessions will help you to understand better the provider's ability to change with the market.

A final pointer to sustainability is the provider's governance structure. What are their internal management practices? What is the quality and importance (to them) of their risk management? What is the structure of their board and audit committee and other functions? Is there a strong institutional investor, which may bring a degree of capital support as well as expertise to their board? The key to a sustainable business is sound risk governance.

SOME TIPS ON SERVICE LEVEL AGREEMENTS

Having made your selection, it is now time to turn to the contract which will govern your future relationship, the SLA. It is your fundamental risk control. It will specify the regular reporting you require of risk and control assessments, relevant key risk indicators and key control indicators. It will also detail the reports you require of incidents and losses, not just those which are for your account, but also those for which the provider is responsible and has suffered the cost.

When you are negotiating the SLA, take a risk-based view of contract development. You will have undertaken a risk assessment, which will have included assumptions about who owns which risks. It is now time to be upfront about the risks you are trying to mitigate and agree a risk ownership matrix. As we have said so often, clarity of roles and responsibilities is a critical element of good operational risk management.

Another tip is to agree the operational details before you get to the legal ones. This is a partnership after all. If you can agree operational and risk issues before you draw up the legal document, you will avoid the risk of undue entanglement with lawyers and legal jargon, and achieve a mutually beneficial deal in a shorter time-frame which you can both sign up to.

Be strong. You have been through all the analysis and assessment. You know what you want and why, so don't allow a provider to dictate what you will receive. Get what you want, which is, after all, what you need. Above all, do not agree to finalise the scope, price or service levels *after* contract signature, or enter into an agreement which relies on benchmarking to keep the supplier 'honest'.

The contract is the deal. What is written down and signed is the service you will receive for the next three to five years, so make sure it is what you want and that as far as possible it is absolutely clear.

When you look at what an SLA typically contains, you will see that practically every clause represents some form of risk control covering the elements of risk management we discuss in this chapter. Table 14.1 shows some typical headlines.

| Table 14.1 | **Contents of a typical service level agreement** |

1. Nature and scope of service	Including all pertinent parameters of agreement such as parties involved, duration, etc.
2. Division of responsibilities over all aspects	
3. Service continuity expectations	Including service availability through business continuity incidents and exclusivity agreements to protect access to outsourced resources
4. Commercial/financial terms	Including freedom of provider to raise fees and penalties for poor performance
5. Metrics on expected level of performance, appropriate to activity	
6. Performance review process	
7. Reporting of performance	Including risk and control assessments, key indicators, incidents and issues
8. Issue escalation process	Including dispute resolution procedures; contingency plans for performance failures
9. Guidelines on accessibility of information for auditing purposes	Including internal and external auditors and regulators, if appropriate.
10. Confidentiality/non-disclosure/ security expectations	Including data protection, systems security and information ownership rights
11. Change control protocols	
12. Exit strategy	Including transition to another managed service

Source: Courtesy of Chase Cooper Limited

Finally, having done your best to achieve an SLA which covers all your needs, avoid over-reliance on it. It is just possible that the provider may be meeting agreed service levels, but the contract is not successful because the wrong things are being measured. Your dashboards are always green, but your customers or staff are seeing red. Be prepared to go back to the table. To help that happen, you need to make sure that the agreement allows for flexibility and is not so rigid that it precludes change. If you are working with a real partner that will not be difficult. After all, both sides want this to work long term.

MANAGING THE PROJECT

Governance

Governance provides the set of guidelines for the relationship and a forum for dealing with legal and service issues. Effective governance will help to ensure that the provider delivers on what they have promised over the lifetime of the agreement. Absence of strong governance results in a lack of clarity about the goals and results of the outsourcing.

As governance typically costs between 3% and 6% of contract value, at the higher end at start-up and lower over time, make sure it is included in the original costings.[5] It is not a peripheral activity.

The governance team

A frequent source of outsourcing failure is that not enough time and energy is given to managing the relationship. Governance of outsourcing operates at many levels – at executive or board level; at project governance level; and within the in-house and provider's own business process teams.

The key to good governance is a good governance team of high-level executives from both organisations who communicate regularly about what is working and what is not. Ideally, outsourcing governance teams should include people with hands-on experience of managing a service provider relationship, and people who understand the needs of the buyer organisation within the context of outsourcing. There must also be somebody expert in the area being outsourced, and representatives from areas such as finance, legal and, if you have them, procurement or (out)sourcing. And especially somebody from operational risk management.

If you have a sourcing or similar department managing all outsourced activities as a portfolio, you will have effectively created an outsourcing centre of excellence which can be used to leverage best practices. Outsourcing requires different types of expertise in its management, so use all the information that is available.

The important thing, though, both within the project and within the firms concerned, is communication and putting in place a full communication plan. Within the project team this will ensure that issues are escalated as appropriate. It will also mean that lessons learnt from monitoring and reporting are fed into the change management process and acted upon.

Within the buyer's firm, good communication should ensure that staff, especially those directly affected, are aware of the reasons why a particular process is being outsourced and the benefits to be gained. As we point out in Chapter 15, Culture and people risk, failure to communicate with staff effectively leads to damaging gossip, rumour and loss of morale. Make sure staff who are being retained know that as soon as possible. As we also point out in that chapter and elsewhere, the key to good management, whether operational risk management or otherwise, is trust.

If the people who are going to be directly affected are brought into the process they can act as a risk mitigant in that their feedback may point to costs or processes which have been overlooked in the financial and risk assessments. And, on the basis that the outsourcing will only be successful if in-house staff are working efficiently, it should reduce middle-management resistance which can drain the project of many of its intended benefits.

Finally, on a staffing point, try to keep people around who were involved in the negotiations. However clear you believe the SLA is, people and circumstances change. It is always helpful to have people available who knew the intent and thinking behind the transaction.

The transition process

The actual transition to the provider is, of course, a high-risk point in the whole project. That risk will be dramatically reduced if the transition works smoothly, which it will if it is well planned and rehearsed. Another problem at transition is that too often unrealistic expectations are placed on the provider, both on the 'go-live' date and in the months immediately following, and are reflected in the expectations of the client's executive management. Be reasonable and realistic and try to ensure there are no surprises. Good communication should help to manage those expectations and act as a risk control mechanism.

The transition is one of the elements which should be explicit in the selection process. Does the partner use a similar project methodology? A smooth transition is what you are aiming for; a troubled transition will cause immediate pain and cost. To smooth the process and reduce the risk both at transition and in the future, it may be a good idea for some of your staff to work in the provider's workplace and to second your staff to the provider as the contract continues. This will ensure that one of your vital controls – the ability to bring the process back in-house if necessary – will have a greater chance of success. That kind of partnership will also make it less likely that you will have to.

Monitoring and reporting

The first thing to bear in mind when considering performance assessment is that you must retain staff with the necessary expertise to supervise and monitor the outsourced activity and provider. The gain of enhanced performance through outsourcing will often lead to the loss of in-house expertise. You cannot allow it also to lead to the loss of your ability to assess performance.

As well as the regular performance reviews – which may be on a daily basis at first and probably weekly or monthly thereafter – allowance has to be made for external and internal auditors to perform their own assessments. But whatever the source, whether it's a performance or audit assessment, document and agree the results promptly and regularly within the governance team. That is your control mechanism for making sure that necessary improvements are made. It is also the process which leads to amendments to the contract, perhaps every quarter, to reflect accumulated changes.

Reporting and monitoring should be risk-based. As we said earlier in Some tips on service level agreements, the provider should be providing regular risk and control assessments, and action tracking of risk indicators, controls, incidents and losses. An integral part of monitoring performance is regularly to reassess the risks within the relationship – at both management and operational level. And, of course, you should constantly monitor the deal against the original objectives in order to check that the transaction continues to meet your requirements, which may themselves change over time.

Finally, if the provider is not carrying out functions effectively or in compliance with regulatory requirements, you must be able to take *action* and put things right. You will have rights of action within the SLA, but you must also have in place an effective and regularly tested contingency plan to cope with major disruptions or process failures (see Chapter 11, Business continuity).

Change

All outsourcing contracts will change. They are never static. After all, the contract is probably for three to five years or longer. That does not mean jumping about and over-reacting in month 1. No outsourced operation is perfect from the start. There will be an efficiency dip in the first two to three months, through inexperience and the additional checking required initially. After that, regular monitoring should point to any aspects which require debate and, if necessary, a change in the contract.

The governance team must be able to deal with change throughout the life of the contract. Change control protocols are the administrative side of that. They will form part of a 'ways of working' document, agreed at the outset, which will also clearly state the goals and expectations of performance reporting and assessment. The human side is that the team should be composed of people who are open-minded and not wedded to the old ways of doing things.

Changes could relate to performance. But they could equally be about differences of interpretation or changes in the environment for either buyer or provider. So keep both the relationship and the contract up to date and make sure the contract works for both parties and is flexible enough to cater for change.

Above all, document, document, document – throughout the duration of the contract and immediately an event happens or a meeting takes place.

Offshoring

Because outsourcing is a partnership, there needs to be full collaboration between buyer and service provider. That can be a particular challenge where collaboration has to be with an offshore team, probably working within a different culture and with a different legal, political, regulatory and socio-economic environment.

To make offshore outsourcing work as effectively as possible, you should first make sure that you have a high-quality local leader for the offshore team. If you can then blend the offshore team with effective onshore specialists, the benefits will be considerable and the risks much lower.

Part of that blending process is training. To be most effective, train the offshore team at the home office first, so that they can become trainers and leaders offshore. They will understand and be able to transmit your values and culture – and, of course, the training will give you a chance to understand theirs. The more onshore people you can involve, the better. The whole team will become ambassadors for the project and make it work.

Partnering in this way will also help to overcome the linguistic and cultural barriers and risks which are all part of offshore outsourcing. People risks such as these are a major element of offshore outsourcing and, apart from language risk (both with the provider and involving local laws and professionals), can include: different HR and employment law requirements; poor communications; different data protection requirements; or different ethical standards regarding bribery and corruption. Many firms have suffered reputational damage when it has emerged that their expensive products have been produced by 'sweatshop' labour. You need to establish in your SLA the standards you expect. In the case of data security, that may be related to international standards, such as those published by BITS or ISO 27001. In other cases you must spell out precisely what your standards are and then make sure that monitoring them is part of your regular monitoring and auditing process.

Finally, and inevitably when considering offshore outsourcing, there is currency risk. In 2008, for instance, the Indian rupee depreciated by over 23% against the US dollar. Since most contracts with firms dealing in the dollar would have been fixed in dollars, that represented a significant additional profit to the Indian provider. Of course, that could work the other way, so where contracts involve volatile currencies – and which currency is not volatile, including the US dollar – one answer may be to include a clause which shares profits arising purely from currency movements above a certain percentage.

EXIT STRATEGY

The SLA will provide for contingency plans to cope with serious problems which arise during the term of a contract. However, there will be times when the contract has to be terminated. There can be many reasons why it may be necessary to exit the contract. Failure of the provider or failure to deliver to the required standard or quality are the most obvious reasons. Action by the provider which causes reputational damage can be another. Less easy to predict – but something which should be monitored as part of regular risk reassessments – is the acquisition of the provider by a company which then either sells it on or merges it with another within the group. That could well justify and require breaking the contract and bringing a process in-house.

Within financial services it is a regulatory requirement that a firm should be able to bring any outsourced activity back in-house. That means, as we have seen above, maintaining appropriate resources, both trained people and infrastructure, and having a clear plan to enable them rapidly to assume the outsourced function. But all sectors must think about their exit strategy. If you do not, you face the risks of becoming dependent on the provider, of losing your negotiating power and of finding it difficult to move elsewhere.

You should also be able to exit for your own reasons and terminate with reasonable notice under softer conditions than those resulting from breaches of the contract by the service provider. That means being clear at the outset, and in the contract, about:

- the circumstances under which the contract may be terminated
- how the activity can be brought back in-house (or passed on to a third party)

- who owns what assets and
- when compensation is due.

Above all, outsourcing is a partnership. If you have managed the relationship as well as you should, even termination can be a collaborative operation.

Notes

1   www.computerweekly.com, 17 April 2007.
2   John-Paul Kamath, *Outsourcing 'derailed by focus on ROI'*, www.computerweekly.com, April 2007.
3   Elizabeth Knight, 'Myths on outsourcing – week 2', www.articlesbase.com
4   Joe Leahy and James Fontanella-Khan, 'Outsourcing clients on the lookout for red flags', *Financial Times*, 22 January 2009.
5   Bob Violino, 'Outsourcing governance: A success story', www.outsourcing.com, 21 March 2008; see also, same date and source, 'Governance: A key to outsourcing success', also by Bob Violino, whose guidance is gratefully acknowledged.

Culture and people risk

WHY IT'S ALL ABOUT PEOPLE

When it comes down to it, most operational risks are ultimately the result of 'people' failure, whether at a strategic, managerial or operational level. 'Our people are our greatest asset', we read at the end of the Chairman's or CEO's statement in the annual Report and Accounts. True. But just as risk is as much about opportunities as threats, so our people are also our greatest potential liability. Yet firms rarely consider people risk management as *the* key element of their overall risk management.

There are two sides to people risk: employees and their managers. Take employees first. People are essentially honest; they do not come to work to defraud or to cause disruption. However, leaving aside risk factors such as individuals' lack of competence, training and experience, there are many aspects of their personal or domestic environment which will affect their reliability from day to day, or even from minute to minute. Times of personal stress – bereavement, relationship break-up, health problems, threats to income (many of which feed off each other) – lead to behaviour, even criminal behaviour, which would be out of character in stable times. Because people's personal circumstances change from day to day, assessing exposure to people risk is difficult. The skill is to manage effectively, rather than to assess accurately, which brings us to the other side of people risk – managers.

People risk is as often caused by poor management and organisation within the workplace: lack of clarity about what needs to be done; too little time to fulfil tasks; too many tasks; the complexity of tasks and work processes; lack of support from colleagues or technology; unreasonable managers. All of these add to stress and unreliability and increase risk. They are symptomatic of an organisation which doesn't rate people management as a priority.

We accept that our employees are not going to be with us 'from cradle to grave'. As Charles Handy has put it: 'Organisations are never again going to stockpile people. The employee society is on the wane.'[1] But we need to ensure that we retain the best people and that all perform to their best ability. If we can create the right environment to achieve that, we will at the same time considerably minimise our people risks.

HOW TO EMBED A HEALTHY OPERATIONAL RISK CULTURE

What do we mean by a risk culture?

Creating the right environment is essentially about creating the right culture. In simple terms culture is 'the way we decide to do things round here'. Not just 'the way we do things' but 'the way we *decide* to do things'. In respect of risk culture, it has been defined as:

> The shared beliefs and assumptions concerning risk and risk management **Definition** which affect and are affected by an organisation's risk-taking and control decisions, and with the outcomes of those decisions.
>
> Source: Institute of Operational Risk

Ultimately, culture is a function of individual behaviours. And since 'no man is an island', as poet and preacher John Donne once said,[2] so our behaviours will be influenced by good examples from the people around us, whether our family, friends or even the football crowd. In a work context, our behaviour will be influenced by our colleagues and actual business practice. Organisational behaviours will themselves be influenced by customers, competitors and other stakeholders. It is similar to the way we manage stakeholders' expectations when we consider reputation risk (see Chapter 16, Reputation risk, A framework for reputation risk management).

The important thing is that those values and behaviours are so ingrained that they lead us to do the right thing even when no one is looking.[3] Before we look at how to make sure that happens, let's first look at why risk culture matters.

Why risk culture matters

Culture is primarily about values and behaviours. And values drive value. Professor Roger Steare, Professor of Organisational Ethics at Cass Business School, has said that 'Business is in the game of making money, but it won't make money for long unless it understands *how* it wishes to make money.'[4] Organisations which do well over time are clear about their purpose: everybody understands why they're there, how they should behave, where they've got to get to and how they're going to get there.[5] A good culture leads to good decision making which is, after all, the main purpose and benefit of risk management (see Chapter 2, The business case for operational risk management).

Your corporate culture is akin to your DNA and is one of the main attributes which gives you competitive advantage. Your technology and your products can be copied, but not your culture.[5]

Like onions, firms which have an unhealthy risk culture go bad from the inside. That is well understood by boards and senior managers. They understand the link between lapses of ethical behaviour and loss of reputation, but it is surprising how little attention is paid by them to the sources of behavioural risk and therefore how to prevent serious damage to reputation.

Indeed, few boards discuss standards of behaviour, codes of conduct or ethical training, let alone undertake it themselves.

The lesson should have at least come home to the financial services industry following the banking crisis of 2007–9. In January 2011 the US Congressional report on the crisis was published. Its key conclusions were that the crisis was avoidable and that one of the primary causes was a 'systemic breakdown of accountability and ethics'.[6] Effectively, a breakdown of operational risk management. Instilling and maintaining a proper risk culture would have avoided much of the subsequent pain.

Getting the culture right is also important when it comes to mergers. A huge percentage of mergers fail to achieve their, often publicly, stated objectives. That is probably because the merged board concentrates on financial aspects, synergies and headcounts, instead of first establishing what the culture of the new firm is going to be. Once that has happened, there is a clear context for strategic and management decisions, not least about risk.

So concentrating on corporate culture, and especially risk culture, is important in preserving business value and gaining competitive advantage. It is easy to ignore and allow the onion to go bad. But what do we mean by a healthy operational risk culture and how do we make sure our firm has one?

Embedding the culture

What do we mean by a healthy operational risk culture?

There is no universal definition of what constitutes a good or healthy risk culture. If culture is akin to your DNA, it is unique. Many would agree that in a healthy risk culture:

- people consider risk naturally, without being told to do so
- people feel free to talk about risk: there is a sense of active learning, rather than a blame culture; bad news is free to travel to where it is needed
- risk is acknowledged as part of everybody's everyday activities, stretching from strategic and business planning, through projects and down to business processes
- risk management and the risk management function are valued and risk management skills are equally valued, encouraged and developed.

But that may not be true everywhere. Any organisational culture will reflect the culture of the society in which it exists. That is why the chairman of the Japanese parliamentary investigation into the Fukushima nuclear disaster, in his introduction to the committee's report, was able to say that the disaster was 'Made in Japan', because a number of the causes and failures were down to behavioural characteristics of individuals and organisations which followed the embedded tenets of Japanese codes of conduct and behaviour.[7]

Fukushima Dai-ichi nuclear disaster (2011)

The Fukushima disaster followed the Tōhoku earthquake and tsunami on 11 March 2011 and resulted in a series of equipment failures, nuclear reactor meltdowns and releases of radioactive materials at the Fukushima 1 Nuclear Power Plant. Immediately after the earthquake the three operating reactors shut down automatically and emergency generators came online to control electronics and coolant systems. However, the tsunami following the earthquake flooded the low-lying rooms in which the emergency generators were housed, causing them to fail and cutting power to the pumps which circulated coolant water to prevent the reactors from melting down. Saltwater flooding of the reactors could have prevented meltdown but the decision was delayed, partly because of a lack of information about the scale of the disaster and partly because flooding with seawater would permanently ruin the costly reactors. Eventually the Japanese government ordered flooding by seawater, but it was too late to prevent meltdown.

In the intense heat several chemical explosions occurred. Concerns about the repeated small explosions and the possibility of larger explosions led to a 20 km radius evacuation around the plant. However, because Japanese government officials did not act on information provided by external agencies, evacuees were in many cases sent to areas of even higher radioactivity. Significant amounts of radioactive material were also released into ground and ocean waters, leading the government to ban the sale of food grown in the area.

Japanese officials initially assessed the accident as level 4 on the International Nuclear Event Scale. It was not until 11 April 2012 that the level was eventually raised to 7 by the Japanese authorities, the highest possible, despite assessments of level 6 or 7 by international agencies almost immediately after the disaster.

The Japanese parliament's Independent Investigation Commission report, published in July 2012, concluded that 'It was a profoundly man-made disaster – that could and should have been foreseen and prevented. And its effects could have been mitigated by a more effective human response.'

The operational risk failures identified by this and other reports included:

- Business continuity planning:
  - lack of effective threat assessment, resulting in little or no preparedness for a disaster of this scale;
  - poor communication and coordination between nuclear regulators, utility officials and government, including deletion of meeting records;

▶

- poor crisis management, including failure to use a logical chain of command;
- failure to instruct and train plant workers on their roles in the event of a disaster.
- Scenarios:
  - inadequate assumptions about the potential for loss of power, the severity of a tsunami and its effects.
- Risk culture:
  - national culture: 'our reflexive obedience; our reluctance to question authority; our devotion to "sticking with the program"; our groupism; and our insularity' (Commission report); a need to save face
  - rigid bureaucratic and hierarchical management structures militating against effective decision making
  - lack of effective independent risk oversight: regulatory agencies and the electric power company TEPCO, which maintained the plant, were not sufficiently independent of industry and tended to side with and promote the nuclear industry
  - lack of communication from the top to the community as a whole and amongst authorities during management of the crisis
  - reluctance to send bad news upwards
  - lack of trust between the major actors: the Prime Minister, TEPCO and managers at the plant.

The key, then, is to understand and articulate what your own risk culture actually is (see Testing the tune in the middle, p. 304). That may sound easy, but the world looks very different from the top of an organisation as it does from the bottom. Once you have agreed on what your risk culture is, you must then ensure that it is actually embedded in the organisation.

Committed leadership

Of course, it all starts with the tone from the top. And the top is where many of the biggest operational risks in terms of impact can lie: a bad acquisition decision, losing the trust and support of investors, lack of strategy or, if there is a strategy, failure to implement it effectively.

To embed a risk culture successfully, there has to be commitment from the top to embrace the values which have been agreed and good behaviour from the board and senior management. Bad board behaviour soon cascades down through the organisation. Good behaviour from the board and senior management means no infighting, no over-dominant individuals or groups of individuals, no obfuscation – so that risks or products are too complex to understand. These characteristics emerged when Equitable Life, the oldest mutual insurer in the world, had to close to new business in 2000.

Equitable Life   Case study

The Equitable Life Assurance Society (Equitable Life) was founded in 1762. At its peak, it had 1.5 million policyholders with funds worth £26 billion under management, but it had allowed large unhedged liabilities to accumulate in respect of guaranteed fixed returns to investors without making provision for adverse market changes. Following a House of Lords ruling in July 2000, and failed attempts to find a buyer, it closed to new business in December 2000 and reduced payouts to existing members.

In October 2010, the UK's coalition government announced compensation to policyholders of £1.5bn, well below the £4-4.8bn loss calculated by consultants Towers Watson in advice to HM Treasury.[8] In a report[9] about the collapse of the society, published on the occasion of its 250th anniversary, Professor Richard Roberts of King's College, London highlighted, amongst other things:

- an autocratic, domineering chief executive;
- a risky business model;
- non-executive directors who failed to control an ambitious management or to understand the risks they were running;
- complex and opaque products;
- inadequate crisis management: over-confidence in the mutual's ability to overcome its problems.

Good board behaviour also means a group of individuals who trust each other, embrace healthy challenge and are open to different thoughts and ideas. Above all, having established the culture they say they want – the values and behaviours going beyond a code of conduct or the staff handbook – senior executives have got to walk the talk. Employees must see their managers actually following the values and behaviours which have been laid down.

Strategy and objectives

The next essential is to be clear about your corporate objectives and communicate them throughout the firm. Without clearly articulated strategy and objectives, there is no context for risk management, risk culture or risk appetite. If risk is a threat to objectives, you can't manage risk unless you have clarity about those objectives and everybody in the firm knows what they are. And we're not talking about a vague mission statement, excellent as that may be as a first step. It may be true that 'culture eats strategy for breakfast', but there's not a lot you can do to move risk management forward unless your strategy is clear and understood by everybody in the firm.

Values and behaviours

Once the firm's strategy and business objectives have been established, the next step is to identify the values and behaviours which will enable them to be achieved and define the firm's culture. Those behaviours, what we mean by excellence, will form the basis of the selection, appraisal and reward systems which, as we shall see, are amongst the key controls of people risk. But what will excellent performance look like?

As examples, key behaviours will almost certainly include teamwork and providing high-quality client services. Teamwork can be expressed through actions such as: cross-function collaboration; collective responsibility; and group decision making. Providing high-quality client services may involve: establishing client relationships; responding to client demands; aligning contact with client needs; monitoring client progress; and dealing with problems and complaints.

Having established the basic headings, we can then detail what constitutes excellent behaviour or performance. For collective responsibility, for instance, high performance might be described as:

> Promotes and supports the decisions of the group even when these may not fit with the priorities of his or her own function or sector and accepts and encourages others to live out collective responsibility.

High performance in dealing with client problems and complaints may be described as:

> Acts as a highly trusted adviser/counsellor and client confidant – not only in good times – but also when things go wrong for the client. Willing to go the extra mile – including 'taking their part' to resolve difficulties or complaints.

Key behaviours will also specifically include ethical behaviours, which are fundamental to all employee-related dealings both within and without the firm and should be written down in the staff handbook. As an example, in February 2005, the Worshipful Company of International Bankers in the City of London published *Principles for Good Business Conduct*, to which all its members subscribe:

- act honestly, fairly and with integrity at all times in dealings with colleagues, clients, customers and counterparties;
- observe applicable laws, regulations and professional standards;
- manage fairly and effectively any conflicts of interest.

Ensuring that everybody in the firm understands and is comfortable with the values and behaviours which are being encouraged has to go further than just writing them down.

Employees need to hear clear, strong and repeated messages on values and behaviours from management, but there must also be the opportunity for feedback. Culture is an organisational matter so feedback is important. Feedback may also discover values which are important to customers or suppliers, or what might differentiate the firm from its competitors and turn that into competitive advantage.

Clear roles and responsibilities

Good risk management is about clarity of accountability. In a healthy risk culture, everyone is aware of what is expected of them, knows their responsibilities and has freedom to act accordingly. On an aircraft carrier, the relatively junior officer flagging in aircraft to land has the authority to abort a landing without referring to her or his superiors, let alone the admiral on the bridge.

As we have frequently pointed out, every member of staff is involved in operational risk management. Clarity of roles and responsibilities is a fundamental part of the risk management framework. Clarity of roles and responsibilities is also key to making people aware of their position and worth within the firm. Where people can explain how they contribute to the organisation, they will make a positive contribution to its performance. Remember the (perhaps apocryphal) janitor at NASA who, when asked what he did, replied 'I'm helping to put a man on the moon'.

Openness, transparency and active learning

Good operational risk management depends on openness and transparency. That cannot happen in a blame or closed culture. As we have remarked earlier, blame is the enemy of understanding.

A healthy risk culture is one which encourages transparency and communication up and down the firm. Not a place where the CEO 'wouldn't want to hear that', but one where bad news travels early and fast to where it's needed for decisions. To that extent the mediaeval monarch often had the advantage over the modern CEO in that he had a court jester to tell him what his courtiers were too afraid to say. A culture of open communication is one where there are no glass ceilings between, say, risk or audit and the C-suite and non-executive directors. It is one where the management hierarchy is not an obstacle to the flow of truth up and down the organisation.

One of the problems of operational risk is that events, and especially 'near misses', generally have to be reported individually rather than through the financial reporting systems. As a result, many events are not reported, which greatly diminishes the effectiveness of operational risk assessment.

So openness and transparency lie at the heart of good operational risk management.

To overcome reluctance to report events and losses, a first step may mean establishing a system where losses are reported anonymously. In a sense that is an admission of failure. In a culture of trust, the reporting of losses, problems and potential risks is encouraged because as a result future risks can be avoided and the control environment improved.

Extending this form of reporting to behavioural aspects also means that there should be channels for 'speaking up'. Whistle blowing is one thing, and is usually about serious crimes and misdemeanours, but speaking up expresses a culture where poor behaviours can be reported in a secure and trusting environment where no retaliation on the speaker is tolerated. The system can be web-based, anonymous and either internally or externally run. But there should be a guarantee that complaints will be handled and researched within a set number of days, for example anything involving financial matters within 14 days and serious ethical breaches or other 'category A' issues within 24 hours.

'Speaking up' is all part of a culture of active learning, such as that undertaken in the airline industry. All errors on a flight whether on the flight deck or the galley, are placed in a log so that they can be investigated and form the basis of future training or changes to procedures. No blame is attached to somebody who reports their errors if they are the first to do so, because all have a duty to ensure that processes are as safe as possible. It is said that on a transatlantic flight as many as a hundred items may be logged. Some may be concerned at that, but it is evidence of a wish to improve and to learn. It is part of an environment in which everybody's views are valued and they are encouraged to contribute ideas to improve their own and other people's performance.

Reward

A key element of embedding a healthy risk culture is to use the reward system to incentivise good risk behaviour and to deter poor behaviour. We will have more to say on reward later in the chapter, but in considering culture we will just emphasise that business is about stewardship both of human and financial resources, the two key elements of risk management. As regards financial resources, the aim should be to make money slowly rather than to get rich quick. Similarly with human resources, firms should not rent human capital over the short term. Human capital is being entrusted with the firm's capital and brand over the long term.

Testing the tune in the middle

But how do you know that the culture you want is truly embedded? Is the 'tune in the middle' the one you composed and wish to hear? There are a number of ways of testing culture. McKinsey has developed a scorecard consisting of 11 dimensions, which are grouped under five clusters.[10] They consist of such elements as level of care, cooperation, respect for rules, transparency, risk tolerance, acknowledgement of risk and challenge.

Another approach is *The Competing Values Framework* devised by Kim Cameron and Robert Quinn.[11] This allows respondents, via a questionnaire, to place either themselves or their organisation in one of four quadrants: Collaborate (the clan), Create (the 'adhocracy'), Compete (the market) and Control (the hierarchy). Tools such as these allow the firm to assess its current culture, identify where it wants its culture to be and also understand where employees sit within the culture. Highly rated businesses such as General Electric or Coca-Cola constantly reassess their culture and fine tune it to make the organisation more adaptable and ready for change.

Testing need not be so systematic. Firms will already have a number of risk and performance indicators which will give a rough guide as to the state of the firm's risk culture and its direction of travel. These might include:

- on controls and quality: trends in audit issues, compliance matters, claims and legal cases, bad debts
- staff/external: customer comments, supplier feedback
- staff/internal: staff turnover, absenteeism; staff surveys or focus groups; training records, expenses reports.

As with so much work on operational risk indicators, many are already being used in the business. There is no need to re-invent the wheel.

Change and flexibility

Before we leave culture and move on to the specifics of mitigating people risk, there is one important point to be made, which is that no firm is static any more than the external environment remains static. Firms are always at some changing point of evolution and development – whether they are growing or contracting. Growth may mean that the entrepreneur culture at the outset has to be tempered by a more structured, control environment. The original close-knit team gives way to a larger organisation which, for some, may be uncomfortably bureaucratic. At a time of contraction, the effects of down-sizing, restructuring and redundancy will have to be managed.

All of these factors mean a changing operational risk environment and operational risk exposure which need to be constantly reassessed, as well as the effects on the operational risk culture. From a people risk point of view, a changing risk profile and risk environment may require different skills being developed or brought in. It is management's job to be aware of changed conditions and to be able to adapt quickly. In this way, risks can be anticipated and their impact limited before they arise. Organisations need to keep fit to remain healthy, just as the people within them.

The temptation at times of economic trouble is to cut staff, cut training and hope the storm will blow over. It may well be that staff have to be made redundant, but losing trained and skilled people will undermine future competitiveness and increase risk. It may be better to devote time to managing people costs more efficiently, for example by: improving absence management; being more rigorous with expenses; imaginative use of contractors, secondments, or flexible and part-time working.

In any case, have you established a clear enough picture of where you want the firm to be in two or three years' time to be able to assess the skills you will need to get you through? And do you have an assessment process which identifies those people with the requisite skills? They may not be the people doing the best job today, but could be your salvation in the future.

A healthy operational risk culture will encourage continuous improvement and be open to change and flexibility. Employees should be encouraged to be creative and innovative and not allow work processes and practices to be rigid, inflexible and stale – in other words unfit for purpose, exposing the firm to more risk. The watchwords should be fitness and agility.

MITIGATING PEOPLE RISKS

Creating the right risk culture will do much to reduce people risks. After that, the fundamental way of mitigating those risks is by effective controls. Controls protect the firm from risk, but also help to protect people from themselves, especially when times are difficult. But there are other elements of people risk mitigation beyond internal process controls. To see them in their context, Table 15.1 gives some typical people risk events, their probable causes and the methods by which those risks can be reduced.

Table 15.1   **People risks and their mitigants**

Risk event	Cause	Mitigant
Employee criminal activity; fraud; unauthorised activity	Lack of integrity, dishonesty	Healthy culture Selection
Errors	Lack of competence	Selection Training/development
	Lack of training	Training/development
	Poor process culture	Healthy culture Appraisals/assessment

Risk event	Cause	Mitigant
Employment law failures (hiring, firing, discrimination, health and safety, etc.)	Lack of training Lack of legal awareness and knowledge Poor people culture	Training/development HR policy and process Healthy culture Appraisals/assessment
Poor (high-risk) business/ transaction decisions	Inappropriate incentives Incompetent staff Autocratic top management/lack of challenge Poor risk culture	Remuneration policy Selection Training/development Healthy culture Governance Environment Risk policy and appetite
Labour relations failures	Poor people culture Inexperienced managers	Healthy culture Training/development Selection Appraisals/assessment
Loss (or lack) of personnel, talent	Poor people culture Inadequate remuneration Failure to recruit	Healthy culture Training/development Appraisals/assessment Retention Remuneration policy Selection
Loss of intellectual property	Poor people culture	Retention Employment contract

Selection

People risk often starts at the beginning with selection and choosing the wrong people. Poor selection leads to cost and wasted management resource. Effective selection is an opportunity to add benefit to the firm.

Who do we want?

- Go for fit rather than capability. If you really want to place a piece of grit in the oyster because you know you're about to embark on a period of serious change and need somebody who will effect that change, fine. Otherwise, consider behaviours and choose the person who fits your culture, rather than the person who appears to tick all the boxes of expertise and experience. You can teach people competencies, but you can't change personalities. Or as Peter Schutz, former President and CEO of Porsche AG, has put it, 'Hire character. Train skill'.[12]

- Psychometric tests. They undoubtedly have value, especially if linked with the excellent behaviours you identified at the outset, but they should be an aid to judgement, not a substitute. If your gut instinct contradicts the test, go with your gut.

■ Recruit with one eye on the future. We are often too certain about what and who we are looking for. Have we really thought about the future and where the firm and the industry is going? The world and the firm will change – and sooner than we may think or like. Another reason to go for fit – and flexibility.

Who does the selecting?

■ The line manager. But does he or she have the skills necessary to interview a potential employee? Do they have the technical knowledge of HR policy and legislation? Is it clear what aspect of the selection process they are dealing with? Too often, when HR is asked to draw up a contract for a new employee, commitments given by the manager to the recruit emerge, which diverge completely from the pay and benefit structures around the firm. So take care about who plays what role in the process and make sure they are clear about their role and the limit of their authority.

■ Do you have a cadre of senior managers who understand the firm and its culture and have proved their worth as good selectors? Develop them into a panel to oversee all appointments over a certain level. They will ensure that you select for fit.

The process

■ Develop selection processes which attract and identify candidates with high potential. Employment may not be for life, but nor is it only for the immediate future or problem.

■ The process may include an outsourced recruiter. There's nothing inherently wrong with outsourcing aspects of selection. But if you do, make sure the search firm thoroughly understands your business and doesn't just rely on the specification given. If it's a first assignment – whether for the firm or a particular department – at least the first third of the recruiter's time should be spent inside the firm, working from there to get a clear understanding of its culture, as well as the assignment itself. Only then can they go out to the market (the next third) and sort through the candidates (the final third).

■ There is, of course, one other informal selection process, which goes back to the comment about selecting for fit – that is referral, contacts or recommendation. You may not have a current vacancy, but if you do come across somebody that way, create a role to get them on board. As Henry Grunfeld, co-founder of bankers S.G. Warburg & Co, once said: 'Recruiting is like buying a tie – you buy one when you see one you like; you do not wait until you need one.' The selection process can be imperfect enough.

Appraisals and performance management

Appraisals are a critical part of performance management, reviewing performance against agreed targets. Since risks are threats to objectives, the firm's or unit's objectives should form the basis of the performance targets, which should be based on both financial and non-financial behavioural factors. Appraisals are the opportunity to reinforce the excellent behaviours which will increase the firm's chances of sustained success and reduce its risks by confronting poor behaviours.

To do that, they have to be fair and based on clear criteria. Fair appraisals reduce the probability of a number of people risks occurring or, if they do occur, being resolved at an early stage and reducing their impact. We have already emphasised the importance of trust to support a culture of honesty and openness and so improve risk management. Fair appraisals are part of that process.

But how do we ensure that appraisals are fair? Compare them. Does the department which appears to have a remarkable cohort of A individuals actually outperform the one which seems to be dominated by down-the-middle Cs? It's more likely that the appraisers are differently motivated than that the mix of individuals is so divergent. Appraisals are a control on behaviour and part of the process of maintaining a good risk culture. That is why they should be validated across the firm to ensure consistency of this vital control.

Do you genuinely check and analyse for gender or race bias? Once it's known you do, it will be surprising how quickly staff become confident in the system and maverick managers are brought into line.

And are those above average scores really justified? Too often, when a department head comes to HR to say that, for whatever reason, Mr X or Ms Y has to be fired, they invariably find that the last couple of appraisals have been glowing to the point of excellent. How strange that 'good' people become 'bad' when there are problems. Dishonest appraisals disproportionately increase the cost of dismissal. If poor staff had been honestly appraised and identified sooner, when times were good, the costs of dismissal would have been lower and recruiting a replacement would have been easier than it will be in a downturn.

One reason for dishonest appraisals is that they continue, despite all the rhetoric, to be an annual formal event. If so, they cannot provide a forum for criticism which should have been made months before. We should be looking at our staff – and our superiors – all the time and providing continuous feedback so that the firm benefits from the resulting openness. That openness will improve performance and develop potential, not just for the individual, but inevitably for the firm as a whole. It should also mean that the formal appraisal, when it comes, will contain no surprises.

Finally, appraisals point to ways in which an individual can be developed further, which may include training, to improve risk management or reduce risk exposure. Staff are like diamonds; they require constant polishing.

Training and development

Just as objectives (and risks) lie at the heart of the appraisal process, so objectives help to frame a firm's learning and development needs and those of individuals. What's next on the agenda of the firm and therefore for the individual? Objectives also form the basis of assessing the success of training and development. There is little point embarking on a training or development programme without assessing whether it succeeded in what it set out to do.

Risk indicators are a critical part of risk assessment and can point to training and development needs. Table 15.2 gives a few typical examples.

Table 15.2 **People risks as indicators of training and development needs**

Risk	Indicator
Poor throughput	Error rates; productivity
Employment law failures; discrimination	Claims by staff
Loss of talent (through poor people management/culture)	Resignations of experienced/senior staff

Training and development may involve courses, but can also mean changes in responsibility or environment. You never know when somebody will be missing. At a higher level, leadership should be developed within the firm. Firms which don't nurture their talent will see it leave to the competition, who have spotted new opportunities. If personal and professional development is switched off, firms will find themselves with an even more desperate shortage of talent when it is needed – whether for a downturn or an upturn.

But appraisals are not the only guide to personal development. The firm's objectives over the medium term will point to the skills required, so that a skills audit should be regularly conducted to make sure the firm has a reservoir of the right kind of both technical and leadership talent to fulfil its strategy and develop its human capital accordingly.

Reward – or what does your bonus system say about your values?

Given the reams which have been written about the impact of remuneration structures on behaviours which appear, to the public and politicians at least, to have been at the heart of the banking crisis, it would be hard to consider people risk without discussing reward and remuneration.

Before we deal with bonuses, let's establish a few principles of good reward policies. Reward is not just about remuneration. Remuneration – base pay, variable pay, share options, other benefits – is the financial aspect of reward. But there are non-financial aspects of reward which can be just as important to employees: recognition, the opportunity to develop skills, career opportunities, the quality of the work–life balance. They all form part of the overall reward package and may be decisive in retaining a valued employee or recruiting a new one – just one aspect of people risk mitigation.

But let's return to the core of reward – remuneration. Remuneration, like appraisals, with which it is obviously closely linked, should reinforce the performance and behaviours we require and discourage unwanted behaviour. It should be based on what the firm considers to be good performance and help the business achieve its strategic objectives, which should themselves be rooted in sound risk management and a healthy risk culture.

If remuneration is linked to performance targets which are closely allied to business objectives, you will have gone a long way to linking remuneration also to risk appetite. On an oil rig, managers are rewarded primarily for the quality of their safety management. Hitting production targets comes second.

Remuneration is not simply a market wage. It is also a balancing act between reward and risk. In the recent financial crisis, did remuneration encourage 'bad' and overly risky behaviour? Probably. But was that, in fact, the publicly visible reflection of a poor risk management culture? Or even lack of any recognisable risk management culture? They were evidence of a remuneration policy which had lost any connection with business strategy and objectives which were allied to risk management, including especially the people risks within operational risk.

Another reflection of the balance between reward and risk is the balance between fixed and variable remuneration. Bonuses are not an evil in themselves, but they should be used to drive non-financial behaviours and performance as much as respond to the achievement of targets and profitability.

The word 'bonus' is, of course, itself emotive in the eyes of the public and politicians. Following the banking crisis, guidelines were published on remuneration for banking and financial services. In the guidelines, it was suggested that where a significant proportion of remuneration is in the form of a performance-related bonus, the majority should be:

- deferred for a minimum period (which will reflect the risks involved in the transactions giving rise to the bonus)

- subject to claw-back (on the deferred element)
- risk-adjusted, through quantitative criteria and human judgement, and reflect all types of risk.

Incentives are intended to distort behaviour. As a result, they can be a force for bad as well as good. In principle, awarding performance bonuses in the form of shares should align reward with shareholder value, but it can mean that executives spend more time trying to manipulate the share price than running the business properly and profitably over the medium to long term. Management is about stewardship of the firm's assets on behalf of the owners, not an opportunity to get rich quick.

Deferring bonuses for an appropriate period should help to discourage short-term risk taking. It also has the merit of aligning remuneration to actual ultimate performance, with that performance based on the whole range of judgements, including risk.

Whether the post-crisis guidelines will improve the quality of risk management in financial services remains to be seen. They should, however, lead to longer-term incentive plans, which is a step in the right direction. Traditionally, incentives have been too short term. That is partly because they tend to focus on things which are easy to measure and tie in with the firm's (usually) annual reporting cycle, whereas the effect of an employee on the firm's future performance is longer term and not easy to assess in the short term.

However, in times of crisis it may be more appropriate to call on the reservoir of trust you have built up with your staff and revert to short-term plans. At such times you need tactics rather than strategy. Longer-term plans can come when times are calmer.

One final point made in the guidelines is that there should be greatly increased public disclosure of the basis for remuneration. Of far more importance from a people risk management point of view is that the internal culture of openness and transparency should extend to remuneration. People are entitled to know the basis on which they and their peers will be remunerated so that they see the process as being fair and open. There has to be differentiation in pay, otherwise remuneration loses its power to incentivise good performance and drive out bad behaviours. The reaction is often to shroud remuneration in secrecy. The risk of upsetting people by paying them at different levels is, however, dwarfed by the negative impact of being secretive.

A clumsily managed or crudely applied remuneration policy risks losing staff and may be seen as tolerating under-performance, under-rewarding people who have behaved excellently or even of rewarding people who threaten to leave. Flexibility is important, though. What counts as good performance in the future may be very different from what counted as good performance in the past.

Finally, who polices remuneration and remuneration policies? Apart from externals such as investors, the media and legislative committees – all of whom seem reasonably ineffectual – there is, of course, the board and the remuneration committee. Ensuring that their senior executives are in a top 'quartile' or similar cohort means that inflation is built into the system and does little to ensure that reward is genuinely linked to the performance criteria which reflect the particular circumstances of the firm at a particular point of time. Boards must tie remuneration back to performance criteria which are transparent. Not only will that mean that excellence will justifiably and publicly be rewarded, but poor performance, including that of the CEO, can be immediately dealt with, again both justifiably and publicly.

SUCCESSION PLANNING

Staff retention

The simplest form of succession planning is, of course, not to lose staff in the first place. Retaining trained and experienced staff is a key to excellent risk management. You cannot afford to lose both the commitment and the intellectual capital of your best employees.

Since the human brain is the easiest way to carry information (and secrets) out of a firm, you should look at how corporate knowledge has been developed, documented and converted into intellectual capital. Has corporate knowledge been compared with competitor knowledge to identify your intellectual as well as your competitive advantage – and the risks if you should lose it? That's one strategy to reduce the risks which an ex-employee can cause either maliciously or if, for instance, they can exploit their knowledge of your systems or strategy. Employment contracts and gardening leave can get you only so far. The opening of Heathrow's new Terminal 5 in March 2008 was a good example of how lack of a skills audit and failure to retain people with knowledge caused untold financial and reputational damage.

Another risk mitigation strategy to reduce the possibility of losing staff is, wherever possible, the exit interview. It may be too late for the employee who is leaving, but the interview may be able to give pointers which will help you retain those who remain. What were the *real* reasons for resignation? Which were inevitable or acceptable? Or avoidable?

| Case study | **Opening of Heathrow, Terminal Five (2008)** |

When Heathrow's new terminal opened, the state of the art baggage handling system failed. To exacerbate the problem, critical baggage handling staff were prevented from reaching their work stations because of new security measures. What is less well known is that British Airways had gone ahead with a redundancy programme which anticipated that the system would work and took effect immediately before the terminal opening. The result was that knowledge and experience which would be needed perhaps only once in 20 years were unavailable just when they were needed. A skills audit conducted with the redundancy programme, together with realistic scenario planning, would have significantly reduced the impact on BA's finances and the reputation of both BA and the UK in terms of industrial relations.

Your best employees will always be in demand. If you do not nurture your talented people, they will leave for competitors who spot new opportunities. Nor is it just the people themselves who go. It is the valuable IP they take with them.

In the end, the best risk control technique is a pro-active human resources policy which seeks to create an environment in which people are valued, and there is a strategy for retaining talented employees and for minimising the damage that occurs when key people leave.

Succession planning beyond the crisis

But if they do go, can they be replaced? At its most basic level, in an appraisal, you should be able to answer the question, who would replace you – and when? In other words, have you developed your subordinates so that you are effectively expendable, or at least expendable in your present position? Of course, if the system works properly, your superior should be in the same happy state, with you pencilled in to fill their shoes – which is another question worth asking in an appraisal.

Whilst that may represent a robust succession plan for your job, it's of little use if the same person has been pencilled in to fill a number of gaps around the firm. In fact, you should have at least two people for each position because in practice only 40% of people actually fill the roles for which they are pencilled in.

So, as senior executive, make sure you look across your area and have a plan which will survive the loss of more than one of your key people. 9/11 was a tragic example of firms losing a number of staff at the same time, just as they might, albeit temporarily, with a virulent pandemic. And, of course, keep the plan under constant review. Almost by definition, it may need to be activated at very short notice, whether from natural causes such as illness or even death, or from the fact that a person or team simply resigns and walks out of the door.

Crisis management is generally as far as most plans go. A crisis plan is fine, but a true succession plan should be a plan for the longer term, not just an immediate crisis. Is the crisis replacement expected to be the permanent replacement or merely a stop-gap? In any case, if somebody leaves, will the job and skills required remain the same, or will a different organisational or skills structure better reflect the firm's strategy and objectives? Perhaps the most sensible approach is to develop a pool of talent, because circumstances will almost certainly be different when the event happens. That paid dividends for McDonald's in 2004 when they managed to replace not one but two CEOs in 12 months from within the firm, following the deaths of two CEOs within 9 months of each other.

True succession planning involves drawing up a skills matrix, performing a gap analysis and then acting on what it tells you. That may mean re-thinking the firm's medium-term strategy, or it may mean re-thinking your view of current employees and whether they really are the best people in the medium term. Succession planning is a classic control to minimise the risks of a sudden absence of personnel.

THE HUMAN RESOURCES DEPARTMENT

Of course, we all know what HR does. HR coordinates appraisals and organises training courses. With luck, it may also sort out remuneration and selection policies, fire people when managers can't face doing it themselves, and above all make sure firms don't fall foul of an increasing tide of employment legislation. Those are all aspects of operational risk management, which should be the responsibility of line management. If they are all down to HR, then HR is being poorly used and people management is probably poor also.

HR should be the driver of good people management within the firm, promoting good – and better – behaviours. It should be a critical friend to the board by providing guidance and minimising reputational risk. It should also partner line managers to build resilience in to workforce planning. They should be the experts in considering flexibility of contract, skills or location to allow business to respond to changing circumstances.

In fact, HR should be seen as one of the key risk management functions. We expect the head of risk management to put in place a risk framework which will cover all the standard risks. Do we ask the HR director to put in place a 'people risk' management framework? Perhaps we do not because, as with operational risk management, managing people is 'what we do'.

HR needs to ensure there is a strong HR strategy and policy, allied to risk and business objectives, and that the policy is fully communicated and implemented consistently throughout the firm. Like risk management, much of people risk is delegated to line managers but HR is there to maintain oversight of the process.

Again like risk management, HR will only add value if it is in tune with the firm's commercial needs and objectives. It does not need to be a large function. Indeed, in a well-run firm, it will not be because line management operates good people management. But it should be central to a firm's management. In a survey by Mercer[13] of 500 HR Directors in Europe, the Middle East and Africa, 65% saw themselves as strategic partners to the business although in practice only 15% of their activities related directly to strategy. To what extent do firms see or develop their HR Directors as potential COOs?

That leads to one final question – does the head of HR have to be an HR professional, or would a good line manager be able to do the job just as well? Given the scale of financial and reputational risks of non-compliance with legislation – employment, discrimination, health and safety and so on – it's probably best that they should have extensive experience of dealing with these issues and with all the ramifications of hiring and firing.

Recruiting that kind of expertise to support a good, though HR inexperienced, senior manager, could be an expensive option. If s/he is good, s/he will be cheap, but if not, no matter how cheap, s/he will be expensive. However, you may have the expertise in your in-house legal team or might choose to rely on external advice when required. The other side of the coin is that no head of HR is going to be a good head of HR without a good knowledge of the business whose emotional health, in the shape of its people, he or she is responsible for.

KEY PEOPLE RISK INDICATORS

If people are, as a category, a firm's biggest potential risk, it's fair to ask what indicators are available to monitor that risk, and in particular to monitor the constituent risks and their controls. When you look at the chain of cause and effect, many indicators relating to process and systems risks and controls in the end come back to some form of people risk. They tell you much about levels of competence in the firm, as well as vulnerabilities, which may point to the need to strengthen controls in the form of training or simply better people management.

But with people, it's not just about competence as expressed, say, by IT failures. We need to dig into the softer environmental issues. Do we use staff morale surveys? Or count the times the 'speaking up' hotline is used for significant governance failures? Do we use human reliability assessments, of the kind used in 'safety critical' industries such as nuclear or space? How do we monitor issues such as stress or bullying and all those other critical, environmental factors? We can aggregate the marks given in appraisals for the various behaviours mentioned earlier, and use them as a temperature gauge for whether the firm as a whole is on target to meet its objectives or whether there are certain behaviours which are not being met.

One good indicator of stress – or unhappiness with the working environment – is sickness. The problem with sickness figures, as we shall see shortly with key staff turnover, is that the raw number is not a good indicator. One of the problems with sickness in the UK's National Health Service is that much of it relates to experienced and dedicated staff whose conscientiousness means that they exhaust themselves in the face of lack of adequate support. So, as with all operational risk data, it is essential to get beneath the headlines and discover the true cause.

National Health Service (2009)
Case study

In August 2009, Steve Boorman published his interim report on the UK's National Health Service, NHS Health and Wellbeing.[14] In it he noted that sickness absence in the NHS, at 10.7 days a year on average, was greater than the public sector as a whole (9.7 days) and the private sector (6.4 days). Reducing absence through sickness by a third would result in a gain of 3.4 million days a year (14,900 whole-time equivalent staff) and an annual direct cost saving of £555m.

More specifically, and related to risk management, hospitals with high staff sickness had poor patient satisfaction rates and higher infection rates. The report concluded that reducing reliance on transient agency staff by reducing NHS staff absence through sickness would lead to a considerable improvement in patient satisfaction and patient outcomes.

Looking at some of the people risk mitigants discussed above, we can see that indicators concerning training and development can be developed: how many staff have been identified with training or development needs? How many of those needs have actually been fulfilled?

As with all indicators, the key is to get to quality rather than mere numbers and to understand what the numbers are telling you. Staff turnover is probably the most common people risk indicator to appear on risk dashboards and management reports. But staff turnover alone is a very blunt instrument. It is not the number of staff, but the quality of staff leaving and the knowledge and experience they take with them which is the issue, so do the turnover data indicate loss of staff by experience and by appraisal grading? Is there a target for turnover? In some areas, we might be concerned by turnover of, say, less than six months. In a new project area, we might be devastated by the loss of anybody in the team.

And what if we appear to be retaining more staff than we expect? Does that reflect our excellent work environment and leadership – or are we retaining staff who are below average, but who are being paid above the going rate for their competence so that there is no incentive for them to leave?

Which brings us back to where we started – selection. If we choose the right people; make sure they are clear about their role and the importance of their job; give them opportunities to develop and learn; pay them according to clear and transparent performance criteria which reflect the behaviours of the organisation; give them regular feedback and dialogue with their superiors; and make sure there is effective internal employee communication, we shall have a successful business in which our people risks are being successfully managed and mitigated.

Good people management is good management is good *operational risk management*.

Notes

1 Charles Handy, *Beyond Certainty* (London: Hutchinson, Random House (UK) Limited), 1995.

2 John Donne, *Meditations upon emergent occasions and seuerall steps in my sicknes, Meditation XVII* (1624).

3 Quoted in the Group of Thirty's report, *The 2008 Financial Crisis and its Aftermath: Addressing the next debt challenge*, June 2011.

4 Roger Steare, 'The Board's role in establishing the right corporate culture', in *Business Risk: A practical guide for board members* (London: Institute of Directors), 2012; www.iod.com/mainwebsite/resources/document/iod-directors-guide-business-risk-june12.pdf

5 How do you embed a winning corporate culture?, *Director*, March 2011.

6 Financial Crisis Inquiry Commission, *The Financial Crisis Inquiry Report: Final report of the national commission on the causes of the financial and economic crisis in the United States* (Washington, DC: Government Printing Office), 27 January 2011.

7 Investigation Committee on the Accident at the Fukushima Nuclear Power Stations of Tokyo Electric Power Company, final report, 23 July 2012.

8 HM Treasury, The Equitable Life Payment Scheme Design, May 2011.

9 Professor Richard Roberts, *Did anyone learn anything from the Equitable?*, Institute of Contemporary British History, King's College, 7 September 2012.

10 McKinsey working papers on risk no. 16, *Taking control of organizational risk culture*, February 2010.

11 Kim Cameron, Robert Quinn and others, *The Competing Values Framework: Creating value through purpose, practices, and people*, 1999/2009; http://competingvalues.com

12 Quoted in Roger Steare, *Ethicability* (Roger Steare Consulting Limited), 2009, p. 72.

13 Mercer, *2010 EMEA HR Transformation Survey*, January 2011.

14 www.nhshealthandwellbeing.org

Reputation risk

WHAT IS REPUTATION?

Good name in man and woman, dear my lord,

Is the immediate jewel of their souls:

Who steals my purse steals trash; 'tis something, nothing;

'Twas mine, 'tis his, and hath been slave to thousands;

But he that filches from me my good name

Robs me of that which not enriches him

And makes me poor indeed.

[Othello, III, iii, 155–61]

As ever, Shakespeare got it right. Iago may have been cynically manipulating Othello, but he was right in the one key element of reputation – it is all about perception. It exists in the minds of others, and you neither own nor control their perceptions – which makes it difficult to manage.

PR can get you so far, but any reputation has to be genuine and based on reality. If the credibility gap gets too wide between what a firm does and what those who deal with it expect, its reputation will suffer and its business will inevitably decline. Reputation risk management is about recognising the size of the gap.

People evaluate a firm's reputation on the basis of available information. Some of that information may be controlled by the organisation, such as annual reports or marketing materials. Other information may take less obvious forms: a customer's experience of service; the opinions of customers in general; staff surveys; the views of all kinds of commentators from parish-pump gossip, to blogger, to syndicated journalist, to campaigning activist. Reputation is a subjective, composite assessment resulting from a number of factors, amongst which *trust* will be the key ingredient.

As Morgen Witzel has put it: 'A reputation is, in effect, the combined experiences that many people have of an organisation over time.'[1] Those experiences and perceptions are dynamic and change all the time. Often that change is caused by the actions or attitudes of others. If your peers and competitors raise their game, your relative reputation will decline. If one of them behaves especially badly, your reputation may suffer through guilt by association. It can also change in response to social and other trends affecting how key constituencies, the reputational stakeholders, understand these actions. The perception you thought you had given may turn out over time not to be the one the stakeholder sees.

STAKEHOLDERS

The stakeholders are not just those with whom you deal directly. They include others, such as regulators and opinion formers, who effectively have in their hands your licence to operate. They not only influence your direct stakeholders but also those who may potentially become directly involved with you and, of course, they influence each other.

Typical stakeholders

Table 16.1

Direct	Licence holders – the influencers
Customers/clients	Regulators
Employees	Trade unions
Suppliers	Opinion formers
Investors	Broadcast, print and social media
Business partners	Politicians
	Political or other lobbyists
	Consumer advocates
	Local communities

Reputation is about meeting the expectations of all these people, many of whom you may never meet. Whether it is good or bad depends on the comparison stakeholders make between how a company and its employees are expected to behave and how they actually do. That was the main reason behind the public outcry in a number of countries concerning the phone-hacking scandal within News International.

News International phone-hacking scandal (2011)

Case study

The News International phone-hacking scandal had its origins in 2005–7 when voice-mail relating to the British royal family was intercepted by a private investigator working for a *News of the World* journalist. Investigations at the time concluded that the paper's phone-hacking activities were limited to celebrities, politicians and members of the British royal family. However, in July 2011, it was revealed that the phones of murdered schoolgirl Milly Dowler, relatives of deceased British soldiers and victims of the London bombings of 7 July 2005 were also accessed. Further revelations showed that phone hacking was far more widespread than had at first been thought and included allegations that the newspaper had bribed police.

▶

> Public outcry and advertising boycotts resulted in the closure of the *News of the World* in July 2011 after 168 years of publication. Continued public pressure also forced News Corporation to cancel its proposed takeover of the British telecommunications company BSkyB. In the same month, British prime minister David Cameron asked Lord Leveson to conduct two enquiries, one into the specific allegations of phone hacking and police bribery by the *News of the World* and another to look into the culture and ethics of the wider British media.
>
> The affair led to a number of high-profile resignations including News International chief executive Rebekah Brooks and the Commissioner of the Metropolitan Police Sir Paul Stephenson.
>
> In separate international developments, the FBI has launched an investigation of News Corporation's activities in the USA and an enquiry is underway in Australia into the country's media, including the protection of privacy.

Unfortunately, each stakeholder has a different expectation. So, if 'a reputation is no more than delivering on a promise', as Sam Mostyn, Group Executive, Culture and Reputation, for Insurance Australia group put it,[2] it actually means delivering on many promises. What your reputation is worth – whether it is a help or a hindrance to you – depends on what matters to your stakeholders and whether they see and experience your business as rising above or falling short of expectations.

This was demonstrated in the Sony PlayStation outage in 2011. On 20 April, Sony became aware of a cyber-attack on its PlayStation network and closed down the service. After forensic examination, it announced that credit details for 77 million accounts had been compromised. Services began to be restored towards the end of May. Whilst Government and other agencies were concerned about data protection, the overwhelming complaint from PlayStation customers was that their games were not available for three to four weeks.

Of course stakeholders' views also change over time, as do groups of stakeholders. They are interest groups which may come and go. If you wish to build a new factory or office block, the local planning department may appear as a stakeholder for the first and only time, together with local residents, who may then remain as a critical group.

To complicate matters further, an individual stakeholder may be in a number of groups. For example, an employee may also be, and commonly is in financial services, a customer and an investor, and possibly a member of one of the influencing groups. Stakeholders are a constantly moving target. Reputation risk management is a slippery beast.

REPUTATION AND BRAND

Is reputation the same as brand? Emphatically not. A brand is an identity created and controlled by its owner for commercial gain and for sale to consumers. It can be closed down if its reputation is sufficiently damaged, such as in the case of the *News of the World*. By contrast, a reputation cannot be closed down. Reputation is about the perception of all stakeholders, not just consumers, and in a broad sense is all about engendering trust. That may be part of a brand, but the point about a brand is that the customer experience leads to differentiation with rival brands.

There are obvious parallels. Reputation and brand are driven by values and behaviour; both depend on experience. However, with brand, the customer is key, whereas with reputation the customer is a sub-set of the stakeholders, albeit a significant one.

A strong brand can protect a company against intensifying price competition and help to protect its reputation. But brand alone will not protect a company from all the reputational risks to which it is exposed. To understand this difference, we need now to look more closely at reputation risk.

WHAT IS REPUTATION RISK?

Reputation risk is the risk that a latent problem of reputation, typically of public trust, will become an actual reputational problem. It is the skeleton, or more realistically all the skeletons, in the cupboard. Following the definition of reputation, it is the risk that the firm will act in a way which falls short of stakeholder expectations.

Is reputation risk a risk in its own right? It is, in the sense that a threat to its reputation has a direct effect on an organisation and it consistently registers as one of the key risks a firm faces. But reputational damage is almost always a *consequence* of a risk event, usually an operational risk event, involving a failure to deliver products and services as promised or behave as expected. Even if it is a second-order risk, reputation risk is nevertheless a critical element of operational risk management.

VALUING REPUTATION AND REPUTATION RISK

If you could insure against reputational damage you might be able to put a price on it. But that's not possible, other than in being able to cover PR and similar costs if a crisis occurs. As we saw in Chapter 12, insurance, like reputation risk, depends on a cause. So insurance may cover the operational risk cause of the reputation risk event, but not the reputational damage itself. If we can't then look to insurance, we must look to other means of measuring or valuing it – apart from the libel courts, that is. And courts are notoriously volatile, partly because of the very good reputation risk reason that reputation is in the mind of the stakeholder and, for these purposes, a libel jury is a randomly selected group of stakeholders, each with his or her own prejudices and backgrounds – and expectations.

We can look at various economic measures of the effect of reputational damage – drop in sales, loss of earnings, the cost of managing the crisis or changes in share price and market capitalisation, but it is difficult to make direct correlations between these and a perceived loss of reputation or the long-term impact on trust. There are too many assumptions and variables to make it meaningful. In any case, can behaviour and expectations be measured in terms of money?

The simplest economic measure is probably the significant intangible, goodwill, a key component of which will be reputation. For a service business it may even represent its total value. As Alan Greenspan put it: 'Manufactured goods often can be evaluated before the completion of a transaction. Service providers, on the other hand, usually can offer only their reputation.'[3] But goodwill can be properly valued only when a business is sold and, even then, reputation is just one of a number of factors in its valuation.

Another approach is to use a scorecard. Here again, the variables are many and their weighting is notoriously subjective. As a basis for a scorecard, many firms use the factors identified by Charles J. Fombrun, founder of the Reputation Institute, shown in Table 16.2.

| Table 16.2 | Harris–Fombrun model of corporate reputation quotient |

Drivers	Attributes
Emotional appeal	Good feeling about the company Admire and respect the company Trust the company
Products/services	Offers high-quality products/services Offers good-value products/services Develops innovative products/services Stands behind its products/services
Vision and leadership	Has excellent leadership Has a clear vision of the future Takes advantage of market opportunities

Drivers	Attributes
Workplace environment	Is well managed Looks like a good company to work for Looks like it has good employees
Financial performance	Record of profitability Looks like a low-risk investment Strong prospects for future growth Tends to outperform its competitors
Social responsibility	Supports good causes Environmentally responsible Treats people well

Source: Reputation Institute

Fombrun devised it as a ranking model, by which the Institute can assess and report publicly either on the universe of companies or on those in a particular industry. It is therefore akin to a rating system. As such, it is possible that it can be self-reinforcing and affect corporate behaviour. Firms will game the system. But it does provide helpful questions with which a firm can self-diagnose its perception in the eyes of its various stakeholders.

In the end, the measure of reputation risk is the gap between stakeholder expectations and actual performance. The value of reputation is, fundamentally, the cost of risk, which is the cost of recovering the trust formerly enjoyed. That cost can be considerable. A survey by Burson-Marsteller of business leaders, journalists and financial analysts in the US suggests that it takes four years for a company to restore its reputation following a major incident.[4]

HOW CAN REPUTATION BE DAMAGED?

The stakes for not getting it right are high. In a survey by PricewaterhouseCoopers,[5] reputation risk was seen as a key threat to success and in a similar survey conducted by Aon,[6] reputation risk was the most frequently noted concern across all industries, and amongst the most serious concerns, in terms of its impact, by financial services firms.

Reputational problems and poor handling issues Table 16.3

Reputational problems	Examples of poor problem handling
Difficulty in raising capital	Poor investor relations
Losing key employees	Not listening; poor internal communications
Losing suppliers and customers	Poor marketing communications
An inability to access new markets	Poor dialogue with licensing authorities, customers and prospective customers
Litigation and more intrusive regulation	Lack of control over operational risks

Some of the problems which arise if reputational issues are poorly handled are given in Table 16.3 (above). It requires a considerable amount of resource and effort to restore the trust of the various stakeholder groups identified in that list. At worst, loss of reputation can lead to the complete destruction of the business, as in the Enron/Andersen case.

Sadly, for some firms, the comfort of a filtered version of reality is preferable to the real thing. One of the greatest threats to reputation risk is what might be called institutional conditioning, a culture in which the organisation hardly knows it is moving the boundaries between acceptable and unacceptable behaviour. Another description of it might be 'ethical creep'. Or firms behave badly, get away with it and so go on and do 'it' again. Of course, in the case of Enron, some senior executives knew exactly what they were doing. It has been argued that institutional conditioning was at the root of the NASA *Challenger* and *Columbia* space shuttle disasters.[7] In the case of the *Columbia* disaster, there was the added failure to learn the lessons of *Challenger*, perhaps another symptom of institutional conditioning. NASA, in common with other firms – and with UK Members of Parliament in 2009 – clung for too long to the belief that its own interpretation of 'acceptable behaviour' was all that mattered.

Case study   **Enron/Andersen (2001)**

Enron was founded in 1985 following the merger of two gas pipeline companies. It thrived on the deregulation of the sale of natural gas in the USA in 1985. By 1992 it was the largest merchant of natural gas in the USA and, by 2001, it had become a conglomerate that both owned and operated gas pipelines, pulp and paper plants, broadband assets, electricity plants and water plants internationally. The corporation also traded in financial markets for the same types of products and services.

In achieving this, Enron accumulated a huge mountain of debt. It managed to hide this and report artificially inflated profits through a complex web of special purpose entities and accounting treatments which stretched the limits of accounting practice. Its audited statements were famously opaque. Although it used derivatives to hedge its liabilities, the hedges were predominantly with its own special purpose entities, so that it was effectively entering hedges with itself.

The company failed to satisfy mounting concerns amongst analysts and investors during 2001 and confidence collapsed after the announcement of an SEC investigation into the company following accounting restatements covering the previous four years of US$1.2bn, and the discovery of a number of problematic transactions.

A sale of the company fell through and its paper was downgraded to junk status. It filed for bankruptcy and sought Chapter 11 protection on 30 November 2001.

During the ensuing investigation, Arthur Andersen, its external auditor, was discovered to have shredded tonnes of documents relating to its audit of Enron. Andersen collapsed with the loss of around 80,000 jobs.

Operational and reputation risk issues

Enron:

- a culture of fraud amongst senior executives at Enron;
- complete lack of transparency with regard to investors and markets;
- complex corporate structure, full knowledge of which was confined to a very small number of senior executives.

Arthur Andersen:

- authorising employees to shred incriminating documents destroyed trust in it as an auditor and so destroyed the firm;
- timing is often important – the damaging revelations about the shredding emerged just before the audit renewal season.

Columbia space shuttle disaster (2003)   Case study

The *Columbia* space shuttle disintegrated on re-entry into the Earth's atmosphere on 1 February 2003 with the loss of all seven crew members. The disaster was directly attributable to damage sustained at launch when a piece of foam insulation the size of a small briefcase broke from the shuttle's main propellant tank, hit the leading edge of the left wing and damaged the Shuttle's thermal protection system.

During the flight, some engineers suspected damage, and wanted to use imaging to investigate the state of the shuttle. Investigations were limited on the basis that little could be done even if the problems were found. The engineers were also thwarted in their requests for external astronaut inspections.

NASA safety regulations stated that strikes by foam or other debris were safety issues which should abort a flight, but flights were often given the go-ahead despite foam shedding. Earlier risk assessments had estimated the damage of small ice impacts, the only impacts recognised as threats to the leading edge wing panels. It was considered that impact from the less dense foam panels would be less. The risk of damage from foam, despite engineering concerns, was reduced from 'possible complete penetration' to 'slight damage' in the risk assessment process.

▶

Perhaps more significantly, the Columbia Accident Investigation Board (CAIB) concluded that NASA had failed to learn many of the lessons of the *Challenger* disaster. In particular, the agency had not set up a truly independent office for safety oversight, nor had it maintained a culture and organisational structure which gave sufficient weight to safety issues. The CAIB believed that 'the causes of the institutional failure responsible for *Challenger* have not been fixed,' and that the same 'flawed decision making process' that had resulted in the *Challenger* accident was responsible for *Columbia*'s destruction 17 years later.

The *Challenger* disaster led to shuttle flights being put on hold for 32 months. The *Columbia* disaster led to a further suspension of two years; construction of the International Space Station was put on hold and depended on the Russian space agency for re-supply and crew rotation.

Operational risk issues

■ despite the *Challenger* disaster, a culture and organisational structure and process remained in place in which safety was compromised in the effort to maintain the launch programme;

■ acceptance of design deviations as normal when they happened on several flights and did not lead to mission-compromising consequences;

■ failure to stress-test scenarios beyond actual past experiences;

■ inadequate crew survival systems, which relied on manual activation.

Source: Based on Volume 1 of the CAIB report, http://caib1nasa.gov/news/report/volume1

In the cases of both NASA's shuttle programme and UK parliamentarians' expense claims, deep reforms and public humiliation were perhaps the most obvious costs for those involved. At a higher level, both episodes carried the greater, if less measurable, cost of lost public faith in institutions which had been held in a position of trust which they abused. In operational risk terms, the risk of loss of public trust resulted from a failure of the control of behaving in an acceptable manner.

Assuming deception is not ingrained, where can it all go wrong? We might expect business leaders to be most worried about hazards to reputation arising out of events beyond their control. In fact, reputation risk is seen largely as a product of business operations – at least in the shape of their performance or non-performance. When asked by the Economist Intelligence Unit in 2005,[8] international senior executives cited the following as their top reputational risks:

■ non-compliance with regulatory/legal obligations (66%)

■ exposure of unethical practices (58%)

■ security breaches (57%).

It is interesting that all of these (to which could be added failures in service delivery, poor crisis management and failure to hit financial targets, which were well up the list) were either wholly or to a great extent within their own gift, and indeed responsibility, to control.

To those directly controllable reputational risks can be added behavioural risks, such as:

■ accounting practices – are they appropriate and subject to truly independent review?

■ corporate governance – is the board and its committees truly independent? Are conflicts of interest properly handled?

■ discrimination – in all its guises

■ data privacy/protection

■ employee relations.

Then there are areas which are only indirectly under a firm's control but may at least be managed through dealings with third parties:

■ client's clients

■ agents

■ partners, suppliers, outsourcers

■ subsidiaries, affiliates

■ regulators and regulatory actions

or even third parties it does not wish to deal with, such as money launderers or hackers.

Finally, there are external events which cannot be controlled, but which can have a serious reputational impact, for example:

■ the activities of a few fellow industry members which can have an impact on the industry as a whole

■ unwarranted allegations, whether supported or not.

A key point to remember is that reputation is damaged by *perceived* failures, even if they are not grounded in fact. Unfortunately, perception is reality. A firm can be punished not because of any failure on its part, but simply because it is being held to the wrong standard or even to one of which it is unaware. If public expectations are simply 'wrong', because of factual misunderstanding or misinformation, you need to take the initiative to redress this. A word of warning, however: managers of many a collapsed brand have blamed public 'misunderstanding' for their own demise. You may not find sympathy if you offer the public a rationale which is deeply unpalatable, or seen as out of step with changing standards of acceptable behaviour.

Given the myriad causes of reputation risk and its ever-changing nature, how do we manage and mitigate it?

A FRAMEWORK FOR REPUTATION RISK MANAGEMENT

Governance

Reputation risk is, at heart, a behavioural issue, both on the part of the stakeholders and the organisation. You may remember the words of Professor Mervyn King (quoted in Chapter 1) about the critical importance of 'the tune in the middle'. The point is not to hand down board initiatives for reputation, but to ensure that everyone understands and lives up to the plain truth that your firm's reputation is in the hands of all your employees and all those who act on your behalf. As they act in your firm's name, people will behave as they think appropriate. They will respond not to formal policies but to 'tone'; to the attitudes and behaviours of those around them, and those they observe coming from board level. If those are ethical and open, then you have a good chance that your employees' and agents' behaviour will be also.

The other reason why reputation management is in the hands of all management and employees is that, as we said earlier, the stakeholders are many and various. In the Economist Intelligence Unit survey of international senior executives quoted above, the question was asked: 'Which of the following have major responsibility for managing reputation risk within your company?' Unsurprisingly, the top answer, with 84%, was 'CEO/President/Chairman'. There was then a sharp drop to 40% where we find the board; CRO/Head of Risk Management; heads of business units, and a further drop to 35% to find the communications officer and compliance officer. Very surprisingly, when the individuals were asked who in fact managed reputation risk, it emerged that few of the executives surveyed took actual responsibility. There was no formal reputation risk management process.

Perhaps that is because, although the CEO may personify the values and conduct which ensure a company's good standing, he or she should not have the sole responsibility for reputation risk management. And nor should corporate communications for that matter. Responsibility should lie with whoever is most responsible for the stakeholder group which may be affected by reputational damage. Table 16.4 gives some examples.

The advantage of ascribing responsibilities for reputation across the firm is that everybody takes the issue seriously. In fact, as BP will tell you, after the Deepwater Horizon disaster there was as much pressure from employees as anybody else for the company to work to protect its reputation.

The danger is that each part of the firm operates in its own silo. There needs to be coordination. Given the number of areas which are directly involved in protecting a firm's reputation, it is probable that the CEO's role – or better that of the board – is one of coordination.

Stakeholders and reputational relationship managers

Table 16.4

Stakeholder	Reputational relationship managers
Customers	Business line
Customer interface	Support functions, e.g. IT
Employees	HR
Suppliers	Procurement
Third-party agents	Appropriate business line
Investors	Investor relations
Regulators	Compliance
Press	Press and public relations; corporate
Politicians	Public affairs or CEO
Trade unions	HR

Of course, the CEO or chairperson can single-handedly destroy a firm's reputation, either by conduct or speech. One of the most salutary examples is probably retail jeweller Gerald Ratner, who at a private dinner famously described one of his firm's products as 'crap' and suggested that some ear-rings were cheaper than a 'Marks and Spencer prawn sandwich but probably wouldn't last as long'. The remarks were reported; the market value of Ratner's group plummeted £500m, nearly destroying it and Ratner was forced to leave.

An interesting follow-up to the incident came from Ratner himself in his book, *Gerald Ratner: The rise and fall ... and rise again*, where he pleads: 'I had worked bloody hard for 30 years, making millions of pounds for shareholders and creating thousands of jobs for the company I loved, and I suddenly had it taken away from me. Not for doing anything criminal. I hadn't embezzled. I hadn't lied. All I had done was say a sherry decanter was crap.'[9] To which one might say 'Absolutely.' If the gap between reality and perception is that great, the result can be devastating.

Many firms have taken the issue of coordination to another level by establishing a senior reputation and brand committee, whose mandate is to ensure that their brand is protected and enhanced and to consider issues which might affect their reputation. It is, perhaps, ironic that Barclays, which had been one of the first to establish such a committee in early 2004, had disbanded it before the Libor-fixing scandal engulfed it in summer 2012.

A committee like that can become the place to hammer out policy on such issues as conflicts of interest, counterparties with which the firm does not wish to be associated, and a code of behaviour within and without the firm, especially if it operates in a variety of countries and cultures. It will make decisions on policy and on conflicts, where a proposed transaction may potentially contravene existing policy or guidance. If that kind of committee can be put in place and supported by a reputation risk competence centre, so much the better.

A proper governance structure will mean that everybody directly responsible for reputation risk management has clearly defined roles and responsibilities. Whether they are customer-facing or back office, they will have well-defined criteria by which events can be assessed, supported by appropriate policies and guidelines. They will also have a clear structure to identify and escalate issues as they arise. And of course, the whole process should be regularly audited.

Identification and assessment of reputation risks

As reputation risk is an indirect effect of an underlying event, each risk identified in the risk identification process or risk register should be examined for both the direct loss to the firm and the indirect loss which may arise through damage to the firm's reputation. This will show whether it will have a reputation impact and which stakeholder groups will be affected. Identifying stakeholders can be done simply, using a table such as Table 16.5. Identifying reputation risk and new reputation risk stakeholders should also be considered as a standard item during discussions on strategy, or about new projects or products.

Table 16.5	Using the risk register to identify possible reputation risks						
Risk	Employee	Customer	Suppliers	Investors	Agents	Press	Regulator
1							
2							
3							
4							
5							

Once you have identified who might be affected, you can assess the likely scale of reputation risk. Since that represents the gap between expectation and reality, you first need to have a thorough understanding of the awareness of your firm by all its various stakeholders. How well known are you? How much do they trust you? How do they rate the quality of what you offer? What expectations do they have of you? What promises do they believe you are making?

When something happens which may harm your reputation, the impact will, in part, be affected by the goodwill you have with the relevant stakeholder groups. So you need to establish a benchmark against which to assess potential reputational damage. If you truly know what all of your stakeholders are looking for in your business, you can reasonably assess whether the reputational damage, if realised, is likely to be significant or not.

The best way to do that is to conduct surveys amongst your various stakeholder interest groups. The surveys will establish not only your own reputation but also how you compare with your competitors, since reputation varies as a result not only of your actions but also of those of your competitors. The surveys can take a variety of forms – face-to-face interviews, questionnaires, e-mails – depending on how many stakeholders you have, how many of them are considered to be key, or how many you may need for a representative sample.

The next step is to establish your appetite for reputation risk, which is probably best done by establishing a scale of damage to measure the impact of an event on your stakeholders. One example, which evaluates trust, is given in Table 16.6.

Levels of reputational damage (example 1) **Table 16.6**

Stakeholder reaction	Trust damage
1 Disappointment	Trust questioned – but recovered speedily
2 Surprise	Trust dented – recoverable with time and good PR
3 Concern	Trust diminished – recoverable at considerable cost
4 Disgust	Trust severely damaged – never fully recoverable
5 Outrage	Trust completely lost – not recoverable

Source: Garry Honey, *A Short Guide to Reputation Risk* (London: Gower), 2009

Another example, which is used in the banking industry (see Table 16.7) focuses mainly on a number of key stakeholders such as customers, regulators and investors.

Levels of reputational damage (example 2) **Table 16.7**

Level	Reputational damage
1	No external effect
2	No media coverage; increase in customer complaints
3	Limited local or industry media coverage; large-scale customer complaints; possible account closures; no negative effect on share price
4	Limited national media coverage; large-scale customer complaints; some customer loss; informal regulatory enquiry; potential negative effect on share price; possible senior management involvement

▶

Level	Reputational damage
5	Sustained national and limited international media coverage; serious customer loss; formal regulatory investigation or enquiry; negative impact on share price; senior management involvement
6	Sustained negative national and international media coverage; large-scale customer loss; formal regulatory intervention and fines; significant effect on share price; direct senior management/board involvement

Source: British Bankers' Association Global Operational Loss Database

The important thing is to establish a scale, involving your own key stakeholders, against which to test both your risk appetite and potential reputational damage.

Having done the groundwork, you can now revisit the risk register and determine the likelihood of suffering reputational damage, the adequacy of your controls and whether an event would be likely to exceed your reputational risk appetite.

Using scenarios

A highly effective method of considering potential reputational damage is to use specific reputation risk scenarios as an assessment tool. They could be one or a combination of incidents such as:

- loss of a licence
- adverse media campaign
- legal dispute
- loss of employees' trust (e.g. following a whistle-blower event)
- adverse perception of selected products and services by customers
- investigation by the regulator and resultant publicity.

In building scenario outcomes, consider each stakeholder and how they interact with each other, as we did during the exercise on identifying reputation risks (see Table 16.5). What are the information flows between them as well as the information flows between them and you? Consider the incident or incidents against the background of your risk and control assessment. A control failure which you identify in the scenario exercise may affect other risks than those directly related to the incident itself. Either method – risk register or scenarios – will produce a hierarchy of reputation risk events or scenarios and point to an effective action plan.

As suggested earlier, the scale of possible reputational damage may well not present itself solely as a financial number, although significant costs may be involved in restoring a stakeholder group's trust in the firm. Reputational impact is difficult to assess, since the range of impacts is large and much will depend on the true causes, whether the problem is systemic or individual and, crucially, on the speed and effectiveness of response to the problem.

REPUTATION RISK CONTROLS

Just as with the controls discussed in Chapter 5, Risk and control assessment, reputation risk controls can be either detective or preventative. With reputation risk, the best control is to manage expectations. Stakeholder surveys are detective controls which not only provide a benchmark with which to assess potential reputational damage, but also act as a basis for establishing preventative controls to reduce both the likelihood and impact of reputation risk events.

The corporate communications department is not the sole repository of reputation risk management (see Table 16.4), but it nevertheless has a critical role to play in managing expectations. Apart from press and similar communications, the annual report can be a useful part in the process – or a source of reputation risk, given the increasing need to articulate management of non-financial risks.

As was pointed out in Chapter 3, Governance, there is a reputational gain in explaining the nature of risks which a company faces and the processes it has in place to manage those risks. Against that, the prudent auditor may well suggest that the important thing is to release into the public domain only that information which has to be revealed, and to make sure it is relevant, reliable and accurate. Has the information been properly audited? Whatever is released, however, it is important that there is a process which assesses the tone of the reporting and its probable impact on stakeholder groups.

TRACKING REPUTATION RISK

Reputation risk can arise, broadly speaking, in two ways: degradation of a firm's reputation over time; or its ability or failure to handle a sudden crisis or catastrophe, whether or not it was the author of the crisis. Planning for a crisis will come from working through scenarios and drawing up an appropriate plan, as we show later (see It won't happen to me: what to do when it does).

The threats to a firm's reputation often come from the drip, drip of an accumulation of small shifts in perception. A small event can be seen as symptomatic of a wider malaise. Monitoring perceptions of a firm's reputation is a critical part of reputation risk management. So the surveys described earlier, which act as controls when they are used to assess the changing perceptions of stakeholders, are also indicators of changing exposure to reputation risk.

The surveys, including self-assessments, perhaps based on the Harris–Fombrun reputation quotient (see Table 16.2), are 'soft' indicators of changing reputation risk. It is difficult to refine these softer indicators down to precise financial measurement, but they do provide the means to an analysis and index of reputation. If you can identify indicators for sources of greatest potential damage to reputation, you are then able to direct policies and resources to manage these.

Apart from these 'soft' methods of tracking reputation risk, there are numerous 'hard' indicators which may point to a changing reputation and can be tracked over time. Amongst them are:

- decline in revenues
- decline in market share
- difference between the market value and liquidation value of the firm (effectively the movement in the value of goodwill in the firm)
- number of customer complaints
- number of product recalls
- increase in regulatory attention
- firm's position on a publicly recognised reputation index.

Finally, when it comes to reputational risk tracking, the social media are key.

Social media

The rise of social media means that stories and comments about you can be in the hands of millions of people within seconds. Facebook has a billion active users each month and Twitter over 200 million.[10] News travels fast, especially bad news, but now it travels in milliseconds. Trends develop very quickly.

So firms have got to follow the media, plug in to customer dissatisfaction or plain untruths, and react quickly before the untruth becomes a 'fact' or the dissatisfaction becomes a serious threat to the business. In 2011 Bank of America and Verizon Wireless introduced 'convenience fees', the bank for direct debit payments and the wireless operator for telephone and online bill payments. Following storms in the social media, the decisions were reversed within 24 hours.[11]

On the other hand, using the media can be a good way for businesses to provide an excellent customer experience as was demonstrated by Domino's Pizza.

Domino's Pizza (2009)

In 2009, two Domino's Pizza employees posted a video on YouTube of the ghastly things they claimed they did to pizzas. Within 24 hours a million people had seen the video and the story escaped the social media and into broadcast and print media, with devastating effects on the company's reputation and share price. Having thought the storm would pass, the company quickly changed tack and responded by launching a transparency campaign, with people saying how horrible the pizzas were. They announced that they had stopped retouching photos of their products. Within a short while, the share price had risen by over 230%.[11]

The Domino Pizza story also highlights the reputation risk arising from employees, or even family members of employees. Most companies now have a social media policy for employees, which may mitigate risk to an extent, and certainly aims to ensure that the same behavioural norms should be applied in social media as apply in normal human interaction.[12] However, given that recruiters and head-hunters routinely trawl the social media when considering candidates, it's not just your own Facebook page or Twitter account which may be revealing, but also those of your friends and children, with those highly embarrassing snaps of the prospective CEO.

So companies have to be better at listening and responding quickly to social media, whether comments are being made from inside or outside the firm. But before dealing with what to do if there is a reputational crisis, it's worth looking for a moment at relations with third parties.

MANAGING INTERMEDIARY RISK

One of the problems of reputation risk is that often your reputation effectively lies in the hands of others, whom you cannot directly control. That is especially true of those who sell your products or services. An important control here is to ensure that good-quality advice is given to the customer to avoid any risk of mis-selling. Whilst an intermediary is primarily responsible to the customer, your reputation can also be damaged, however unfairly. It is the perception which matters, whatever the truth.

The key is to engage in thorough due diligence before you take on an intermediary, and then to make sure you continually review progress through continuous dialogue and more formal reporting. The following checklist provides a useful list of topics.

Checklist	Checklist for using intermediaries

Due diligence for new intermediaries

- CVs of key individuals
- professionalism, expertise and experience
- business plan
- financial standing
- banking/credit control procedures
- compliance procedures and controls, especially Treating Customers Fairly (if appropriate)
- complaints and analysis
- press and advertising
- product information and marketing strategies
- remuneration strategies
- business continuity plan
- previous audits.

Review of existing intermediaries

- continuous review of most of the above
- inaccurate or untimely reporting by intermediary
- management information
  - business volumes
  - prospect types and volumes
  - business outside intermediary's norm
  - business outside agreed business plan
  - cancellation rates
- complaints – volume and analysis
- audit
  - purpose: to enhance the intermediary's performance and development
  - conducted by approved audit partners
  - consistent approach across all intermediaries.

But it's not a one-way street. The intermediary also has a reputation to protect and needs to ensure that any interaction with the product provider does nothing to harm it. The following is a checklist for intermediaries.

Checklist for intermediaries

The initial due diligence will be complementary, but in addition:

- Does the provider provide clear product information and training?
- What do customers say about interaction with the provider?
- What does the industry say about the provider?
- New products – what is the product design process: focus groups, stress testing, product training?
- Where has the provider had problems in the past and were they rectified speedily and satisfactorily?

One point common to both checklists is that the results of both due diligence and ongoing review should be clearly documented. For the intermediary it is especially important to document why the provider's product has been chosen.

As with all aspects of reputation risk management, this is not only about the down-side. Where providers and intermediaries work together, their reputation can be enhanced.

IT WON'T HAPPEN TO ME: WHAT TO DO WHEN IT DOES

Reputation risk management is different. Dealing with a reputation risk event is not the same as activating the business continuity plan we considered in Chapter 11, Business continuity, although it may be part of it. That is because reputation is in the mind, whether it is the mind of the public, the media or any other constituency.

The reason for the problem may be operational, and that can be fixed, but reputational damage is a separate effect, with potentially far more expensive consequences, which must be treated separately – and fast. The impact of reputational damage is measured in time in a similar way to business continuity planning (see Chapter 11, Business continuity, Business impact analysis). How long will it take to restore trust and reputation? That partly depends on existing goodwill, your prior state of trust with stakeholders, as well as the nature of the event. To what extent was it foreseeable and preventable, or was it truly unpredictable? These factors, as well as how not to handle a reputational crisis, were evident in the *Deepwater Horizon* disaster in the Gulf of Mexico in 2010.

Case study

Deepwater Horizon (2010)

The Deepwater Horizon oil spill in the Gulf of Mexico followed an explosion on 20 April 2010 on *Deepwater Horizon*, a mobile off-shore drilling unit owned by Transocean which was drilling from BP's Macondo oil well. The explosion killed 11 men working on the unit and injured 16 others. It also caused extensive damage to the Gulf's tourism and fishing industries as well as to marine and wildlife habitats. It took until 15 July for the well-head to be capped. Although, by September 2010, the federal government declared the well 'effectively dead', in July 2011 the Louisiana Department of Environmental Quality had extended the state of emergency and roughly 500 miles (800 kilometres) of coastline in Louisiana, Mississippi, Alabama and Florida remained contaminated by oil.

After its own internal probe, BP admitted that it made mistakes which led to the Gulf of Mexico oil spill and in June 2010 it set up a $20 billion fund to compensate victims. In November 2012, BP was fined a record $4.5 billion for criminal failures and the US Environmental Protection Agency announced that the company had been barred from bidding for new contracts, citing 'BP's lack of business integrity'. Civil suits continue.

The commission appointed by President Obama, in its report in December 2010, stated that the disaster could have been prevented and 'can be traced to a series of identifiable mistakes made by BP, Halliburton [which was responsible for capping the well with cement] and Transocean that reveal such systematic failures in risk management that they place in doubt the safety culture of the entire industry'. There were 'recurring themes of missed warning signals, failure to share information, and a general lack of appreciation for the risks involved'.

They blamed BP and its partners for making a series of cost-cutting decisions and the lack of a system to ensure well safety. They also concluded that the spill was not an isolated incident, but that 'the root causes are systemic and, absent of significant reform in both industry practices and government policies, might well recur'. The commission believed that their findings highlighted 'the importance of organizational culture and a consistent commitment to safety by industry, from the highest management levels on down'.

Operational risk issues

The joint investigative report of the various responsible federal agencies which reported in September 2011, pointed, amongst many items, to gas detector systems being bypassed to prevent crew being woken by false alarms, ineffective evacuation training, numerous safety failings, poor maintenance and follow-up on audits.

Reputational risk issues

The key issues were that BP had a very small reservoir of trust in the eyes of the American public following the Texas City oil refinery (2005) and Prudhoe Bay, Alaska pipeline (2006) disasters. The Gulf accident was seen to have been preventable and, perhaps more importantly, took months before the well was capped, partly because BP and Halliburton underestimated the task of using cement at the depth required. But perhaps the reputational final straw were the comments of CEO Tony Hayward, who was the public face of BP immediately following the explosion, who appeared first to avoid blame on behalf of the company, then made a statement which appeared to trivialise the scale of the problem and finally made the comment that 'he'd like his life back', which appeared to suggest that he was more anxious to go home rather than to manage the problem until it was under control.

Sources: National Commission on the BP Deepwater Horizon Oil Spill and Offshore Drilling, 11 January 2011; Deepwater Horizon Joint investigation, 4 April 2011; *Financial Times*, 29 November 2012.

The news media no longer report on a daily basis. Journalists are required to file stories instantly, through blogs and websites, leaving less time than ever to think and challenge a version of events. It is a sad truth of modern commercial news media that journalists now have little, or even no, time to check a given version of the 'facts'.[13] News journalists are not specialists. And yet they shape the agenda, often by framing the charge in the court of public opinion. Unfortunately, in that court, lawyers are of little use. The lawyer's advice to 'admit nothing' is at best irrelevant, and at worst can significantly harm your business value. By all means retain lawyers for legal advice, but do not make them your first source of counsel on crisis communications matters.

In a crisis, when there is the threat of catastrophic loss of trust, you have limited time to start communicating. If you leave a vacuum, other organisations and stakeholders will assert their own agendas and write a script for you, which will rarely be flattering. At a time of crisis, all parties involved will engage in a contest to stake a claim to ownership of the debate or issue, to 'frame the dialogue'. It is up to *you* to frame the debate. A good example was the Democratic presidential primary campaign in 2008. The Obama team successfully framed the debate about Hillary Clinton, the clear front runner, and used unprecedented means – the Web, text messages – to get their message across. Another aspect of this approach is to polarise the debate. 'Only an unreasonable person would disagree with us', or 'if you're not for us you're against us', as George W. Bush did on the 'war on terror'.

However, if you can at least communicate quickly, the chances are that those running the business may get stakeholders to give them the benefit of the doubt, granting some valuable extra time to exert control over the underlying problem. The worst thing executives can do is to be afraid to speak to the media or make any public pronouncement in case their words are misinterpreted or taken out of context.

So what do you say, when you're in the eye of the storm? Be transparent. Be truthful. Tell it all and tell it quickly. Media stories can come from whistle blowers and malicious tip-offs. Companies that keep silent often become the subject of rumours and speculation. What are they trying to hide? The longer it takes to deal fully and openly with a problem, the greater the impression of foot-dragging, whilst a series of forced disclosures keeps the issue in the media longer.

The BP *Deepwater Horizon* case is a good example. The lessons to be learnt from that and other cases are:

- don't hide the truth;
- be straight with the media (because your employees will be if you're not);
- recognise where trust lies and don't breach it (contamination was the worst possible crisis to afflict a brand associated with natural purity);
- make sure you have a coherent and consistent communications policy.

And above all, don't make light of the seriousness of the situation or imply that 'these things happen'. Deal with the problem as quickly as you can and follow the 3 Cs[14] shown in Table 16.8.

Table 16.8	The 3 Cs of reputation risk communication
Concern	Acknowledge something has gone wrong
	Accept responsibility
	Apologise
	Express regret and concern
	Offer remedies
Commitment	Commit to fixing the problem
	Explain in detail what you're going to do
Control	Show that leading figures in the company:
	– are in control of the situation
	– are working to make sure it won't happen again

Remember your own employees. They are key stakeholders and crucial advocates in defining your reputation. So make sure they are involved in the communications exercise from the start.

As to who does the communicating, you should ideally provide one spokesperson, with one message, certainly in dealings with the media. Otherwise there is the danger of mixed or conflicting messages which will only make the situation worse. Equally important is to make sure that whoever appears for you knows what they're talking about. Accept that for some purposes a line manager simply *will* be a better communicator than the chairperson, although the latter should be seen to be involved.

Certainly, the board will want to be kept aware of, and possibly involved in, the strategy for responding to a crisis of reputation. But the most important thing is to keep an eye on the various stakeholders, and to communicate with each of them in the way they would most expect and appreciate, preferably through the relationship manager (see Table 16.4). Any reputation crisis plan should ensure that crises are tackled by the appropriate person in the firm, with a consistent message, and soon.

Finally, it is a fact of life that in the court of public opinion you have *no* right to remain silent – although anything you say may, and probably will, be used against you. You must answer the charges as presented, however unreasonable. The court of public opinion also operates a harsher regime than a court of law: you are guilty until you can prove you are innocent. Sentencing and punishment, in the shape of public vilification, start immediately. Regarding the Enron case discussed earlier, Andersen eventually won its battle in the legal courts. But by then the clients had long since deserted, and the firm and its reputation were destroyed; the legal victory was hollow.[15]

Let Shakespeare have the last word:

The purest treasure mortal times afford

Is spotless reputation: that away,

Men are but gilded loam or painted clay.

[Richard II, I, i, 177–9]

Notes

1 Morgen Witzel, 'The terrible cost of reputational loss', *Financial World*, July/August 2009, pp. 53–55.

2 Quoted in Stuart Fagg, 'Reputation risk management beyond the spin', *Risk*, 18 August 2006.

3 Commencement address at Harvard University, 10 June 1999.

4 Alison Maitland, 'Barclays banks on a good name', *Financial Times*, 19 February 2004, p. 11.

5 8th annual CEO survey, PricewaterhouseCoopers, 2005.

6 Aon, Global Risk Management Survey, 2007.

7 See Diane Vaughan, *The Challenger Launch Decision* (Chicago and London: University of Chicago Press), 1996.

8 Economist Intelligence Unit white paper, *Reputation: Risk of risks* (London: EIU), 2005.

9 Gerald Ratner, *Gerald Ratner: The rise and fall ... and rise again* (Chichester: Capstone Publishing), 2007.

10 Facebook company announcement 5 October 2012; Twitter company tweet reported on http://mashable.com/2012/12/18/twitter-200-million-active-users

11 *Director* 20 June 2012.

12 See, for instance, www.informationshield.com

13 Nick Davies, *Flat Earth News*, 2006.

14 The 3 Cs themselves are fully discussed in Judy Larkin, *Strategic Reputation Risk Management* (Basingstoke: Palgrave Macmillan), 2003.

15 Tim Prizeman, Director of PR Advisers, Kelso Consulting, in *Internal Auditing*, December 2008, p. 33.

Resources and further reading

Chapter 1 What is operational risk?

Peter L. Bernstein (1998) *Against the Gods,* New York: J Wiley & Sons.

Michael Power (2009) *Organized Uncertainty,* Oxford: OUP.

Chapter 10 Business continuity

Tony Blunden and Tim Landsman (2003) *The Business Continuity Lifecycle,* Complinet, www.complinet.com

British Bankers' Association and KPMG (2003) *A Guide to Business Continuity Management,* www.bba.org

British Standards Institute, *BS 25999-1: Business Continuity Management: Code of Practice,* 2006; *BS25999-2: Specification for Business Continuity Management,* 2007.

Business Continuity Institute website: www.thebci.org

Chapter 12 Internal audit

Institute of Internal Auditors website: www.iia.org

KPMG Audit Committee Institute website: www.kpmg.co.uk/aci

Chapter 13 Outsourcing

The Outsourcing Institute website: www.outsourcing.com

Outsourcing Leadership website: www.outsourcingleadership.com

Chapter 15 Reputation risk

Garry Honey (2009) *A Short Guide to Reputation Risk,* Farnham: Gower Publishing Limited.

Index

THE MASTERING SERIES

9780273759034

9780273772255

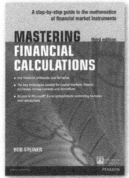

9780273750581

9780273735670

9780273730330

9780273732815

9780273757177

9780273734970

9780273744795

9780273724544

9780273725206

9780273719298

Practical. Comprehensive. Essential